writing poetry

'You're wrong, Oscar Wilde: those who can are often the most inspiring teachers. John and Matthew have produced a sensible, lively apprenticeship course in poetry, with insider tips no non-practitioner could have conceived.'

LES MURRAY

'It's sharply and freshly written, tough, funny, companionable, practical, and full of ideas for welcoming and handling poems. Poets and their teachers will find Writing Poetry blissfully indispensable.'

RUTH PADEL

'An essential text for would-be writers and readers of poetry. Matthew Sweeney and John Hartley Williams have given us a look inside the hows and whys and wonders of their craft. As always, it is generous and genuine and uniquely instructive.'

THOMAS LYNCH

'This is the book we have been waiting for. Hartley Williams and Sweeney have assembled a cornucopia of sound advice and ingenious starting points for writing. With so many exhilarating examples from the liveliest of poetry and poets, this book makes you immediately want to grab your pen and write.'

JO SHAPCOTT

'What Hartley Williams and Sweeney have produced is an excellent manual for the craft of writing poems.'

JOHN STAMMERS

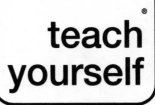

writing poetry

matthew sweeney

and john hartley williams

Launched in 1938, the **teach yourself** series grew rapidly in response to the world's wartime needs. Loved and trusted by over 50 million readers, the series has continued to respond to society's changing interests and passions and now, 70 years on, includes over 500 titles, from Arabic and Beekeeping to Yoga and Zulu. What would you like to learn?

be where you want to be with **teach yourself**

For UK order enquiries: please contact Bookpoint Ltd, 130 Milton Park, Abingdon, Oxon OX14 4SB. Telephone: +44 (0) 1235 827720. Fax: +44 (0) 1235 400454. Lines are open 09.00–17.00, Monday to Saturday, with a 24-hour message answering service. Details about our titles and how to order are available at www.teachyourself.co.uk

Long renowned as the authoritative source for self-guided learning – with more than 50 million copies sold worldwide – the **teach yourself** series includes over 500 titles in the fields of languages, crafts, hobbies, business, computing and education.

British Library Cataloguing in Publication Data: a catalogue record for this title is available from the British Library.

First published in UK 1997 by Hodder Education, part of Hachette Livre UK, 338 Euston Road, London, NW1 3BH.

This edition published 2008.

The **teach yourself** name is a registered trade mark of Hodder Headline.

Copyright © 1997, 2003, 2008 Matthew Sweeney and John Hartley Williams

Typeset by Transet Limited, Coventry, England.
Printed in Great Britain for Hodder Education, an Hachette Livre UK Company, 338 Euston Road, London NW1 3BH, by CPI Cox and Wyman, Reading, Berkshire RG1 8EX.

The publisher has used its best endeavours to ensure that the URLs for external websites referred to in this book are correct and active at the time of going to press. However, the publisher and the author have no responsibility for the websites and can make no guarantee that a site will remain live or that the content will remain relevant, decent or appropriate.

Hachette Livre UK's policy is to use papers that are natural, renewable and recyclable products and made from wood grown in sustainable forests. The logging and manufacturing processes are expected to conform to the environmental regulations of the country of origin.

Impression number   10 9 8 7 6 5 4 3 2 1
Year   2012 2011 2010 2009 2008

contents

vi

acknowledgements

Every effort has been made to trace the copyright for material used in this book. The authors and publishers would be happy to make arrangements with any holder of copyright whom it has not been possible to trace by the time of going to press.

On behalf of the authors, Hodder Education would like to thank the following for permission to reproduce copyright material quoted in this book: The University of California Press via Copyright Clearance Center for 'Stop Press' by Blaise Cendrars, from COMPLETE POEMS translated from French by Ron Padgett; 'Get the Money!' by Ted Berrigan, from THE COLLECTED POEMS OF TED BERRIGAN, University of California Press 2005. Faber and Faber Ltd for 'The Pisan Cantos' by Ezra Pound from *The Pisan Cantos*; W H Auden's 'In Memory of W B Yeats' from *Another Time*, 'The Shield of Achilles' from *The Shield of Achilles*, 'Consider' from *Poems 1927–1931* and 'In Due Season' from *City Without Walls*; Seamus Heaney's 'The Flight Path' from *The Spiritlevel* and 'A Postcard from North Antrim' from *Field Work*; 'Land Love' by Douglas Dunn from *Elegies*; 'Popular Mechanics' by Charles Simic from *Frightening Toys*; and Theodore Roethke's 'My Papa's Waltz' and 'Child on top of a Greenhouse' from Collected Poems. Faber and Faber and Farrar Straus Giroux for 'Metamorphoses' by Ted Hughes from *Metamorphoses*; '7 Middagh Street' and 'Sushi' by Paul Muldoon from *Meeting the British*; 'Considering the snail' by Thom Gunn from *Selected Poetry* and 'Dream Song 14' by John Berryman from *The Dream Songs*. Marianne Chipperfield, on behalf of the author, for 'Sonnet for Dick', 'Pride' and 'The Magic Box' by Kit Wright. Random House Inc for W H Auden's 'In Memory of W B Yeats' from *Another Time*, copyright 1940, renewed in 1968 by W H Auden, 'The Shield of Achilles' from *The Shield of Achilles*, copyright 1952 by W H Auden, 'Consider' from *Poems 1927–1931*, copyright 1934 and renewed in 1962 by W H Auden and 'In Due Season' from *City Without Walls* © 1976 by Edward Mendelson, William Meredith and Monroe K Spears, Executors of the Estate of W H Auden; one haiku from AN INTRODUCTION TO HAIKU by Harold G Henderson © 1958 by Harold G Henderson. Used by permission of Doubleday, a division of Random House Inc; 'My Papa's Waltz' © 1942 by Hearst Magazines Inc, 'Child on Top of a Greenhouse' © 1946 by Editorial Publications Inc, from

COLLECTED POEMS OF THEODORE ROETHKE by Theodore Roethke. Used by permission of Doubleday, a division of Random House Inc; and 'The Race' by Sharon Olds from *The Father*, Knopf 1992. Random House Group Ltd for an extract from 'Birches' and 'The Runaway' by Robert Frost, from THE POETRY OF ROBERT FROST edited by Edward Connery Lathem, published by Jonathan Cape. Reprinted by permission of the Random House Group Ltd © 1916, 1923, 1969 by Henry Holt and Company © 1944, 1951 by Robert Frost, Reprinted by permission of The Random House Group Ltd and Henry Holt and Company LLC; an extract from 'Three Things Enchanted Him', from POEMS OF AKHMATOVA by Anna Akhmtova, translated by Stanley Kunitz and Max Hayward, published by The Harvill Press; and an extract from 'I like you to be still', from TWENTY LOVE POEMS AND A SONG OF DESPAIR by Pablo Neruda, translated by W S Merwin, published by Jonathan Cape and Viking Penguin © 1969 by W. S. Merwin, Reprinted by permission of The Random House Group Ltd UK and Viking Penguin, a division of Penguin Group (USA) Inc. Farrar Straus Giroux for 'Crusoe in England' and 'The Bight' by Elizabeth Bishop; and 'During Fever' by Robert Lowell from *Life Studies*. David Higham Associates Limited for 'Ars Poetica' by John Heath-Stubbs, from COLLECTED POEMS 1943–1987; extract from 'Soap Suds' by Louis MacNeice, from COLLECTED POEMS published by Faber and Faber; and 'Death of a Farmyard' by Geoffrey Grigson, from COLLECTED POEMS 1963–1980 published by Allison & Busby. Dalkey Archive Press for two short quotes by Flan O'Brien, from THE BEST OF MYLES Flann O'Brien. Carcanet Press for two lines from 'The chances of rhyme' by Charles Tomlinson, from SELECTED POEMS 1955–1997 published by Carcanet Press; 'The Red Wheelbarrow' and 'The Great Figure' by William Carlos Williams, from COLLECTED POEMS published by Carcanet Press; 'The Video Box' and 'Alpha' by Edwin Morgan, from COLLECTED POEMS published by Carcanet Press; 'Cat-Goddesses' by Robert Graves, from COMPLETE POEMS IN ONE VOLUME published by Carcanet Press; and an extract from 'The Idyll Wheel' by Les Murray, from COLLECTED POEMS published by Carcanet Press. Houghton Mifflin Harcourt Publishing Company for extract from 'Ars Poetica' by Archibald MacLeish, from COLLECTED POEMS 1917–1982 by Archibald MacLeish © 1985 by The Estate of Archibald MacLeish; and 'Popular Mechanics' by Charles Simic, from UNENDING BLUES, POEMS by Charles Simic, published by Harcourt. PFD www.pfd.co.uk on behalf of Roger McGough for an extract from 'Shooting Stars' by Roger McGough, from LUCKY © Roger McGough 1993. Anvil Press Poetry for 'In The Village of My Forefathers' and 'Imminent Return' by Vasko Popa, translated by Anne Pennington, revised and expanded by Francis R Jones VASKO POPA: COLLECTED POEMS, published by Anvil Press Poetry in 1997. The Estate of Randall Jarrell for 'Protocols' by Randall Jarrell from *Little Field, Little Field*, Dial Press. Trident Media Group for 'Sweet Like a crow' by Michael Ondaatje, from *Running in the family*. Museum on the Seam, Jerusalem for 'Jerusalem' by Yehuda Amichai from *A Touch of Grace*, Museum on the Seam 2000. New Directions for 'Red Wheelbarrow' and 'The Great Figure' by William Carlos Williams from *Collected poems*. John Murray (Hachette Livre UK Ltd) for 'Hamnavoe Market' by George Mackay Brown, from SELECTED POEMS 1954–1983 by George Mackay Brown. Suhrkamp Verlag GmbH & Co for our authors' translation of 'Unkraut', from GEZAHLTE TAGE by Peter Huchel. Allen Ginsberg Estate for one line from 'America' by Allen Ginsberg, from COLLECTED POEMS 1947–1997 HarperCollins USA, Penguin UK. Macmillan for 'At Dusk', from A PAINTED FIELD by Robin Robertson, published by Pan Macmillan; Pan Macmillan London for 'Mrs Midas' by Carol Ann Duffy, from THE WORLD'S WIFE © Carol Ann Duffy. Tomaž Šalamun for 'Who is Who' translated by Tomaž Šalamun and Anselm Hollo, from THE SELECTED POEMS OF TOMAŽ ŠALAMUN. George Braziller for 'My Shoes' by Charles Simic, from SELECTED EARLY POEMS (New York, George Braziller, 1999). Gray Wolf Press, Saint Paul, Minnestota for 'Black Silk' by Tess Gallagher, from AMPLITUDE: NEW AND SELECTED POEMS © 1987 Tess Gallagher. Sheil Land Associates Limited for 'Laughter in Hell' by George MacBeth © 1992 by George MacBeth. Wesleyan University Press for 'Lying in a Hammock at William Duffy's Farm in Pine Island Minnesota' by James Wright, from COLLECTED POEMS © 1971 by James Wright. Gordon Dickerson on behalf of the author for an extract from 'A Cold Coming' by Tony Harrison, from COLLECTED POEMS, Penguin 2007. The Estate of W S Graham for 'Loch Thom' and extract from 'Johan Joachim Quantz's Five Lessons' by W S Graham © Michael and Margaret Snow. The Literary Trustees of Walter de la Mare and the Society of Authors as their representative for 'The Sea Boy' by Walter de la Mare, from The Complete Poems of Walter de la Mare 1975. A P Watt on behalf of Grainne Yeats for four lines from 'The Man and the Echo' by W B Yeats. A P Watt and Simon and Schuster for 'Autobiographies' by W B Yeats. W W Norton & Company for 'Buffalo Bill's' Reprinted from COMPLETE POEMS 1904–1962, by E E Cummings, edited by George J Firmage © 1991 by the Trustees for the E E Cummings Trust and George J Firmage and 'A Note on the Rapture to his True Love', from BODIES IN MOTION AND AT REST by Thomas Lynch © 2000 by Thomas Lynch, Richard McDonough, Literary Agent. The author c/o The Gallery Press, Loughcrew, Oldcastle, County Meath, Ireland for an extract from 'Entropy' by Derek Mahon. The Estate of Michael Hartnett and The Gallery Press, Loughcrew, Oldcastle, County Meath, Ireland for an extract from 'Death of an Irishwoman' by Michael Hartnett, from COLLECTED POEMS, 2001. The Tate Gallery London, and Paula Rego for 'The Dance' by Paula Rego. The Tate Gallery, London and DACS © ADAGP. Paris ad DACS London 2008 for 'The Reckless Sleeper' by Rene Magritte. The Tate Gallery, London for 'The Kiss' by Auguste Rodin.

preface

It is an unusual thing for poets like us to have a book go into a third edition, so we thought we'd write a brief preface to mark this occasion. Over the last ten years we've bumped into many people who've read the book and found it useful. Even poets of our acquaintance have told us they like using it for workshops. Not everyone is completely positive, though.

MS: I was coming off the platform, after doing a reading at the Ledbury Poetry Festival when one man came up to me. 'I've read your *Writing Poetry* book and enjoyed it, but the exercises don't work.' 'Oh, yes they do,' I said. 'You're just not doing them right.' Then I carried on to the bar for that much-needed glass of red wine.

As a matter of fact, the exercises really do work – we've tried them ourselves and every now and then we have found, to our surprise, real poems emerging. So we can confidently pronounce, as chefs do of their recipes – tried and tested! In fact, the man at the Ledbury Festival later confessed he'd noticed that one of the poems he'd heard had indeed come out of one of the exercises. He announced he would go back and try the exercises again.

The book you're holding is a revised and expanded edition. We have introduced more exercises that we have tried out in workshops. These new exercises (in the previous update as well as this one) are ones we evolved to connect specifically with writers new to poetry. We have updated and developed the chapter on the internet and added one on poetry prizes and festivals. There are also numerous other small additions embedded in the text that have come from our thinking and reading about the craft of poetry. The book has developed a life of its own, which is perhaps natural, seeing as we're both practising poets who continue to produce new work and to reflect on the process.

JHW: One of the nicest things to have happened to me was to encounter a woman after a reading who was holding a copy of the first edition of this book. It was so well-thumbed it was falling apart, practically everything had been doubly underscored, there was scribble everywhere in the margins. 'I'm so happy with this book,' she said. 'I don't know how many times I've read it. It's my bible.'

We certainly didn't set out to write a bible. We started writing this book with all the uncertainties and doubts you'd expect. Maybe by the tenth edition we'll have perfected it.

Forget about Piers Plowman, *forget about Shakespeare, Keats, Morris, the English Bible, and remember only that you live in our terrific, untidy, indifferent empirical age, where not a single problem is solved and not a single Accepted Idea from the poet has any more magic.*

FORD MADOX FORD

01

what does it take to be a poet?

Louis MacNeice had this to say:

> *Speaking for myself I should say that the following things, among others, have conditioned my poetry – having been brought up in the north of Ireland; having a father who was a clergyman; the fact that my mother died when I was little; repression from the age of six to nine; inferiority complex on the grounds of physique and class consciousness; lack of a social life until I was grown up; late puberty; ignorance of music (which could have been a substitute for poetry); inability to ride horses or practise successfully most of the sports which satisfy a sense of rhythm; an adolescent liking for the role of enfant terrible; shyness in the company of young women until I was twenty; a liking (now dead) for metaphysics; marriage and divorce; Birmingham; an indolent pleasure in gardens and wild landscapes; ... a liking for animals; an interest in dress.*

He's not suggesting, of course, that you have to have a clergyman father to be a poet. You certainly don't have to be a man. But perhaps somethings in this list might be fertile ground for the poetic vocation, for example, a taste for intellectual pursuits, a liking for animals, and a deep sense of the quirks of fate. Interestingly, MacNeice omits one vital conditioning factor from his list: the encounter with poetry itself.

You've probably opened this book because you already have poetic stirrings. You've tried your hand at writing poems. Perhaps a few have found favour with friends and peers. But what can you tell us about *your* encounter with poetry? What poetry do *you* read? Do you *listen* to poetry? Do you take an interest in other people's poetry, or just your own? Do you keep up with the contemporary scene? Just as it's impossible to be a professional footballer if you never watch football matches, it's impossible to write poems if you don't read them, but it's surprising how many people don't seem to appreciate this. Although we'd readily admit that poetry competitions are pretty much a lottery, we can also tell you, from experience of judging them, that most of the poems entered haven't a chance of winning. Why? Because it's obvious the writers haven't read anything written since the mustard gas attacks of the First World War.

The American poet Robert Frost said, 'Poetry is a fresh look and a fresh listen', by which he meant, of course, a fresh look at the world around us, and a fresh listen to the language people are using. This may seem obvious but it's something that has to be said again for every generation. Wordsworth and Coleridge said it for *their* generation with a famous remark about the need to describe incidents and situations from common life 'in the language really used by men'. Ezra Pound said it again for the generation that survived those mustard gas attacks: 'Make it new!' Many people can't accept this. They think the language of the age should never be the language of poetry. They yearn for a golden, pastoral age, and a language that will bathe everything in a romantic glow. What this leads to, if they are writers, is cliché, stale archaism and bathos. To those people, we'd say this: if you want to write poems for yourself alone, you can do it anyway you want to, but if you want to write for publication, if you want others to read your work, you have to see the world you live in – and see it in a fresh way – as you write.

What will you need to learn?

An extreme view of poetry holds that its source is inspiration. A sort of divine welling-up – no further training needed. Another view holds that to write poetry what you chiefly need is craft. Our view is that you will certainly need some inspiration – and we aim to suggest, at various places in this book, where you might find it – but you will definitely need a lot of craft. What does this word suggest to you? A blacksmith's forge? A potter's wheel? Certainly the idea of a traditional skill that can be learnt. We aim to give you some of the basics of the poet's craft in this book.

Another thing. Wordsworth said it better than we can:

> *There neither is, nor can be, any* essential *difference between the language of prose and metrical composition.*

Does that surprise you? In the public mind poetry is often associated with the effervescence of powerful (or incomprehensible) feelings and not much else. Now the public may have no training in pottery, but it can recognize a well-wrought urn when it sees one. The public likewise knows when a piece of prose is murky and confused. Where poetry is concerned, however, the public is uncertain. How can one tell if a poem is good or not? If there is no *essential* difference between the language of prose and that of poetry, well, there's still a difference, isn't there?

Yes indeed. The language of poetry is, as the French poet Paul Valéry put it, a language *within* a language. And you have to learn to read the language of poems before you can respond to it properly, let alone use it to write poems. Furthermore, that language within a language which poetry is has its rules and proprieties just as prose does. Many people, through insecurities bred by the certainties of teachers perhaps, never do learn to feel quite comfortable with it. But if you want to be a poet, you will need to acquire for yourself the language craft with which poems are written. This learning of the 'language within a language' is really a pretty straightforward business. Don't be put off by people who try to blind you with science. It really isn't difficult to acquire the basics, and we hope you'll find most of what you need to know in this book.

To strike a keynote, though: the word 'craft' implies an activity that is carried out in the public domain. If you make a serious attempt to write a poem you should be making, or attempting to make, a public communication. And if you want to get published and get read – as people who write seriously do – you have to ask yourself certain questions. Are you prepared to take criticism that might lead to your improvement? Are you serious enough to learn techniques that will enable you to compete successfully in the publishing world? Are you willing to stay the course, given that the way to publication is often littered with rejections and disappointments?

What are your chances of getting published?

In the last decade more poets of all kinds – young poets, black poets, women poets, white, middle-aged male poets – have been published than ever before, and this pluralism is good for poetry. And there are many routes to publication. You may, for example, start with publication on a platform or reading aloud at a poetry slam. Or you may get a poem into a local magazine, or church gazette, or the smallest of small poetry magazines, or you may find a magazine willing to publish you on the net. Maybe someone you know with artistic and printing skills would be willing to publish a broadsheet poem of yours. The steps onward from there would involve a progression to more established poetry magazines, higher circulation literary weeklies, a volume, perhaps, from one of the countless small presses who are willing to take on newcomers, and finally, if you're lucky and persistent, to publication by a major London publishing house. To achieve this, you'll need to build up your confidence, read widely, and try to moderate the demands of your ego. Don't assume that if no one responds to your work it's because it's too original and brilliant. It might just be written in such an obscure and self-indulgent manner that only you can understand it.

What we think is this: if you are willing to consider your readership, if you are willing to think about how people other than yourself and your most intimate peer group might respond to what you write, there are definitely more opportunities for getting your work in print these days than ever before. But you'll need to develop a capacity for self-criticism, and develop your self-confidence as well. It's a difficult balancing act. After years of practice, and years of honing instinct, a tightrope walker, high up, without a net, steps out on to the wire. To do this, a vital ingredient is needed: confidence. Without it the walker would fall. This book will aim to help you develop your craft, but also your confidence. Nine tenths of the battle for confidence is knowing what you're doing and *why*.

What will publication bring you?

No money to speak of. Very little fame for most of us. The satisfaction of seeing your name in print, and the hope that people – however few initially – will read your work. That is, after all, the point of publication, to gain readers. Better than that, it may gain you friends.

Even a successful poet cannot expect to live on his or her royalties alone, but many live indirectly from their work. This can take many forms – invitations to give readings from published work, or to run workshops or writing courses; school visits in which the writer encourages children to write; writer-in-residence jobs; bursaries and grants from funding bodies; radio and reviewing work. None of this would happen, of course, had the writer not been published. At the outset of a writer's career, he or she has to take a decision on whether to take a job and make writing a spare time occupation or whether to do it full time. This latter option – especially where poetry is concerned – is risky, unless you're lucky enough to have a private income. There won't be much money; there's no guarantee, in fact, that there will be any at all.

Actually, the situation for contemporary poetry – if you measure it in sales of books – looks somewhat dire. In 1999, the Arts Council of England commissioned research into the market for contemporary poetry, and commented that: 'The image of contemporary poetry, lack of awareness and knowledge, cultural factors and factionalism within contemporary poetry [are] seen as major barriers to widening its appeal.' In February 2003 a report appeared, commissioned by the Poetry Book Society. It was entitled: 'Growing the Market for Poetry – A Review', and was prompted by a concern that the market for poetry books is in decline. It showed that: 'Poetry is increasingly a part of national life, particularly at moments of crisis (the attack on the World Trade Centre, for instance, resulted in a surge of interest in, and use of, poetry) but also showed that: 'the overall volume of poetry book sales has declined over the last five years by 11 per cent.' Furthermore: 'Publishers report that sales are increasingly hard to achieve and that the rise in the profile of poets and poetry has not converted into sales of collections of contemporary poetry.'

There's nothing exactly new in this. In the 1960s, Stephen Spender wrote: 'A modern poet launching forth his slim volume today is like a person dropping a feather over the edge of the Grand Canyon and then waiting for the echo.' Spender, though, might have been surprised to hear that a rendering of the poem 'Funeral Blues', by his old friend W.H. Auden, in the 1990s film *Four Weddings and a Funeral*, would have the surprising effect of selling two hundred thousand copies of Auden's lyrics in a paperback version. It's a confirmation of the fact that people do respond eagerly to the heightened language of poems when it is presented to them in a context they can understand. But it's also the exception that proves the rule: poetry will never be a bestseller, in the *Harry Potter* sense. However, the success of *Poems on the Underground* has demonstrated that people occasionally prefer to read something true instead of advertising. Perhaps, too, this is making a dent in the commonly held belief that poetry doesn't connect with the world we live in, or that even if it does connect, it's written in such an obscure or pretentious manner that no one wants to read it.

If you are seriously interested in improving your writing to a level where you may be published, and read, the rest of this book is for you.

02

bump-starting the poem

How do you make inroads on the blank page? Where do poems come from? How can you hook them and reel them in? Robert Frost has an excellent and very persuasive answer to these questions – it certainly fits our experience of how poems generally come about. This is what he says:

> A poem is never a thought to begin with. It is at its best when it is a tantalising vagueness. It finds its thought and succeeds or it doesn't find it and comes to nothing.

There it is, as cleanly put as a sweetly struck golf shot. What he's talking about, in that 'tantalising vagueness' reference, is the old idea of inspiration. Something bubbles up in your memory, or catches your attention as you're walking around or reading, or simply jumps into your head from nowhere, and sticks like a burr, until a thought train is set in motion. Think of it as some germ that gets you going. Afterwards, you either arrive at a new piece of writing, or – as Frost says might happen – you crunch up the piece of paper and drop it in the bin. This possibility of failure is always likely, but it shouldn't deter you from having a go.

So do you wait for these 'tantalising vaguenesses', or can you encourage them? Yes, and no. Certainly the best poems often arrive out of the blue, taking you by surprise. You can be going out to post a letter and an image or phrase can jump into your head, so strange you nearly get run over by a taxi. At that stage you'll have no idea what it means, or where it will lead, only that you can't wait to get back to your notebook and your writing desk. Sometimes it'll feel as if the poem has been offered to you – all you have to do is hold the pen and the poem writes itself. Unfortunately, poems are rarely so co-operative, but at least you can be set firmly on your way.

MS: I was invited to give a reading at an Irish literary festival a few years ago. When I checked into the hotel in which I was staying, I found they'd put me in the bridal suite. Somehow, the combination of this and having no bride with me provoked a poem. I have no idea why, but it happened – the poem got written.

You may have to wait for your best poems, but that doesn't mean you sit there idle and let mildew grow on your notebook. Practising does no harm whatsoever – at the very least you'll develop certain techniques that will come in useful later, and you'll get a feel for language. This facility cannot be overvalued.

Imitating models you've particularly admired, for example, is a way to develop that feel. Most poets at some stage in their early development 'piggyback' on other poets to whom they are drawn. Philip Larkin records that he began his writing career with a volume of Yeats open on the kitchen table, and a notebook open next to it. It took him a while to find his own way of writing and escape the influence of his model, but without a genuine and sincere admiration for a master it seems doubtful if the poetic process can make any headway. A schoolboy wants to imitate his favourite bass player, a schoolgirl dreams of emulating her favourite Olympic swimmer. As budding writers, you'll need to decide who your models truly are. Finding out who they are, and what it is exactly about the way they write which so appeals to you, is an all important part of the process of becoming a writer.

Sometimes people are anxious that too much imitation will make it impossible for them to find their own voice. This is a groundless fear because you'll be developing your technique in readiness for when your own personal style emerges, and remember: you won't be influenced by everyone you read, you'll be drawn to only those poets to whom you're temperamentally suited.

It's worth mentioning here that the model doesn't have to be one of those idiosyncratic literary geniuses who have put their stamp on the century. W. B. Yeats is probably not a good example for a beginner who is still wondering how to proceed. The mixture of high-flown rhetoric and odd philosophy could swamp a beginner's ideas. Try someone good but more approachable: Elizabeth Bishop or Robert Lowell, or more contemporary poets like Simon Armitage and Carol Ann Duffy.

The next thing to remember is that imitation will take you only so far. If you're a skillful mime, you may quickly learn someone else's tricks and make them your own, but you won't convince anyone else that what you're doing has validity – least of all, probably, yourself – until you've found a way of writing that is individually yours.

The first thing that will be individually yours is your notebook and what you put in it. This may well provide material to spark off poems. Its contents will be full of observations of things that have struck you as you move from day to day. It may record experiences you've had, or encounters, both pleasant and unpleasant. It may record your successes and setbacks. It's likely, however, that it is your setbacks which will prove to be the most productive of writing, as it's only when you experience a rebuff that you can truly be said to be learning. W. H. Auden was of the opinion that it is the poet's capacity for experiencing humiliation that makes him or her a poet. Certainly, it's worth thinking of a poem, sometimes, as enacting what the French call *l'esprit d'escalier* – that tendency to think of exactly the right, devastating riposte to an insult as you are on the way downstairs and out of the house.

The way to start a poem, then, is to think small; begin with the scraps or fragments you've accumulated in that notebook. Don't start with the idea that you're going to write an epic for our time, however much you might think our time needs one. Nor should you assume that a poem can put the world to rights, however indignant you feel about ecology, animal rights, atomic tests and so on.

Your subject matter is all around you, but to develop your powers of expression you'll also need to increase your awareness of the surprising possibilities of language. One useful way of doing this is playing poetry games.

MS: A game I used to happily engage in over a bottle of wine or so was one a friend and myself concocted from the surrealist painters' 'Exquisite Corpses'. What we did involved writing a line of a poem and folding it over so it couldn't be seen, then handing the page to the other person who had to add a line of his own (without knowing anything about the previous line), fold it over in turn, and hand the page back to the first person. This process continued for a pre-determined number of lines. Sometimes we'd reveal the last word of the line so the other person could find a rhyme for it. It was a game we never tired of.

JHW: It looks to me as though Matthew and his friend invented a development of the game *Consequences*. The surrealist painters' game he mentions was actually derived from a surrealist writers' game called *The Exquisite Corpse* in which you choose a grammatical string and produce very arbitrarily constructed sentences. For example, each player writes an article (definite or indefinite) and an adjective on a piece of paper and folds it over. Players swap papers and then write a noun. Papers are folded again and passed back, and each player writes a transitive verb. The same procedure happens again, only this time another article plus adjective is added, then a final noun. (The sequence art/adj + noun + verb + art/adj + noun can be extended or varied as the players want.) Then complete sentences are read out, after slight grammatical adjustments have been made for consistency. We've just played the game and got:

The far off taxi-driver swallowed the obese horse

and

A luminous tortoise tore open the lopsided pyjamas

It's the chance element here which produces sentences you couldn't think of yourself.

The serious pay-off of such light-hearted scribbling is that it might encourage you to develop a playfulness in the writing you do for yourself. This needn't move your writing away from the serious, but what it will do is move it from the over-serious straining that spoils the efforts of most beginning writers. It's also very easy to do, being a game, but even here you are practising with language and that can only feed positively into your 'real' writing.

Exploiting the possibilities of chance and random occurrence in this way opens a window on your unconscious mind, and writing poetry usually involves your conscious and unconscious minds working together. It's important to practise using your unconscious because good poems often come from the writer's willingness to be receptive to unknown parts of the self. There are times when you are more receptive, with your verbal antennae up, and times when your brain won't tune into the opportunities for poetry. Mood is as important in writing as it is in the rest of life. There are ways, however, to develop in yourself an increased receptivity. The kind of games we've been mentioning help to keep you alert for any poems that might be coming.

One of the most powerful devices for unlocking the route to the unconscious is automatic writing. Quite simply you write without using any conscious control. How do you do this? Take a piece of paper and pen, forget about your genius and your desire to win the Nobel prize, and start scribbling. If you can't get going, choose a letter – say B – and use a word beginning with B to start you off. Keep your pen moving and don't attempt to censor what you're doing. If you get blocked, use the letter B again and off you go. It's a way of sleepwalking through the language and, as sleepwalkers know, you can often end up in very surprising places by doing this. We're not suggesting you use this method for serious composition, but as a freeing-off technique it can be enormously helpful. An analogous situation from the world of performance is illustrated by the following:

JHW: I once heard a musician on the radio describe how he interpreted a piece of music. He first played the piece according to a literalist interpretation of the notes – it was a jerky and peculiarly arhythmic rendition – then gave a performance in which he quite deliberately suppressed his knowledge and technical knowhow in favour of a kind of 'sleepwalking' – a playing by instinct – and immediately the music became smooth and fluent.

Your memories are located in both your conscious and your unconscious mind. Some you'll be able to recall, some you won't. Even when you can recall things, your memories are often somewhat fictionalized by your unconscious. You won't be aware of this – you'll take bets you remember things exactly the way they happened, but you'll often be wrong. From a writing point of view, however, factual accuracy is irrelevant: the fictionalizing can actually help the writing. Being able to recreate detail and mood, however, takes practice. You have to think yourself back into the exactness of a situation to get its feeling right.

JHW: I had a problem with a commission I was given to write a poem for Bosnia, protesting against the war. Staring at news programmes gave me no ideas for a poem at all. Emotions of shock and anger merely blurred my ability to write. I had to focus on what I knew about the country, my own personal experience. I remember driving through Bosnia in late autumn and seeing people standing by the roadside selling mushrooms. We stopped and bought a basketful of huge ceps, and later my paranoia persuaded me they were toxic mushrooms and shouldn't be eaten. Other members of my family ate them and suffered no ill-effects. There was nothing wrong with the mushrooms, only me. Much later that gave me a kick off to John Bosnia:

> We have the biggest mushrooms in the world.
> If you're lucky enough to collect a basketful,
> Take them home and cook them.
> Wait a year or so. If you're still alive
> Buy some more and try again. Either way
> The process is definitive.

The mushrooms became an image, not only of a boastful nationalism, but also of long-maturing hatreds, of long-premeditated folk-revenge. I was aware, from having stayed in Sarajevo for a while, of the high degree of local chauvinism that existed in the region. I also became very aware of my own

Western-ness, and how odd my pretensions to being liberal and democratic seemed in that place. Yet I loved the warmth, vigour and crankiness of the people. Somehow those mushrooms seemed to encapsulate all my feelings about the place, and about my character: John Bosnia.

Place is one of the first aspects of the relationship between you and the world that you can explore in a poem. Start with where you live, for example, or where you grew up. Other possibilities are places you've visited, or places you've just read about. Remember that places are usually associated with people (even the moon since 1969) and the happenings that take place there.

So think of people you know: friends, lovers, relations. Explore other areas: hypochondria, your fears of mortality, your thoughts on food and music. Focus on television, water polo or anything that takes your fancy. William Carlos Williams once remarked: 'Anything is fit material for poetry.' You ought to be cautious, however, when dealing with the self-consciously 'poetic' subjects beginning writers often start off with, such as 'time', 'life's vale of tears', 'autumn sadness', 'my darling cat', 'fading beauty', '*chiaroscuro*', 'peace', and 'daffodils'. We haven't made this list up. We've come across appalling poems on these subjects in competitions. You may object that these are perfectly valid themes for poems, and it's true we could find good poems on our bookshelves dealing with some of these topics. It's not so much the subjects that are the problem, but the vagueness, abstraction and cliché they seem to encourage beginning writers to produce. The successful poems on our bookshelves will all have found fresh angles on their subjects.

People often ask us in workshops: 'Why must contemporary poetry be so relentlessly ugly?' (or some related form of this question) and our answer is that it isn't; we don't believe that good poetry ever sets out to be ugly. It sets out, rather, to transform and revive the commonplaceness of unlooked at surroundings. It grasps the mysterious logic behind ordinary, even banal situations. Poetry is to be found by seeing everyday things afresh.

Coming to grips with subject matter is really a matter of looking hard at it, and what is important is the degree of attention paid to detail. William Carlos Williams' infamous little poem 'The Red Wheelbarrow' is not just a piece of plain realism; it's a brilliant example of the art of selection, and the response of many readers (So what? How can that be a poem?) is simply a failure to respond to the delicate juxtaposition of detail. It's like a miniature canvas in an art gallery – you don't read it, you just stand in front of it and look at it.

> so much depends
> upon
>
> a red wheel
> barrow
>
> glazed with rain
> water
>
> beside the white
> chickens

This may seem so obvious as to be risible, but first of all, read the opening phrase again: 'so much depends'. Some people completely overlook this line, but the poem would be diminished without it. It emphasises the importance of a precisely focused image in a poem. It also suggests the uses to which a wheelbarrow can be put. Notice how the line-breaks, too, have the effect of controlling each step in the seeing process, mimicking the way your brain takes cognisance of the various details of an object or a scene, additively. First you see the colour red, then the wheel becomes part of a wheelbarrow, and the word 'water' being dropped down seems to add wetness to the rain. The white chickens finally locate the whole scene as a detail from a smallholding or a farm, and in this way the whole farm is suggested.

So accurate detail is the key to realist writing. But what happens when the writing goes beyond realism? We would argue that this is where well-observed detail is critical if you're going to carry the readers with you and get them to suspend disbelief. The writings of Franz Kafka come to mind immediately here. Think of his story 'Metamorphosis', with its preposterous opening sentence: 'Gregor Samsa awoke one morning from uneasy dreams to find himself transformed into a gigantic beetle.' How can you be expected to believe such a statement? Kafka gradually persuades you by the accumulation of detail. When Samsa, the beetle, falls off the bed and onto his back, he can't turn over again, just as beetles we've observed can't turn over. When he does get right-way-up again, he bangs his soft underbelly on the bed corner, gouging a deep wound, then when he reaches the wall, insect instinct takes over and he scurries happily across the ceiling, forgetting for the time being his predicament. After a few pages of this, his situation seems no more unnatural than waking up with a bad hangover.

MS: When I first encountered Kafka's work, I thought it was fantasy, but I realized later that although he was operating in non-realist territory, he was meticulously applying the methods of realism in the way we've outlined above. I began thinking of this type of work as 'alternative realism'.

Here's a contemporary poem that seems to us to work superbly in a similar way. Again, realist techniques convince us of the plausibility of a bizarre situation:

Popular Mechanics

The enormous engineering problems
You'll encounter by attempting to crucify yourself
Without helpers, pulleys, cogwheels,
And other clever mechanical contrivances –

In a small, bare, white room
With only a loose-legged chair
To reach the height of the ceiling –
Only a shoe to beat the nails in,

Not to mention being naked for the occasion –
So that each ribbon muscle shows,
Your left hand already spiked in,
Only the right to wipe the sweat with

To help yourself to a butt
From the overflowed ashtray,
You won't quite manage to light –
And the night coming, the whiz night.

Charles Simic

Even though both the poem and the Kafka story might be seen as weird, they both connect back to the world in which we live; they are both still earthed. In each case there is a distinctive angle on the subject matter. Each can be said to have a clear and individual vision.

The indirect, oblique approaches to the world these examples provide are sometimes found to be confusing by readers. 'Why can't you poets say what you mean?' they ask. The answer is that poetry is always and eternally restating common human problems and it can be very flat and boring to parade the obvious. The essence of poetry lies precisely in finding solutions to problems of expression through interesting uses of language and a fresh approach. You have to find a different way to present the basic human desires. The unexpected angle can make the reader see something as if for the first time.

At the very beginning, you won't have a recognizable vision, but you'll have your own distinctive personality out of which your vision will later come. How will you get there? Your technique is not yet formed, and you feel a natural uncertainty. It's quite a responsibility, after all, this 'writing a poem' business. You will be aware that the poet's 'voice' which so many people talk about, that immediately recognizable stamp of identity which seems to be the watermark in an assured poet's writing, is something you don't yet have. How can you develop it?

The answer is: with practice and hard work it will come. You must be determined not to be deflected from what you feel is the truth you want to express. You must take the world and everything in it as your subject matter, but concentrate on the detail, especially the intimate detail with which you're familiar. You'll need ambition and you'll need to be willing to accept that ambition can entertain small scale projects to begin with. You should seek out others doing the same thing and exchange criticism and commentary. There's no other way to improve. Above all, you shouldn't forget what Robert Graves called 'the reader over your shoulder', or what Seamus Heaney calls 'the second reader', i.e. everyone except you who will read what you write.

03

a challenge to the reader: groundwork exercises

We hope you've already been busy scribbling in your notebook. Whether you have or not, you'll need to keep it with you while you read this chapter because we're going to throw some groundwork exercises at you. Maybe you don't want to do exercises, maybe you just want to be spontaneous – but just as an improviser on the piano had to start out by doing five-finger exercises, you too will have to develop your technique. No one is born with it.

In the previous chapter we introduced poetry games. All writing exercises contain elements of games playing, and because you're usually asked to do them in a ridiculously short time, any serious expectation that you might produce something good is removed – or, to put it more bluntly, the blank page on which you do an exercise is not as terrifying as the blank page on which you are about to write this week's big poem. Writing done in an exercise, of course, is not the same as the writing you do for yourself – although, occasionally, a real poem can develop out of what you produce. The poet Michael Baldwin relates a story about the Romantics:

> *There are those who say nothing good will come of poets challenging one another, that the Muse does not like games. Keats, Leigh Hunt and Shelley once played such a game, by proposing a sonnet on a set subject, the Nile. Leigh Hunt and Keats each produced admired sonnets which were afterwards published. Shelley wrote 'Ozymandias'. Naturally he did as all poets do when they are midway through a writing exercise and find the Muse taking over: he let her. He allowed her to lead him from the rules a little, in this case the strict subject matter.*

Even when this doesn't happen, what an exercise will do is zero in on different aspects of the techniques that are necessary to the writing of poetry. Working through these exercises should give you a better chance of coming up with something worthwhile whenever you actually write.

EXERCISE 1 Spying

Let's start with a small-scale spying exercise. The history of literature is full of examples of poets who were spies; Christopher Marlowe was one. What is it that a poet and a spy have in common? The ability to observe, remember and record.

So try to be a spy for a day. Keep your eyes and ears open; make notes of anything you see and hear that's interesting or different.

Do this in a much more deliberate and focused way than you ordinarily would. Notice the everyday things around you, things you might pass without ordinarily looking at them. Look for odd juxtapositions and surprising sights. Have you been to the seaside and seen cows at the water's edge, or seen a surprising piece of graffiti scrawled across an advertisement? Listen to what people are saying, even if you have to eavesdrop. Trains and restaurants are good places to do this; it need be only the merest scrap of conversation.

MS: I was changing trains one day, for example. These two young women walked past me and I heard one say to the other, 'Me and Benjy, my teddy bear...' I heard nothing more, they were gone, but the phrase stuck in my head, and when I got home I wrote it in my notebook. Over the next few days I poked it with questions, asking in what other context someone might say that. I came up with a situation where a child is trying to get to sleep while her parents are having a party and making an awful racket, and that's what my poem 'Me and Benjy' is about.

Sometimes a tiny fragment like that can lead to a piece of writing. Here's a similar example:

JHW: I was standing in an empty Greek amphitheatre, trying to imagine what it must have been like to be a gladiator. My companion was watching me from the stalls. Then a crowd of Italian schoolchildren poured in, and began to practise their English on me. I used their questions ('Ello! All right, mister?' 'You like Liverpool? Rangers?' 'E mister? She lady yr wife?') in a poem called 'Teatro Greco', which isn't really about Greek amphitheatres at all, but about an illicit relationship.

What has *your* day of observation yielded? Pick out what seems to you to have the most possibilities and ask yourself questions about it. If it's a cow on a beach, how did it get there? Does it like being there? Does the farmer know? If it's a piece of graffiti, who wrote it and why? How did they get it that high up on the wall? Were they using stilts? When did they do it, and have they done this before? Answering these questions for yourself will start your piece of writing.

EXERCISE 2 Fly on the wall

Another observe-and-record exercise you can try is this: take your notebook and sit yourself down at an interesting vantage point – a harbour, the concourse of a railway station, a trendy outdoor café, or this could be just a looking-through-your-living-room-window exercise. Look at what is in front of you and try to record it as precisely as you can. Make yourself notice detail. Here are two examples from our own poems.

MS: I observed this out the window of my fourth floor flat in central London:

> But who's this back so soon
> wheeling her case alone
> up the concrete path, waiting
> at the lift door, stretching
> her back, till she disappears
> up to whichever floor
> her empty flat is on?

(from 'Calais')

JHW: This was written sitting in a deckchair in the garden of my wife's parents' house in Yugoslavia:

> I wish
> I were a fat
> dirty white & ginger Jack
> pussycat
> > prowling...
> or a bicycle
> leaned against the drainpipe
> in the sun
> > I wish
> > > upright behind the shed
> > > I had been that
> > > particular
> > > > green rake
> > > for at least 20 years/ no one
> > > > has raked with

(from 'A Corner of the Garden')

When you feel you've done enough recording, sift through what you have and select the most interesting and evocative details. Use these to kick off a piece of writing. Don't feel you have to stick to what you've observed. Speculating about what might be going on, or filling out the picture with imaginary details that would fit the details you've noted, will move your piece of writing into another dimension.

If you want to look at poems that clearly arise from observation, read *Terry Street* by Douglas Dunn, 'The Bight' and 'The Moose' by Elizabeth Bishop, and poems by C.K. Williams such as 'From My Window', 'The Dog' and 'Tar'.

EXERCISE 3 News items

Part of being alert to the world around you, of course, is being alert to what you read. Often it's not the headline stories which prove interesting, but the smaller quirkier items.

MS: Sometimes what you come across in a newspaper can frogmarch you to the writing desk. For example, I once saw a piece in a local newspaper about a sign pinned up in an office in Derry's City Cemetery saying, 'Those who don't believe in life after death should be here after closing time.' Later, in the correspondence column of the same issue, I came across a letter from a woman complaining about the flowers she put on her late husband's grave ending up on another grave. If this practice continued, she wrote, there would soon be a fresh corpse. How could you not want to write a poem after reading those two?

So go through some newspapers yourself, taking care not to overlook the smaller, tucked-away items, and pick out the odd story. Then set your imagination on it to see what piece of writing might emerge.

EXERCISE 4 Hell

Now we'd like to jump into a more speculative area and ask you what you think of when you think of hell. Devils with hooves and forked tails and plenty of nicely hissing flames, or is your idea of hell closer to home? For this exercise we would like you to locate your hell on this earth, in our time. No demonic clichés are permitted. Think of what you are afraid of, of situations that terrify you. Be as detailed as possible. Here's a stanza from George Macbeth's poem 'Laughter in Hell':

Imagine buttons
That won't go into their holes. Shoelaces
    You can't untie. Fancy going to bed
    In your brogues? And a zip
You need two hands for. A scenario.

The man stumps into a lavatory
    On his dog-headed stick. Leans the stick
In a corner. Leans on the wall
With one hand, and fumbles. Meanwhile, the piss,
    Growing tired of waiting, comes
With a gush. Over the seat,
Over the whole world
    It sometimes seems. And he has to wipe it up.

This is about the awful effects of the motor-neurone disease
from which George Macbeth eventually died, and is a very
obvious hell for the sufferer. Other hells might be more
imaginary – the thought of your partner leaving you, the threat
of nuclear holocaust, being involved in air or sea disasters, or
maybe having picked the right lottery numbers but forgetting to
buy the ticket. There are, unfortunately, many more hells than
those we have mentioned. We would like you to ransack your
imagination and come up with hells of your own, then write
about them in as detailed a way as possible.

What this does is force you to **show** your hell, rather than have
us take your word for it that it is hell. This is an important
element in writing poetry – it's always better to show than to
tell. Even storytellers bring out the dramatic possibilities of their
stories through the use of particular detail and incident rather
than descriptions of emotions. We often ask people in writing
courses to describe orally a time when they were frightened.
This introduces a narrative element in which the narrative
emphasizes the 'showing'. By the time the groups have finished
their stories, no listener has any doubt that the more persuasive
speakers, at least, have experienced fear. We do not need to be
told that the speaker has been frightened, we know from what
we have heard. If you, as readers, keep this dictum *show, don't
tell* in mind, many of the points we will be making in the
remainder of this book will be clearer for you when you come
across them.

What points of technique will you have been focusing on as you
do these exercises? Well, for a start you'll have learned to keep
your eyes and ears open and to make notes about what you see
in a much more scrupulously attentive way than you might
ordinarily have thought of doing. Just as a photographer has to
learn to notice the cactus growing out of his sitter's head and
move the cactus out of sight, you'll have learned to register the
kind of detail most people simply fail to observe. As a

consequence of this, you'll not only begin to notice things more acutely, but also – something you have to learn to do – how to select the most interesting and evocative detail, the detail which seems to carry something of the whole picture in itself. If you've managed this, the next stage is to start speculating about what's going on – why is that man sitting on the roof of that car? – and try to fill out the picture or the story with something that might fit. Asking yourself questions about what you've noted will help you to do this. Through developing your faculty of observation, you'll learn to put your trust in the carefully selected detail; you'll begin to recognize when enough is enough, or, even better, when less is more, and this will help you to bring off the effects you want without spelling things out too much.

04

getting started: working arrangements

Where is the best place to write? Your own study is a good idea but not everyone has one.

JHW: I do. MS: I don't!

Somewhere silent, but that's difficult to come by. We have worked at poems on train or boat journeys. Some writers go off to artists' colonies to finish books, and others do most of their writing at workshops or on writing courses. Oscar Wilde is a famous example of someone who wrote poetry while in prison. We hear from writers who've worked there that increasing numbers of today's prisoners are writing. The captain of at least one U-Boat during the Second World War instigated regular poetry competitions to keep his crew from being bored. In Anthony Burgess' *Enderby* novels, the eponymous poet writes all his poems while sitting on the toilet. The fact is that you can work anywhere. Be prepared, wherever you are, to jot lines down when they come to you.

In the last chapter we advocated using a notebook that you can carry around with you, and don't forget your pen.

JHW: I always use a Harley Davidson fountain pen. The Australian poet Robert Gray introduced me to them. They're good for riding poems down long highways.

Most poets still like to draft by hand, but laptop computers are becoming increasingly popular because of their mobility. Drafting with a typewriter has the disadvantage that every new version has to be retyped, and it's for this reason that people who draft by hand wait until they feel a poem is finished before typing it up. Some writers worry that, if they type a poem up before it's finished, they'll ruin it – it'll 'set' prematurely and they won't be able to change it. However you draft is your business, but the final version should be produced on a typewriter or word processor. This is especially relevant if you're thinking of sending your poem to a magazine or into a poetry competition. The way in which your poem is presented will be taken as a measure of your seriousness.

The amount of time you will need to produce a poem varies enormously from writer to writer. Some people have the mistaken idea that poems, because they're usually short, can be dashed off in five minutes.

JHW: I was once at a poetry reading in Berlin given by the British poet D. J. Enright. After the reading a German professor of English literature asked him, 'Have you written a poem since you arrived in Berlin?' Enright replied, 'Well, I

only got off the plane two hours ago.' The professor smiled. 'Come now, Mr Enright,' he said. 'How long does it take you to write a poem?'

There is no answer to that question, and a professor of literature ought to have known that. Some poems get completed in a matter of hours, others take five years. You wouldn't know from looking at them which was which. However long your poems take, you'll need to organize your time. That means finding gaps and spaces in your busy schedule. Holidays afford an obvious opportunity to get some writing done. We mentioned trains earlier – the advantage there is that you're stuck in the one place for hours. Some people like to get up early in the morning and write for a few hours before going to work. (There's a popular belief that your mind is at its sharpest in the morning, and the most productive work gets done then.)

Don't feel, though, that unless you end up with a completed poem in these periods of writing, you've failed. George Barker said: 'Writing a poem is like having a long-distance telephone call with someone on a bad line.' Most likely you will bring away from these sessions nothing more than scraps, images, isolated phrases or combinations of words you like the sound of. All these can be worked on further at a later time.

What you will find, to begin with, is that your work is full of false starts. You will not be focused. You may not have a clear idea of what you're doing, but you'll need to keep writing until an idea begins to gel. The process is analogous to a photographic print taking form in the developing tank – at first you can see only blurs of white, grey and black, blocks of contrasting material which finally cohere into a face or a landscape.

EXERCISE 5 Two versions of an image

To test this process of gradual focusing, here is an exercise we would like you to try. We have suggested previously that a poem is more likely to begin with an image or phrase, rather than with an idea. Let's put this into practice.

The image we are giving you comes in two versions, rural or urban, in case you have a strong preference for either. First the rural image: dusk, a deserted country road, and suddenly goats. The urban alternative is this: dusk again, a long empty corridor at the end of which a human figure suddenly appears. That's all we're giving you – a choice of two related images. Pick one and focus on it. Try as hard as you can to visualize the situation. Ask yourself questions about it, in the way we suggested at the end of the previous chapter, and speculate on what might be going on. Establish a context in which that image might be seen. (This will involve thinking of what happens before and after.) Try not to use too much conscious control when you do this – let yourself go.

EXERCISE 6 Houdini

You might be alarmed by how little you had to go on in that last exercise. This second exercise we want you to try comes with more rules – and rules, whether self-imposed or traditional (the sonnet, for example), are an important element in poetry. You may think rules are a hindrance, that they stop you from getting what you want on paper, but actually they help you to get beyond the first easy thoughts, to reach further and get to something more interesting. Some would put it more strongly. When W. B. Yeats was asked where he got his ideas from, he said 'The rhymes'.

There's a famous anecdote about the Irish poet Austin Clarke meeting Robert Frost at a reception in Dublin. After a while Frost asked Clarke what kind of poems he wrote. Clarke replied, 'I load myself with chains and try to get out of them.' He never loaded himself with chains such as the ones we're going to give you in an exercise we call the 'Houdini exercise'.

First you get five words: **plain, shadow, mountain, light, glass**.

Your task is to produce a piece of writing in two stanzas, each stanza of which contains the five words and as many other words in the English language as you want.

There are two conditions:

1 The two stanzas must be two parts of one whole, and not two separate entities.
2 What's written must contrive to make sense, yet be as surprising as possible.

The piece should be written out in lines, as a poem. Ideally, the two stanzas should be the same length. The five words are deliberately chosen so that inventiveness is needed to avoid clichéd writing. You will notice that some of the words can be nouns, verbs or adjectives and can therefore be used in one form in the first stanza, and in another form in the second. Words can occur as different parts of speech – for example, 'light' could be a noun or a verb, it could be singular or plural, or even embedded in another word (e.g. enlighten), as long as it is clearly there. A word with a different spelling but the same sound can also be used (e.g. 'plain' and 'plane').

The fact that five words are given is a real plus for the inexperienced writer. The page is not blank. The words are giving their shadowy suggestions. The beginnings of a story, or a situation, are forming. If people are stuck or hesitant we urge them to pick on one of the words and tease it into revealing something – prod it, turn it over, ask questions such as:

- Is it plane or plain?
- Whose or what's shadow?
- What mountain – what's going on there?
- How can I get a fresh approach, a surprising angle?

One of the most common faults to look out for is vagueness, or lack of focus. This exercise involves the building up of the piece of writing, detail by detail, until it's almost three-dimensional. As this is a process that should go on in some form or another – consciously or unconsciously – in all areas of creative writing, it is an important one to practise.

You should spend no more than 30 minutes doing this. The piece you'll come up with won't be a finished poem, but it will have something distinctive about it – what we call the 'essence' – so think of it as a starting point that may be redrafted and crafted into a poem.

MS: Here is one of the many texts I have come up with while running this exercise in workshops – very often writers try to lead by example and join in the exercises they set.

> He lay on the verandah, holding
> the magnifying glass
> over the sugar mountain he'd made
> that morning, asking the sunlight
> to make toffee
> (which he preferred plain)
> cursing the shadows
> the clouds dropped
> like a spoiling curtain.

> His mother brought him a glass
> of iced coffee, shaking
> her blonde head that the light
> played on, while his father
> at that moment
> (unknown to him) struggled to coax
> his spluttering aircraft
> over the mountain
> the plane's shadow grew on.

The poem that developed out of this is the first poem in my book *Cacti*. It's called 'Sugar'. I should add that it's the only occasion I got what I considered to be a poem from this exercise.

There are obvious contrivances in the above draft – the chains of the five words and the conditions of the exercise are hampering naturalness – but there is an essence there: the tropical, probably colonial setting; the solitary child; the hint of menace. Given the chance to develop this piece, these are areas on which you might concentrate. Through the constraints and rigours of the 'chains', the imagination is unlocked and images are suggested that one might not necessarily have even considered in the initially hasty process of construction.

You can stop at this stage or, preferably, you can try to isolate the essence of your piece – it might be a single image – and develop it into a second piece of writing, free from the constraints of the five words. The process of drafting, of trying to develop an idea, of exploring language and form and images, is one we encourage strongly and will come back to again in this book.

EXERCISE 7 The rules

An easier exercise in using rules is one which allows you to invent your own. It's perhaps more fun to do this with a partner or in a group, but you can also work by yourself if no one else is about or willing to be press-ganged into participating. First of all, determine the line-length of your poem. Is it going to be 14 lines, or 20 – how many people are there in your group? You can now invent a rule for each line to determine its content or shape. For example, line 1 could begin with the words 'I wish'. Line 2 might have to include a crow. Line 3 might have to rhyme with the preceding line. Line 4 might have to include a foreign word, etc. As you can see, the rules can be very wide-ranging and different from each other – some can be language-oriented and some can be content-based. There is plenty of room for playfulness. This is a good warm-up exercise for the beginning of a writing course as it helps to overcome the fear of getting started. It is therefore a very useful exercise for teachers who are encouraging students to start writing.

JHW: The last time I used this exercise was at an Arvon course, with 20 students. Each member of the group devised three rules and these were then voted on until we had a set of 20 altogether. There was a good deal of hilarity at some of the suggestions, but people usually proved to have enough foresight to vote for the most workable ones.

EXERCISE 8 Backwards

We'd like to round off the exercises in this chapter with one that draws on elements of both the previous writing activities. It was inspired by the kind of calamity that can befall any poet, if they're not careful enough, as the following anecdote will illustrate:

MS: I woke up one morning with a poem fully formed in my head, but I was too lazy to get out of bed and write it down. Then the poem started to evaporate, line by line, but I jumped out of bed and caught it by the toe – I had the last line, 'The smell and colour of petroleum', and spent the rest of the week working backwards to recover the poem, although it was undoubtedly inferior to the one I had had in my head.

Here are some lines you can consider to be last lines that have lost the rest of their poems. Can you work backwards until you have a whole poem?

- 'Eating red carnations by the dozen'
- 'Singing, she pedalled over the moonlit bridge'
- 'Back to his underwater home'
- 'And roared for hours at the moon'
- 'To stand, staring into the water'
- 'Then parachuted, roaring, into a bonfire'

Having the last line with which to work involves a very different process than having the first one. The last line of a poem should feel inevitable; everything leads to it. You'll find that, although the possibilities are limitless, the inevitability of your destination is always at the back of your mind, and you keep having to adjust your ideas to this, if that last line is going to be convincing.

How can you get yourself going on an exercise like this? You can start by asking yourself questions again. Take the line 'Singing, she pedalled over the moonlit bridge', and answer the following: Who is she? Why is she singing? What is she singing? Where is she going? What happened immediately before this? You should find out more than you'll use: this will help you to select the most relevant and telling details. You shouldn't use all of this detail, but whatever you don't use will give you a more rounded picture of your character and the situation. Here, again, the principle of **show, don't tell** helps you to avoid flabbiness and redundancy. Narrative in a poem often works austerely, by leaving a lot up to the reader to fill in.

MS: I was doing a reading at a writing course tutored by Simon Armitage and Beryl Bainbridge. After I read a poem about someone being left blue taps in a will, Beryl said: 'You poets are all the same. When you tell a story you leave half of it out. For example, that line "I hoped the taps fitted". I want to know whether they fitted or not.' I told her I couldn't care less if they fitted. That was up to the reader to decide.

The procedures which these exercises involve – focusing on an image or phrase, applying a system of rules to a number of words, inventing a narrative to fit an intriguing sentence – are all useful techniques you can use to start yourself writing. Some people think you have to be inspired to write a poem, but inspiration is rarely a sudden flash of illumination or a vision. It's more likely to be small scale and concrete, a detail which catches your attention and intrigues you. Developing a poem from this detail involves a lot of graft and imagination, and graft is what becoming a poet is all about. Don't be too ready to believe the much-quoted remark 'Poets are born, not made', and assume they're talking about you.

05

I gotta use words when I talk to you

> *I hoped to write poems as pliant as conversation, so clear a listener might get every word, and I would... Life Studies is heightened conversation, not a concert.*

from Collected Prose by Robert Lowell

Talk? Conversation? Wasn't our subject writing?

Robert Frost said:

> *There are two kinds of language – the spoken language and the written language... words exist in the mouth not in books!*

Of course words exist in books – the fact that you're reading this proves that – but Frost means you should use the living language that people speak when you write poetry and not some artificial 'poetic' language.

> *The vocabulary may be what you please, though I like it not too literary; but the tones of voice must be caught fresh and fresh from life.*

Here is the opening to one of Robert Frost's most famous poems, 'Birches':

> When I see birches bend to left and right
> Across the lines of straighter darker trees,
> I like to think some boy's been swinging them.

The language here has the directness of someone engaging you in conversation. The natural word order of English has been kept to, there are no inversions or unusual words. Look at the colloquial ease of the third line, the simple use of the contraction 'boy's' instead of the more formal variant 'boy has' and how right this feels both rhythmically and tonally. Of course, to sound natural and easy requires art and is deceptively difficult to do, but through observation and practice it can be learned.

A fresh use of language needn't always be quite so straightforward. E. E. Cummings is a good example of a poet whose language is often unconventional, even radical, yet it always echoes the patterns of everyday speech:

> Buffalo Bill's
> defunct
> who used to
> ride a watersmooth-silver
>
> stallion

and break onetwothreefourfive pigeonsjustlikethat

                                          Jesus

he was a handsome man

                        and what i want to know is

how do you like your blue-eyed boy
Mister Death

The diction here is artfully simple, yet surprising. Alongside the colloquial 'Jesus, he was a handsome man' you get the romanticism of 'watersmooth-silver stallion', the tough guy talking to 'Mister Death', the deflationary use of the word 'defunct' and the playfulness of 'onetwothreefourfive pigeonsjustlikethat'. These rapid and startling changes of register are nevertheless absolutely easy to follow and understand.

It's worth saying a word or two here about 'register'. This refers to the convention that different situations require different kinds of language. You wouldn't address your brother in the same way you would address your boss. If you met your neighbour in the street and she said, 'I'm so irritated with Fred; he's gone and hanged himself,' you'd think something didn't sound right. E. E. Cummings uses the pedantic word 'defunct' in Buffalo Bill to create an effect of irreverence. It's a good illustration of the way the language of poetry often gives a little twist to the language we normally speak. Notice that this is not some kind of overblown artificiality, as people often imagine poetry should be.

You'll need to read widely to see how poets achieve their effects through changes of register and other linguistic surprises. This will help you to develop the sensitivity to language you'll need if you're going to control it to expressive effect. Particular poems you might look at for the different ways each uses language are:

- 'Balloons' by Sylvia Plath
- 'Autumn Begins in Martins Ferry, Ohio' by James Wright
- 'The Future' by Les Murray
- 'Johann Joachim Quanz's Five Lessons' by W.S. Graham

As you read, notice how well-sustained the manner of address is, how there's no bumpiness or awkwardness, how the diction feels right and is of a piece with the content. If the diction of a poem is not right, the effect will be murkiness, lack of precision and inappropriateness.

Very often it comes down to a matter of the concrete versus the vague. Most poems that fail are only half there. The writer has not imagined well enough and is content with what came too easily. Sometimes if you stop and don't write the first thing that comes into your head, something better will come into it.

What do we mean by 'imagining well'?

MS: I was working in a school, getting children to write. I wrote the names for various feelings on pieces of paper and gave one to each child, asking him or her to illustrate an occasion when they might have felt that way. Don't just say: 'I was unhappy,' I told them. 'Try to imagine what you did when you were unhappy. Imagine what you said. Try to remember specifically what it was that made you feel that way.' One boy wrote: 'I was frustrated because my mother had bought something for my brother's birthday and I wanted to tell him about it, but I wasn't allowed to.' 'That's too vague,' I said. 'What something?' 'A toy,' he said. 'What kind of a toy?' I asked. 'A teddy bear,' he said.

'Something' is the kind of word you use when you can't think or can't be bothered to think of the word you *really* want. 'Teddy bear' is better than 'toy' because it's more distinctive and brings the illustration into focus. It also narrows down the age of the brother – in other words the concreteness of the example supplies more in the way of specific context. As George Orwell said:

> *When you think of a concrete object you think wordlessly and have to hunt around for the right words.*

He also had this to say:

> *As soon as certain topics are raised, the concrete melts into the abstract and no one seems able to think of turns of speech that are not hackneyed.*

In our experience, this comment applies particularly to the bad poems we come across in competitions and workshops – those poems that deal with subjects like 'time', 'life's vale of tears', 'autumn sadness' and so on (see Chapter 02). Many people still think high-flown, abstract words give greater resonance to their writing, but vagueness is always a consequence of using abstract words. We would go further: abstractions should be avoided because they verge on the meaningless. If you think of the word 'sadness', for example, all you get is a blur in your head. If, on the other hand, you ransack your memory and fix on an experience that was a truly sad one, and tell people about this experience, your listeners will not have to take your word for it that you experienced sadness. They'll know because you've shown them.

It would be silly for us to claim there are no good poems that use abstractions (T. S. Eliot's *Four Quartets*, W. H. Auden's 'Lay Your Sleeping Head My Love' among many others). What we *are* saying is that it isn't a good idea to use them unless you're an experienced poet with a developed voice. Think of them as being in an out-of-bounds territory from which you can reclaim them warily as you gain in confidence. Seamus Heaney, for example, talking in a newspaper interview about his book *Seeing Things* said this:

> *I found myself using words like 'spirit' and 'soul', words which I'd disallowed myself for a long time because there was so much prejudice against them in my literary education. Then you realise that's attenuating, and that there's a space that's covered by them.*

We've suggested there are good reasons for this literary prejudice. It goes without saying that Seamus Heaney has reached a stage in his development where he can control such language, but too often the unskilled poet, led by feeling, is rather like an apprentice bus driver who loses control of the vehicle. 'Good writing,' as Ezra Pound said, 'is perfect control.'

A few do's and don'ts from Ezra Pound

- Poetry should be written at least as well as prose.
- Language is an instrument for expressing and not for concealing or preventing thought.
- Go in fear of abstractions.
- Use no superfluous word, no adjective, which does not reveal something.
- Don't use such an expression as 'dim lands *of peace*'. It dulls the image. It mixes an abstraction with the concrete. It comes from the writer's not realizing that the natural object is always the *adequate* symbol.
- A narrative is all right so long as the narrator sticks to words as simple as dog, horse, sunset.

What all this implies is: it's always better to make a particular and specific statement rather than a vague and imprecise one. Better 'the red wheelbarrow glazed with rainwater beside the white chickens' than 'farm implements get wet if left out'. Generalization is the last stop before abstraction.

One of the main ways in which we experience the reality of the world, in our everyday lives, is through our senses. Using them can help us get beyond abstraction and vagueness in our writing.

MS: I became really conscious of this when I led a series of workshops for visually impaired writers. The fact that for most of the participants one of the senses was not functioning properly, if at all, made me look for poems where the other senses were prominent. The selection of poems I accumulated was evidence of how crucial the appropriate use of sensory perception is to good writing. Even when the visual sense came into some of the poems I'd chosen (because it's difficult to keep that one out), it was not a problem for my participants because they said they imagined what a visual sense was like, what different colours were, etc.

One of the poems listened to in those workshops (spoken by the dead poet himself, on a crackly record from the Poetry Library's archives) was the following, by Theodore Roethke:

My Papa's Waltz

The whiskey on your breath
Could make a small boy dizzy;
But I hung on like death:
Such waltzing was not easy.

We romped until the pans
Slid from the kitchen shelf;
My mother's countenance
Could not unfrown itself.

The hand that held my wrist
Was battered on one knuckle;
At every step you missed
My right ear scraped a buckle.

You beat time on my head
With a palm caked hard by dirt,
Then waltzed me off to bed
Still clinging to your shirt.

Just look at how the senses are being used there. The smell of the whiskey, the sound of those pans, the feel of the buckle on the ear, or the beating time on the head, or even the clinging to the shirt, and look at how the mother's reaction is given – visually, like a shot from a film. Together, they go a long way towards creating the vivid, dramatic quality of the poem, and are responsible for its clarity and complete lack of vagueness. The poem is imbued, of course, with strong human emotions – the mixture of fear and love in the boy, the anxiety or anger in the mother, but nowhere are any of those abstract terms used. The poet knows that the concrete images he's chosen, with the help of the senses, will show the abstract emotions, and he doesn't have to step in and tell the reader.

EXERCISE 9 The garden of panic

A workshop exercise we do to help people escape from vagueness and abstraction is to take two envelopes, one containing slips of paper with the names of domestic locations (rooms, mainly, but also a few surprises), and the other containing abstract words. Each participant takes one slip blind from each envelope. They might get 'garden' and 'panic', or 'bedroom' and 'madness', or 'wardrobe' and 'lust', etc. We then ask them to write about the Garden of Panic, the Bedroom of Madness, or the Wardrobe of Lust, showing the panic, the madness or the lust in the details they choose. They are not allowed to use their abstract word, or any other abstract word, although they are allowed to use the domestic location word. However it's not enough to simply write 'garden'. They need to remember it's not their garden at home; it's an imagined garden where panic reigns. They need to ask themselves questions: what *is* panic? In what situations might they experience it? Is it slow or sudden? What does it *feel* like? Can they think of a concrete way of showing how panic feels?

Devise two lists of your own and pick one word at random from each column. Remember that the Garden of Panic is a place where something happened, or is happening, or is going to happen. It's not, perhaps, a happy place, and you'll have to present it that way (although there is always room for humour in your poems, don't forget). Before attempting your poem, it might be an idea to cast your eyes over the Roethke poem again and think about how you might use the senses to make that abstract word concrete to the reader.

Another weakness of careless or unfocused writers is a tendency to rely on clichés and hackneyed expressions, instead of trying to find a fresh and interesting way of saying what they want to say. Frost said:

Clichés and jaded diction carry no insight because they freeze meaning, allowing the mind no new feats of association; an idea has to be a little new to be at all true and if you say a thing three times it ceases to be so.

How can you develop a strategy that pushes you into finding new ways of saying things? How can you develop in yourself a cliché detector? Flann O'Brien used to stand stale expressions on their heads to release their comic potential:

What will your man some day come into?
    His own.

To what should you put your shoulder?
    The wheel.

Look at what the poet Allen Ginsberg does with that rather macho second cliché. He ends his poem 'America' with the line:

America, I'm putting my queer shoulder to the wheel.

In other words, a good way of rehabilitating the cliché is to subvert it. This can also be done, as Roger McGough demonstrates, by taking it literally. His poem 'Shooting Stars', for example, is about being

out here every night
rifle in hand, picking them off.
Trouble is, they're fearless. Kill one
and at the speed of light another takes its place.

This has the effect of making you look again at that trite expression 'shooting stars'. So, a phrase which you've used or read countless times without thinking suddenly acquires a witty twist. Look, as well, at what is being done with the phrase 'speed of light'. If we take some clichés literally and see what effect that produces, the humorous possibilities become immediately apparent. Try to visualize 'grist to the mill' for example, or 'no flies on him'. Do you know what 'grist' is, and what effect it would have on a mill? Is everyone else covered in flies?

EXERCISE 10 Clichés

Here are five common clichés.

- Every dog has his day
- A bull in a china shop

- A game not worth the candle
- Have no axe to grind
- When all's said and done

Can you subvert these expressions and make them live again? What do the dogs do on their day? How did the bull get in the shop? Is candle the local currency here? What kind of game could that be? Where has the axe gone? What's going to be ground instead? What exactly has been said and done?

At the beginning of this chapter we talked about the spoken language and suggested you might aim to capture some of its directness and naturalness in the language in which you write. Another aspect of spoken language, however, is the sound it makes and one of the best ways of checking the language you're using in a poem is by reading it aloud. Yeats did this; his wife George has written about him walking over and back on the floor above, reciting his poems as he wrote them. Ezra Pound, who acted as Yeats' secretary for a while, recalls him back in 1913, humming his poems to himself when they stayed at a cottage in Sussex:

> the noise in the chimney
> as it were the wind in the chimney
>   but was in reality Uncle William
> downstairs composing

(from *The Pisan Cantos*)

What was Yeats listening for, as he chanted there? Certainly for any bumpiness in the rhythm, or jolting dislocations in the syntax. He would have been testing the momentum of what he had written, and hearing whether it was smoothly sustained or whether it faltered. He would have weighed the balance of the phrasing, and listened for one phrase echoing another. If his concentration had wandered during composition, he might have noticed a cliché or a jarring sound. He would have heard if the phrasing closed effectively, or was left in suspension – effects like lifting and falling tones.

It's important to remember that a poem breaks down, essentially, into three different units: the line, the stanza (if it's divided into stanzas) and the poem as a unified whole. Each of these must justify itself as a unit, in the sense that you need to feel there's good reason for this arrangement. The kind of thing you'll be listening for, then, as you mutter your poem at the bathroom wall, is a feeling of balance and roundedness in those different units of the poem. We might sum this effect up as 'cadence'. An ability to control cadence is what is meant when poets are described as having 'a good ear'.

You can check what we mean by this by reading aloud, to yourself, or anybody else who's prepared to listen, this first stanza of a famous poem by Auden:

> Consider this and in our time
> As the hawk sees it or the helmeted airman:
> The clouds rift suddenly – look there
> At cigarette-end smouldering on a border
> At the first garden party of the year.
> Pass on, admire the view of the massif
> Through plate-glass windows of the Sport Hotel;
> Join there the insufficient units
> Dangerous, easy, in furs, in uniform,
> And constellated at reserved tables,
> Supplied with feelings by an efficient band,
> Relayed elsewhere to farmers and their dogs
> Sitting in kitchens in the stormy fens.

(from Poems 1927–1931)

Although the noise of a poem is important, you mustn't become preoccupied with sound to the exclusion of other things; that would be like a football team so committed to attack it neglects defence. Robert Lowell breaks down the different elements that go to make up a poem in these terms:

> *Meaning varies in importance from poem to poem, and from style to style, but it is always only a strand and an element in the brute flow of composition. Other elements are pictures that please or thrill for themselves, phrases that ring for their music or carry some buried suggestions. For all this the author is an opportunist, throwing whatever comes to hand into his feeling for start, continuity, contrast, climax and completion. It is imbecile for him not to know his intentions, and unsophisticated for him to know too explicitly and fully.*

So, a poem can be seen as a little word-machine, in which all the components must be in perfect working order. Only at the level of its language can a poem be critically and usefully evaluated. Anyone ambitious enough to want to write a poem will need to give a great deal of thought and care to the words they use. In our experience of workshops, and judging competitions, it is at the level of language that most poems fail.

06

letters, alphabets and lists

The words we use exist in th.
we write them down we use
referred to as letters; letters spel.
therein lies a problem: literature is
way, or about finding quite (or ne.
much of our day to day conversatio.
rehearses commonplaces. How can you
English vocabulary to find different wa
want to say, and perhaps, in doing so, fi.
Well, you could, for example, impose restr.
them. Take the lipogram. This is a literary
certain letter is disallowed from the text. Th.
Georges Perec, wrote a novel from which th. .s
excluded, (*La Disparition*). It was translated into ...nder
the title *A Void*, by Gilbert Adair. Many of the ...ewers in
France who praised the book on its first appearance failed to
notice the vanished *e*, which is interesting if you consider that
the masculine definite article in French is *le*. Perec only
disallowed one letter, but by doing so, he set himself
considerable problems of expression. Solving them, no doubt,
was a voyage of discovery. You could disallow more than one; a
mock press conference with Ronald Wilson Reagan, using for
the president's replies only the 11 different letters of his name,
begins like this:

> **Q.** *What is your reaction to critics of your Presidency?*
> *How does a former actor feel about the awesome*
> *responsibilities of the Presidency, with all the world his*
> *stage?*

> **A.** *Derision or a dressing-down is as degrading as*
> *dredging sewage alongside a noose on a gallows ladder. I*
> *ignore; no one sees a lone leader's real sorrows.*

In fact, the restrictions that can be imposed on the use of letters
are limitless. You could insist on the same letter appearing in
every word of a text. Or, in acrostical writing (for an example
of this, see Exercise 30, Sex and Death, page 109) you could
insist that an obligatory letter be placed at the beginning (or
end) of each line of a poem. Or you could write a poem for your
beloved using only words that are formed by the letters of
his/her name.

But the most powerful letter-engine we have is the alphabet. It
contains 26 letters and all of us learned it when we were
children from a simple abecedary, a process that was both visual
and oral. Powerful? The alphabet? If we were to say: the literary

44 letters, alphabet lists

et are countless, you might start to
poet, Edwin Morgan, in an introduction
lphabetical and Letter Poems (edited by Peter
the traditional unifying factor of a repeated
and the underlying sense of huge permutations are
ent in such a manner as to suggest that power, and not
merely play, is a concern of alphabets. Creative power can be
expected to manifest itself from the combinative developments
and experiments of 20 or 30 letters, yet there is also, and it can
still be felt, a ritualistic power in the alphabet, very ancient,
transmitted to children, used by poets and composers and
advertising men...'

EXERCISE 11 Simple abecedary

A way to tap into that power and begin exploring what a simple
alphabet can unleash is to compose your own, on the model of
a child's abecedary. Begin 'A is for...' and continue. Use simple
concrete objects that could be illustrated for a book. Do it as
quickly as you can.

EXERCISE 12 Grown up abecedary

Now try the same task using all the vocabulary at your disposal.
You can use everyday words, unusual words, any words you
like, but you must do it quickly, without too much forethought,
and the words should be native to *your* vocabulary.

EXERCISE 13 Alpha poem

The following poem by Edwin Morgan is offered to you as a
model of what can be done with the simple structures of the
alphabet.

Alpha

A is for atlas, but I am not in it.
B is for beehive, but I have the honey.
C is for cheesecloth, but I shall not materialise.
D is for Darwin, but I am a mutation.
E is for ecstasy, beyond your apprehension.
F is for fools – how are you, my friends?
G is for gunfire, all in the day's work.
H is for high altitudes, for some.
I is for invisibility – see?
J is for jailer, but mine is not born yet.

K is for knell, but mine is not tolled yet.
L is for law, but I have none.
M is for mantra, but mine is silent.
N is for nature, but I am beyond it.
O is for owls, but wisdom is for me.
P is for plot, and that you have not got.
Q is for quick, and you had better be.
R is for rust on your trap – look!
S is for sweetness I stole from the stars.
T is for truth, terrible as fire.
U is for untruth, an old yellow tooth.
V is for veil, and mine is of iron.
W is for war, but I do not advise it.
X is for xerox, but I have no copy.
Y is for you as you sink in your grave.
Z is for zero, and that's all your secret.

This has come a long way from a child's alphabet. The tone is superior, arrogant, and menacing. Perhaps the title is meant to suggest the dominance of an alpha male – someone you wouldn't want to go on a date with. Notice how Morgan has hijacked the alphabet for his own devilish purposes. Can you now take the alphabet as your starting point and slant it your way? You don't have to take the tone from the example we've given you; use it to explore a different nexus of feeling and subject matter. It could be erotic, self-pitying, insane, superstitious – whatever. As Edwin Morgan says: 'Depending on the purposes for which letters in sequence are employed, a surprising range of human experience seems to be willing or anxious to cling to this fish-ladder.'

Finally, we'd like to point out that the alphabet can be used (is used) as a fundamental structuring device for anything. The Hebrew bible is alphabetically organized. Anglo-Saxon and Icelandic poems alphabetized their world. You can use the alphabet to list kinds of disaster, types of animals, the attributes of your loved one, the nature of love, Gods and Goddesses, the names of your friends (and enemies), whatever you can think of. The poet Peter Redgrove wrote an 'Alphaladybet' (which is an alphabetical list of women's names, followed by surreal descriptions of them) and a 'Trashabet', which carries at its beginning the following citation: '*Wabi* is the spirit of poverty... appreciation of what most consider to be the commonplace... something hitherto ignored being seen for the precious thing it is', and then goes on to list 26 commonplace and overlooked things. For example:

'**B** is for buttons, which are a cross between numbers and persons. Snip a button from Joey's shirt, and it *is* Joey. Snip six buttons, and you have spots to arrange in an equilibrated pattern of Joey. I possess buttons stolen from everybody I have ever known; they are as good as photographs. I have filled four large grocery boxes with the buttons, and I recognise each one personally.'

That fine and underrated poet, Asa Benveniste, wrote *The Atoz Formula*. The novelist and poet John Updike wrote a poem which uses the alphabet to characterize, adjectivally, all 26 passengers on a bus. The novelist Walter Abish wrote a novel called *Alphabetical Africa* in which the first chapter has only words beginning with A, the second allows A and B, the third A, B and C, until he reaches the middle chapter which allows all the letters of the alphabet, and then the procedure is reversed until he comes back full circle to A. Yes, this is wordplay – games playing. But do remember Edwin Morgan's words: 'power, and not merely play, are a concern of alphabets'. We'd say that all of these literary efforts have tapped into alphabetic power. The possibilities are endless, and we'd like to suggest that you explore any that occur to you.

The alphabet, essentially, is a list of letters. And the list, as a structural device, is often found behind some of the most sophisticated poetry. You may think that the mundane list is too basic a form to hang a poem on. But take a quick look through this book and see how many of the poems have elements of the list about them. If we may direct you to Anna Akmatova's 'Three things enchanted him…' on page 103, for example. Or James Wright's 'Lying in a Hammock at William Duffy's Farm in Pine Island, Minnesota', on page 50. We do not give you all of Michael Ondaatje's 'Sweet Like a Crow' on page 55 but enough, hopefully, to give you the idea that the poem is simply a list of similes. On page 171 there is the beginning of Kit Wright's 'The Magic Box', and our imitative 'The Bad Box'. Even George Mackay Browne's 'Hamnavoe Market', on page 73–74 has, as we say in the discussion of the poem, the structure of a list.

The ancients knew all about the usefulness of lists, with regard to poetry. Anglo-Saxon verse was full of them, something Auden noticed and learned from, most clearly perhaps in his majestic 'Spain'. Early poetry in Irish consisted often of a list of metaphors. The recently deceased Irish poet, Michael Hartnett (who wrote in both Irish and English) draws on this for his poem 'Death of an Irishwoman' which ends in this way:

She was a summer dance at the crossroads.
She was a card game where a nose was broken.
She was a song that nobody sings.
She was a house ransacked by soldiers.
She was a language seldom spoken.
She was a child's purse, full of useless things.

What is it about a list that makes it good for poetry? Well, as these lines show, the items in a list tend to be very concrete and specific. Furthermore, the act of listing has an objectivity about it that is very beneficial for writing.

EXERCISE 14 The list

We want now to introduce an exercise that'll get you writing a list poem. To start with, perhaps we can mention, but not quote, a poem by Neil Rollinson called 'A List of Requirements for the End of the World'. The title itself is enough to start you making your own list in your head. What the poem does is list what the poet thinks he'll need in the few days before the cataclysm – beginning with a barrel of beer and two glasses, continuing through marital aids and 'a girl I've never met before' until it gets to the ending where radiation comes through the window in a day or so. The tone of the poem is funny and somewhat perverse, until the ending reminds the reader of the grim situation that's being envisaged.

A second poem, by Robin Robertson, is very different, and here it is, in full:

At Dusk

Walking through the woods
I saw these things:
a cat, lying, looking at me;
a red hut I could not enter;
the white grin of the snared fox;
the spider in a milk bottle,
cradling the swaddled fly,
rocking it to sleep;
a set of car keys, hanging from a tree;
a fire, still warm, and a bone
the length of my arm, my name
carved on it, mis-spelt.
The dog left me there,
and I went on myself.

The tone here is sinister, mysterious, with some of the qualities of a David Lynch film. Note how specific everything is – the red hut, the spider in the milk bottle, the car keys hanging from the tree, the name carved on the bone, mis-spelt – and how no explanations are given for what any of them mean, or what is going on. It brings Charles Causley's comment to mind – he remarked that 'poetry is more about questions than answers' – and another comment from a student in one of our workshops who asked, 'so the reader of the poem has to, as it were, finish the writing of the poem?'

You will notice that this poem is framed somewhat, at the beginning and end, like most of the poems mentioned above, and indeed like most poems you will find that employ a list strategy. But the framing device used here could not be more simple – 'Walking... I saw these things', then a colon, followed by the seven things he saw, separated by semi-colons. In this it is reminiscent of the list in Louis MacNeice's great poem, 'Soap Suds':

> And these were the joys of that house: a tower with a
>   telescope;
> Two great faded globes, one of the earth, one of the stars;
> A stuffed black dog in the hall; a walled garden with bees;
> A rabbit warren; a rockery; a vine under glass; the sea.

Another example of the simple within the sophisticated.

So we want you to take your cue from one or other of these poems, and write a list poem of your own. You might, like Rollinson, have it simply as a list, and find some specific occasion to hang it on – maybe a very special party, or perhaps things to take with you on being banished into exile. Or you might, like Robertson, want to frame your list somehow, dramatically. The nature of a list is such that, as we've said before, it requires you to be objective; it is always a list of things to do, things to buy, things to send, things to remember etc. It will keep you from straying into the fogs of abstraction.

07

visualizing

The use of appropriate and illuminating detail is one of the keys to good writing, but it's also an area in which many inexperienced writers encounter problems. Too often a poem is overloaded with unnecessary description. The writer hopes, by piling on the facts, to give a complete representation of what he or she saw. What happens, actually, is that the poem becomes blurred. Good description works by scrupulous selection of the telling detail. Here, for example, is the opening of a poem by the Israeli poet Yehuda Amichai:

> On a roof in the Old City
> laundry hanging in the late afternoon sunlight

This is how he sets the scene for his poem 'Jerusalem'. He doesn't bother to mention TV aerials, flowerpots, telescopes, hammocks or anything else you might see on a rooftop in that city. He trusts the laundry image will give you a flavour of life in old Jerusalem.

When a writer accumulates detail in a spare and effective way, as in this next poem by James Wright, what you should notice is how the images build on one another to illuminate, suggest and sum up the mood of the whole. You should also notice how they work together and complete each other.

Lying in a Hammock at William Duffy's Farm in Pine Island, Minnesota

Over my head, I see the bronze butterfly,
Asleep on the black trunk,
Blowing like a leaf in green shadow.
Down the ravine behind the empty house,
The cowbells follow one another
Into the distances of the afternoon.
To my right,
In a field of sunlight between two pines,
The droppings of last year's horses
Blaze up into golden stones.
I lean back, as the evening darkens and comes on.
A chicken hawk floats over, looking for home.
I have wasted my life.

You can read this poem in various ways. You can enjoy the progression of clear and evocative images as they establish a mood of idleness and contentedness – you come to the last line, however, which makes you question what you've just read.

Looking at the poem again, you can see there is a mood of gradual darkening. Are these 'pictures that please or thrill for themselves' as Lowell put it, or do they suggest a deeper meaning? It could be that the progression down through the poem to the final, sinister image of the chicken hawk is suggestive of movement towards death. On the other hand, the associations of the word 'home' and the general easeful mood of the piece may bring in happier connotations. These contrasting readings are made possible by the way Wright restricts himself, up until that last line, to letting the images work for themselves.

Another thing to notice is the clarity of these images. Even when the right details have been selected, careless poets often present them in an unfocused way. Suppose Wright had used an inappropriate adjective in front of the word 'chicken hawk' – 'daydreaming', for example – you'd be trying so hard to work out what it meant that you'd be distracted from the image. If he'd put the adjective 'sinister' in front of 'chicken hawk' it would control your reading of the image too much. The writer has to learn to trust that the image alone is enough.

One area of the arts where this is crucial is cinema. Film and poetry have more in common than is generally supposed. Think of any film that's impressed you in recent years and you'll probably find that it is particular images that come to mind.

MS: In an overlong but often haunting film directed by Theo Angelopoulos (1995), *Ulysses' Gaze*, there was an image that will stay with me always. It is the Sarajevo youth orchestra (made up of Serbs, Croats and Moslems) playing outdoors in the fog that has made the city temporarily safe from sniper attacks.

The immediacy of cinema works powerfully on the viewer. It can leave a visual residue long after the twists of the plot are forgotten, and this can occasionally lead to poems.

JHW: The setting of the 1930s film *L'Atalante*, directed by Jean Vigo, is a barge on the river Marne. The black and white photography, the grainy quality of the print, the fog which also descends at one point in the film, the strangely jumpy, nervy quality of the soundtrack – all of these created an atmosphere which I knew I wanted to use in a poem. You'll find it – it's called 'The Barge' – in a book called *Spending Time with Walter*.

EXERCISE 15 Filmic

We'd now like you to try an exercise based on what we've been saying. See if you can summon to mind a film whose images or mood have stayed with you. Don't bother to remind yourself about the story or the characters, or the actors playing them. Concentrate on the visuals and the atmosphere they created. Let them blow in and out of the crannies of your imagination. Return to the theme from time to time. Nothing may come of this immediately, but it's worth a try. Be persistent and in a few days you may find the beginnings of a poem will be suggested. Even if this doesn't happen, it will be good practice for capturing clear and evocative images in language. Resist the temptation to explain or interpret them – try letting them speak for themselves.

The image of the Sarajevo youth orchestra playing in the fog suggests the whole Bosnian situation in a surprising way. Essentially this way of using an image to suggest more than itself can be called metaphorical – and here, perhaps, is the place to start looking at metaphor in more detail. At its most basic level a metaphor works by referring to one thing in terms of another. If you describe a tall, thin person as a 'beanpole', for example, you are using a metaphor. Nobody would suppose this person has got bean plants growing up him, any more than hearing the expression 'she came catlike into the room' you would suppose she came in miaowing. Quite why one characteristic of something is activated rather than another is not entirely clear – although in these examples, because the expressions 'beanpole' and 'catlike' are so familiar to us, we know what is intended. In fact, they're clichés. Despite this, such expressions still have some life in them (although we hope that, after reading Chapter 05, you'd be careful how you used them in a poem). In addition to half-dead images like these, the English language is also full of metaphors that are so completely dead (flower 'bed', for example, or table 'leg') that we don't even notice they are metaphors at all, until we stop and think about them. Good writers should always be responsive to this tendency of metaphor to lose its force through overuse, and endeavour to shun what is tired, stale and too familiar.

Make up your own metaphors, then; don't simply use what's already been said. When you do this, test them for their plausibility and appropriateness. Check that you have not produced any inadvertent side-effects. The boxer Mike Tyson, in a press interview prior to his heavyweight fight with Frank

Bruno in March 1996, spoke of his baby daughter like this: 'The baby's mother is an extremely beautiful woman, but the baby is so beautiful it makes the mother look like a yard dog.' We're sure he intended no slight on the lovely woman he lives with, but he didn't see how inapt his comparison was.

EXERCISE 16 Things

Here's an exercise you can try which we learned from the poet Maurice Riordan. It might lead you towards generating powerful metaphors by getting you to meditate closely on an object. Some poems have objects as titles – 'My Shoes', for example, or 'Black Silk', or 'The Blue Dress'. (These are titles of poems by Charles Simic, Tess Gallagher and Sharon Olds respectively.) A poem with a title like that is like a flag with a skull and crossbones on it. You know exactly what kind of poem is sailing towards you. What's more, as Maurice says, if you were leafing through an anthology, you'd probably be more intrigued with a poem that has an object in its title than, say, a more philosophical sounding title like 'The Idea of Order at Key West' by Wallace Stevens. No disrespect to Stevens is intended here, by the way – it's a fine poem.

If you look at Charles Simic's poem 'My Shoes', you'll see that it's far from being merely a literal description, but uses objects as a launching pad for a dizzying series of metaphors that seem to encompass not merely the idea of the things themselves, their function, but also the wearer, and the wearer's inner nature. In fact, the poem constructs a kind of crazy theology out of a pair of shoes.

Shoes, secret face of my inner life:
Two gaping toothless mouths,
Two partly decomposed animal skins
Smelling of mice-nests.

My brother and sister who died at birth
Continuing their existence in you,
Guiding my life
Toward their incomprehensible innocence.

What use are books to me
When in you it is possible to read
The Gospel of my life on earth
And still beyond, of things to come?

I want to proclaim the religion
I have devised for your perfect humility
And the strange church I am building
With you as the altar.

Ascetic and maternal, you endure:
Kin to oxen, to saints, to condemned men,
With your mute patience, forming
The only true likeness of myself.

What we'd like you to do is make a list of a series of common
objects you might write about; things that interest you because
of their appearance or personal associations, or because of their
uses or history. You might have 'inside' knowledge of them, or
they might be things you've lost or haven't seen for a long time.
Now choose one of them, concentrate on your list and see if one
of them stands out from the others, magnetizing your attention
in some way. Jot down some phrases the thing suggests to you,
but don't try writing your poem yet. What you need to do is
meditate on the object you've chosen until it begins to take over
your thoughts and you find you can write about it without
letting your subjective awareness of yourself intrude. Try some
lateral thinking or automatic writing on one or two of the
objects. The main thing is not to worry too much about the
weirdness or ordinariness of your thoughts.

Now read some more poems. Look at 'Black Silk' – quoted in
Chapter 11 (page 90) – or 'Mirror' by Sylvia Plath, and then go
back to your list. You need to let the object you've chosen dangle
like a lure for the imagination. With luck, the object itself may
reveal its innate self to you. Be cunning. Stalk it carefully. Try to
mix absolute concentration with absolute absent-mindedness.
Try not to let your subjective state of mind get between you and
it, but let the thing you've chosen dictate the poem to you. Try
not to get in your own way. (This is a gratifyingly non-egotistical
exercise.) As the poem emerges it will begin to make its own
demands and generate its own form. Let it. If the process is
working, you'll find yourself hell-bent on giving the poem all the
solidity and distinctiveness of the object itself.

EXERCISE 17 Like what ...?

For a more frivolous and fanciful exercise, which we hope will
get you thinking about simile, we'd like you to look at this
extract from a poem by Michael Ondaatje, who is a Canadian
poet, originally from Sri Lanka. It's called 'Sweet Like a Crow',

and Ondaatje prefaces it with a quotation from Paul Bowles: 'The Sinhalese are beyond a doubt one of the least musical people in the world. It would be quite impossible to have less sense of pitch, line or rhythm.'

> Your voice sounds like a scorpion being pushed
> through a glass tube
> like someone has just trod on a peacock
> like someone howling in a coconut
> like a rusty bible, like someone pulling barbed wire
> across a stone courtyard, like a pig drowning,
> a vattacka being fried
> a bone shaking hands
> a frog singing at Carnegie Hall.

We'd like you to take another of those objects you noted down above, and compare it with anything and everything you can think of. Be as down-to-earth and off-the-wall as you like. Remember that your similes can work at various levels; they can win immediate literalist assent: 'Yes! That's what it's like!' or they can awaken a sense of unconscious recognition. Sometimes a comparison is difficult to justify from the point of view of logic, yet it still has a common ground with the thing with which it's being compared at an underground, subconscious level. Collect as many similes as you can. Try using nonsense words that seem to echo the meaning in their sound (a vattacka may be a vegetable – but are you absolutely sure?). Don't just compare your object with other objects, but also with dramatic situations, works of art, political figures or events, states of mind, or to absolutely anything you can think of.

For a look at metaphor working in a slightly more restrained, but nevertheless extremely effective vein, you should go to Elizabeth Bishop's poem 'The Bight'. Here are three lines from early on in the poem:

> Absorbing, rather than being absorbed,
> the water in the bight doesn't wet anything,
> the color of the gas-flame turned as low as possible.

At first glance, this is a startling comparison until you think about it, and about the colour of a gas-flame turned down low, and see how true it is. It's very acutely observed. Most people don't look carefully enough at their surroundings to be able to make such an unexpectedly apt comparison. Later on in the same poem, we come across the following:

Some of the little white boats are still piled up
against each other, or lie on their sides, stove in,
and not yet salvaged, if they ever will be,
from the last bad storm,
like torn-open, unanswered letters.
The bight is littered with old correspondences.

Likening the stove-in boats to torn-open letters, and the water
in the bight to a gas flame, bring together the domestic and the
natural spheres. It demonstrates how the ground for any
comparison need not be exotic, but may lie all around you. If
you hunt down and read the whole of the poem (which we urge
you to do), you'll see that Elizabeth Bishop uses this contrast of
the natural and the domestic as a thematic device throughout.
To say the boats are 'like' letters is, of course, a simile. What the
word 'like' does here is to make the ground of the comparison
explicit. There's probably not much difference in truth-value or
persuasiveness between a simile and a metaphor, although some
people may consider that a metaphor is more daring and that a
simile slightly dilutes the force of the comparison. This is a
matter of opinion. We personally feel there's room for both in
good poetry. Anyway a simile is simply a variant on a metaphor.
Look again at the Bishop image we have been discussing and see
how the simile 'like torn-open letters' becomes a bare metaphor
(and a pun to boot) in the next line.

Metaphor and simile of the kind we've been describing are
everywhere. You can't read a newspaper report about anything
without encountering them at every turn. Sometimes, though,
you come across pieces of writing which seem to do without
metaphor altogether; there are hardly any metaphors or similes
to be found in the individual lines. On closer inspection,
however, it turns out that the whole piece is underpinned with a
single metaphor. When a metaphor is extended through the
whole piece of writing like this, the meaning can be said to have
been represented symbolically. Often the terms 'parable' or
'allegory' are used to describe this way of working.

**MS: When I started to write what I thought were poems at the
end of my time in secondary school, I was very struck by an
essay we read in English class called *The Vision of Mirzah* by
Joseph Addison. This was an allegory where a bridge across a
river stood for the human life-span. Crowds of people hurried
across it, and every now and then a trapdoor would open and
someone would fall through. Fewer <u>and</u> fewer people survived**

as the end of the bridge drew closer. I was very struck by how this image of the bridge and of people falling through it made abstract ideas of life and death seem concrete and real. The poems I attempted for years afterwards rarely strayed from the territory of allegory.

Allegory is also a way of approaching forbidden or difficult material in an indirect way, allowing you to say things whose adversarial character you hope the censor cannot determine. It doesn't always work out that way, however. Peter Huchel's poetry earned him ten years under house arrest in the former German Democratic Republic and a total publication ban. This is his poem 'Weeds':

> Even now where the paintwork blisters
> and flakes from the walls of my house,
> and the metastases of mortar
> show themselves in wide streaks,
> I will not write
> with my bare finger on the porous wall
> the names of my enemies.
>
> The trickling soot nourishes the weeds.
> Nettles, chalky and white,
> grow along the cracked edge of the terrace.
> The coalmen who bring me coke
> secretly at night,
> dragging their baskets to the cellar-chute,
> are careless. They tread
> the evening primroses down.
> I straighten them again.
>
> I welcome guests
> who are fond of weeds,
> who are not afraid
> of my overgrown paving stones.
> They do not come.
>
> It's coalmen who come,
> tipping from filthy baskets
> the black, jagged sadness
> of the earth into my cellar.

Translated by John Hartley Williams

Compared with the allegory Joseph Addison employed, this is more riddling, oblique and mysterious. You have to decide for yourself why the coalmen come at night and why no weed-loving guests visit the narrator. In such a short and tightly focused poem, the power of suggestion the images carry in themselves conveys the situation in a much more immediate way than could be achieved through the sequential discursiveness of prose. It's a good example of how the questions triggered off in a reader's mind by a poem can resonate with a kind of implicit meaning which a prose narrative, by contrast, always seeks to make explicit. We quoted Charles Causley in the previous chapter: 'Good poetry is more about questions than answers.' Bad poetry, on the other hand, spells out the message and leaves nothing for the reader to complete.

Two other ways of working that could be described as operating within the general territory of metaphor are symbolism and myth. Symbolism is essentially a private use of metaphor, whereas myth operates in the public domain. In Robert Frost's famous poem 'Stopping by Woods on a Snowy Evening', for example, the woods are clearly symbolic of something, but it's not absolutely clear what. The woods ('lovely dark and deep') seem most likely to be a symbol of death, but could they, perhaps, be symbolic of some prohibited erotic zone? Readers often complain that this kind of imagery is wilfully obscure, but it would be wrong to suppose that the majority of poets set out to baffle their readers. Some poets do, but it's not the kind of writing we're interested in. What's the point of publishing if you don't want to communicate? It is, perhaps, to avoid charges of wilful obscurity that some contemporary poets have sought to reinterpret the problems of our own day through the use of ancient myths. This both revitalises the myth, and provides a public framework for the verse. A good recent poem that does this is 'Mrs Midas' by Carol Ann Duffy:

I served up the meal. For starters, corn on the cob.
Within seconds he was spitting out the teeth of the rich.
He toyed with his spoon, then mine, then with the knives,
       the forks.
He asked where was the wine. I poured with a shaking hand,
a fragrant, bone-dry white from Italy, then watched
as he picked up the glass, goblet, golden chalice, drank.

It was then that I started to scream.

Let us sum up by looking at what can be achieved through the use of metaphor. Anyone who has ever tried to write more than a shopping list has come up against the expressive deficiencies of language. How can you say something memorably? How can you avoid rolling out the same hoary clichés? This chapter suggests that effective use of metaphor, in any of its forms, will go some way towards giving you the answer. The role of visual imagery in the language we speak and write is all-important. Essentially, when you employ any metaphorical caste of language, you give a kind of tonic, a figurative fillip to your writing. Use of metaphor rehabilitates everyday discourse, adding zing. It draws attention to itself, even as it allows the mind to experience a different level of meaning.

Sometimes, it has to be said, indiscriminate use of metaphor can get you into trouble. Inexperienced writers are often tempted to cram their writing with as many metaphors and similes as they can think of, however strained they might be. They can't let a line go by without giving us a flash of their brilliant invention. This is just self-indulgent, a knee-jerk reaction to the problems of diction. Less is more in this instance; metaphor can work powerfully when it's used sparingly. Overuse it and you risk losing control.

A poem you might look at which illustrates the illuminating effect a well-placed metaphor can have is 'Loch Thom' by W. S. Graham. This is a poem about a man returning to the scene of his childhood at the age of 56. We've taken the liberty of putting the metaphor at the end of the poem in bold to draw your attention to it.

Loch Thom

Just for the sake of recovering
I walked backward from fifty-six
Quick years of age wanting to see,
And managed not to trip or stumble
To find Loch Thom and turned round
To see the stretch of my childhood
Before me. Here is the loch. The same
Long-beaked cry curls across
The heather-edges of the water held
Between the hills a boyhood's walk
Up from Greenock. It is the morning.

And I am here with my mammy's
Bramble jam scones in my pocket.
The Firth is miles and I have come
Back to find Loch Thom maybe
In this light does not recognise me.

This is a lonely freshwater loch.
No farms on the edge. Only
Heather grouse-moor stretching
Down to Greenock and One Hope
Street or stretching away across
Into the blue moors of Ayrshire.

2

And almost I am back again
Wading the heather down to the edge
To sit. The minnows go by in shoals
Like iron-filings in the shallows.
My mother is dead. My father is dead
And all the trout I used to know
Leaping from their sad rings are dead.

3

I drop my crumbs into the shallow
Weed for the minnows and pinheads,
**You see that I will have to rise
And turn round and get back where
My running age will slow for a moment
To let me on**. It is a colder
Stretch of water than I remember.

The curlew's cry travelling still
Kills me fairly. In front of me
The grouse flurry and settle. GOBACK
GOBACK GOBACK FAREWELL LOCH THOM.

What's so interesting about this metaphor is the way in which it seems so integral to the basic idea behind the poem. You don't feel it's there to make you think how clever the writer is – it's not flashy or ornamental – but the startling poignancy of it wins the reader's recognition immediately. It crystallizes the feeling of loss that suffuses the poem.

Such metaphors often rise unbidden in the course of writing, as if to help you grasp the nature of what you're writing about. If you're writing well, they'll be just the metaphors you want. If you're writing slackly, not paying attention, you'll get metaphors that'll clutter up your poem with a lot of unnecessary debris. When you learn to recognize those true metaphors, the essential ones that go straight to the core of a scene or a situation like the example we've just quoted above, you'll know that you're writing well, and you'll want to keep fishing in the same pool. Those kinds of image are the ones you want: the ones that can convey in a split second, almost faster, it seems, than the language in which they're written, and sometimes in a way that seems beyond logic, the kernel of the poem.

08
drafting and revision

Good morning, Karl. Sit down. I have been thinking
About your progress and my progress as one
Who teaches you, a young man with talent
And the rarer gift of application...

> (from 'Johann Joachim Quanz's Five Lessons'
> by W.S. Graham)

What W.S. Graham means by 'application' is, of course, not just hard work but concentration and an unwillingness to be too easily satisfied with what you've written. This involves being hard on yourself. You should aim to become your own best critic, but this won't happen overnight. How do you get there?

We've already touched on the subject of using models. Obviously you will be inspired by, and will want to emulate, to some extent, the poets you most admire. You should certainly learn something from reading them, but what you won't get from them is a direct response to your own writing efforts. Lots of people delude themselves into thinking that they don't need responses, that what they write is perfectly OK. The reason they do this is because they're afraid someone will tell them it isn't. This is a perfectly natural fear. How do you overcome it?

Your first task is to find a second reader you can trust. You can start very simply by showing your efforts to a like-minded friend. Perhaps he or she writes too, but this is not necessary. Immediate members of your family may not be the right people to do this. Whoever it is won't necessarily offer much in the way of criticism at this stage. What they will offer is encouragement, and a shared appreciation of the models that inspire you.

You may be lucky enough to find a mentor. This will be a person (usually an older, more established writer) who, in recognition of your seriousness and promise, will know how to blend constructive criticism with encouragement.

MS: I was fortunate enough to be taken up by the Scottish poet Aonghas MacNeacail, or Angus Nicholson, as he was known then. I used to be invited round at least once a week. When I came in he would say, 'So you think you've written a masterpiece. We'll see about that.' He'd take out his red pen and go through the poem. A typical comment would be, 'This bit sounds nice, but if you follow it into a corner, does it stand up?' That way I had to justify every phrase. 'You get better,' he'd say, 'not by comparing yourself with models, but by comparing the good bits of yourself with the bad bits.'

Sometimes, with a special favourite, it wasn't easy to take everything he said. But it disciplined me and I will always be grateful for the way I was pushed in the direction of a greater austerity.

We're not saying it's essential to find a mentor, and you should on no account pester people to adopt you. Poets are pressed for time just like everyone else. If you are taken up by someone, it's likely to be an expression of friendship as much as a recognition of your commitment to your craft. No matter who you find (if anyone) to comment on and encourage your writing, the final decisions on your poems will rest with you.

So what should your red pen home in on? Waffle, stale language, clichés, vagueness, abstractions and generalizations, obvious spelling out rather than suggesting, pomposity, archaisms, derivative/imitative writing, syntactical clumsiness, obscurity, rhythmical bumpiness and clanging rhyme. A lot of these will be familiar to you from what we've already said, but it does no harm to list them again. Any we haven't dealt with will come later.

You may by now be thinking that if you zap all the stylistic lapses listed above there'll be nothing left. It's a bit like the man who puts up a sign saying 'Fresh fish on sale here'. Someone comes up to him and says, 'You don't need the "here". You're not selling them anywhere else.' The man paints out the 'here', so the sign now reads 'Fresh fish on sale'. Someone comes up and says, 'You don't need the "on sale"; you're not giving them away.' The man paints out the 'on sale' so the sign now reads 'Fresh fish'. Someone comes up and says, 'You don't need the "fresh"; you're not selling rotten fish.' The man paints out the 'fresh', so the sign reads simply 'Fish'. Someone comes up and says, 'You don't need "Fish"; you can smell them at the bottom of the street.'

Actually, there is much to be gained from this kind of scrutiny of your work. Even though the anecdote is satirical, there's a degree of sound advice in it, too. Using this kind of approach can get rid of a lot of dead wood, and if there's little left, you'll still be learning habits that will be useful to you later.

You'll find it helpful, as we've suggested over and over again, to fire questions at yourself at every stage in the writing of a poem. You might also remember the words of Robert Lowell we quoted in Chapter 05. 'It is imbecile for him (the author) not to know his intentions, and unsophisticated for him to know too explicitly and fully.' So a kind of balancing is important. The kind of questions you'll ask yourself should help you to check whether you have avoided over-explicitness, or over-determined what you wanted to say. At the same time you'll need to satisfy yourself that the poem makes an interesting and intelligible statement, however obliquely you've approached your subject. Ask yourself: What am I trying to do here? Is what I've written as short as is compatible with what I'm trying to say? Is what I've written new, fresh and surprising enough to resist paraphrase? (i.e. could it be said equally well in prose?)

When you feel you've got a draft that seems finished, it's time for the 'frisk draft'. Think of how international air travellers are frisked before they board the plane to check whether they're carrying anything that might be detrimental to the success of the flight. You need to do the same to your draft poem. Frisk it to see whether you've got any superfluous words. You should be particularly suspicious of adverbs and adjectives. Certain nouns are very often associated with particular adjectives. Take the phrase 'little old woman' for example. There's nothing wrong with the words 'little', 'old' or 'woman' but taken together they constitute a cliché. You should ask two questions of an adjective: is it contributing anything useful or can the noun live without it? Is it a little surprising in connection with that noun, even though a moment's reflection will tell you it fits? The same kind of test can be applied to adverbs. What you're on the lookout for is lazy or automatic use of these words.

You should also be watching for occasions when you've stepped in and explained for the reader what you've already shown. It's perfectly natural to be nervous that you haven't got your point across. We would even say it's a normal part of drafting a poem to put too much in. This is a way of getting your thoughts in order – it should be temporary, though. Think of it as being like the scaffolding you need to build a house which you take away once the house is finished. As the American poet W. D. Snodgrass has said: 'It's what you leave out, not what you put in.' The task of editing your own work as you write it, which is actually what drafting is all about, is not just a matter of checking your grammar and punctuation but also of pruning away excess.

As well as looking for what is superfluous you should, in your frisk draft, be looking to see if everything in your poem is working as well as it could. Does it sound smooth? Have you read it aloud, as we advocated in Chapter 05? If you detect some bumpiness in the rhythms, are there any other words you could use as replacements, without sacrificing your effect? Are some of the lines obscure even to you? Be honest with yourself about this. (Young writers in particular can get carried away with the sound of words; this is perfectly natural, otherwise you wouldn't be a poet, but you should watch out you're not being self-indulgent.) Is the syntax and grammar clear? In your frisking have you come across lines suspiciously like lines you've read elsewhere? Is the tone of your piece consistent? All of these questions and more will be running through your head as you scrutinize your draft. It is unlikely to remain unchanged, if you're thorough.

JHW: I've found that some young poets are persuaded their poem is finished before it is. I remember one girl who came with a sheaf of perfectly typed poems to a four-day workshop in which I was involved. I read them and advised her they weren't quite working yet. Halfway through the course I noticed the sheets of A4 were still unblemished; no handwritten corrections at all. I asked her why and she told me she couldn't do anything more to the poems. I suggested that in that case she had two alternatives: she could either throw them away, or she could think of them as suitcases she'd packed for a journey. You know that feeling you get when you've packed and you're not sure if you've got what you need? Well, the only thing to do is unpack the suitcase and take out the items one by one. When you've done that and checked that you really have got what you need, you'll have to repack the suitcase again – but you'll do it differently this time, and maybe you'll be pleasantly surprised. This time things won't be so crushed, the suitcase will close more easily and it won't bulge.

The girl smiled at my metaphor and left the tutorial. At the end of the four days she stood up to read her poems and they were still unchanged. I asked myself why on earth she'd bothered to come.

Sometimes, of course, as you're revising you simply get stuck. You won't know how to go on. Showing your seized-up poem to a poet friend might be helpful. Often, though, all you can do is put the uncooperative elegy into a drawer and try to forget about it. If you attempt too insistently to fix it, your thoughts will probably get stuck in the same ruts that took you nowhere the first time around. By ignoring it, your unconscious mind may solve the problem.

Imagine a round building with a concealed door, and you're trying to get in. The heftiest sledgehammer-swipes you can manage will do no more than dent the wall. If you're where the door is, however, the merest touch will swing the door open, and a long corridor will take you to the centre of the building.

Assuming you get the poem up and running again, how many drafts will you need? There's no simple answer to this. It varies from poem to poem, and from poet to poet. Sometimes it's just one line or image you get stuck on, while the rest of the poem is all right. This can be sorted out quickly, or it can take a long time – and each of us, unfortunately, has poems that have never reached the stage where they could be published. We're sure any of our colleagues would tell you the same.

William Carlos Williams, in a letter to James Laughlin, remarks:

> *A verse maker should never be in a hurry. The mind is a queer mechanical machine that allows itself to be caught in traps. A rhythmical jig takes hold of us forcing us to follow it, slipping in the words quite against our better judgement sometimes. We grow enamoured of our own put-put and like to see the boat push ahead – even to its destruction sometimes: a heavy figure for a stupid happening... What I really wanted to say is that to make a good poem it is often necessary to wait until we have forgotten the conditions under which we wrote in the first place. Going back, we see clearly (perhaps) where we have been led astray – there is a free field once more, the defects stick out like boulders.*

For most of us, though, it's irritating to have to admit that our poem is flawed, and there's always a temptation to persuade ourselves it's right when it's not. This can happen to experienced as well as new writers. You try to suppress the doubt in your head, but you must learn to listen to it. Solicit the opinion of someone you trust and what they have to say may confirm your doubt. You'll learn to recognize when comments aren't relevant or useful, but don't be too quick to assume that.

Before you finish a poem you must develop an instinct for how it might end. You're unlikely to get drumbeats or a spelt-out moral in a contemporary poem; the end may often seem abrupt. It surprises the reader, but on reflection is seen to be right – nothing further needs to be said. A good ending should flash a light back up a poem so the reader starts it again.

09

using models

Our idea of a true college for poets would be a college for thieves. We don't of course mean seminars in how to shoplift slim volumes, but we do mean lessons in stealing from the contents of those volumes. In Chapter 02 we mentioned the value of using models as a springboard for your writing. We use models a good deal in our workshops, and we'd like to use them here, so think of this as a practical chapter, a bit like being in one of those workshops.

Most poems we use as models tend to be contemporary, for the obvious reason that they employ the language of today. However, older models can provide a different kind of stimulus. Both of us have taken poems from a previous era as a starting point for new work.

EXERCISE 18 Imitation sonnet

JHW: I've always been fascinated by the sonneteers of the Elizabethan age. Their love poems work and rework the same themes, always with a witty twist or sudden reversal in the final couplet. I liked the bravura self-confidence of the following Michael Drayton poem. The idea that he, the poet, could make his beloved immortal simply by writing about her seemed to be such an un-20th century point of view, I wanted to see if I could make the idea work using contemporary language. I did this a long time ago, and looking at it now I can see its limitations – but I still think it was a useful learning exercise.

Here, first, is the Drayton poem:

Sonnets to Idea

(xiv)

How many paltry, foolish, painted things,
    That now in coaches trouble every street,
Shall be forgotten, whom no poet sings,
    Ere they be well wrapped in their winding-sheet?
Where I to thee eternity shall give,
    When nothing else remaineth of these days,
And Queens hereafter shall be glad to live
    Upon the alms of thy superfluous praise.
Virgins and matrons reading these my rhymes,
    Shall be so much delighted with thy story,

That they shall grieve they lived not in these times,
  To have seen thee, their sex's only glory.
So shalt thou fly above the vulgar throng,
  Still to survive in immortal song.

And here's the imitation:

After Drayton

The varnished women from the *coiffeur* sweep
  (In limousines that terrify the suburbs)
To death. No hack would bother losing sleep
  By resurrecting them in vivid words.
You, though, I can make immortal. Think,
  When all this shabby daily flux recedes,
How fêted floozies, belles upon the brink
  Will shiver in their painted loins to read
Of our uncanny passion. Likewise teens,
  And maiden aunts & mums will fret to feel
What they haven't got, we had – which means
  That they are history, & we are real!
    This, my arrogance, that this is true,
    Is adamant as these quick lines for you.

Why don't you pick an Elizabethan love poem and rewrite it for a modern audience? Don't feel you have to use rhyme, but do try to capture the ideas of the original, using a completely up to date language.

EXERCISE 19 Tyrant's garden

MS: At school I remember using Coleridge's 'Christabel' very consciously as a model for a poem. I tried what was in effect a translation from Coleridge's English into the modern idiom. I tried to preserve the structure and feel of the original, while substituting my own invented incident for some of the details in the poem. I hoped by doing this to teach myself a little of Coleridge's craft.

We'd now like you to try a variation on the above. Coleridge's poem 'Kubla Khan' will be familiar to most of you. Here are the opening eleven lines:

In Xanadu did Kubla Khan
A stately pleasure-dome decree:
Where Alph, the sacred river ran
Through caverns measureless to man
   Down to a sunless sea.
So twice five miles of fertile ground
With walls and towers were girdled round:
And there were gardens bright with sinuous rills,
Where blossomed many an incense-bearing tree;
And here were forests ancient as the hills,
Enfolding sunny spots of greenery...

This is all you get of Kubla's garden. The poem goes on to talk
of deep romantic chasms, a waning moon and a demon lover,
not to mention a damsel with a dulcimer and the milk of
Paradise, but what we want you to do is imagine more of
Kubla's garden. Remember, it's not your garden but the garden
of a tyrant. Use your recollection of some recent tyrants to help
you find the wavelength. Ask yourself what tyrants would like
to surround themselves with. We want you to show the
character of the tyrant through the detail you find for the
garden. You might carry on from Coleridge's lines, trying to
keep some of his cadence and rhythmical feel, but making your
language utterly contemporary. The details, likewise, can be as
contemporary as you want. Despite the 18th-century starting
point, make sure your piece of writing has a 20th-century
flavour.

You may feel anxiety that by using models you'll stifle any
originality you might have. This anxiety is unfounded. Most
poets will tell you that, like us, they began with a very conscious
imitation of models. You should look upon this process as a
natural stage of your development, and one you'll pass through.
You might think this is plagiarism, but it's only plagiarism if you
crib whole lines and poems and pass them off in print as your
own. Besides, after this initial learning period, you'll find that
the thieving happens unconsciously. You'll suddenly realize, for
example, that the line you like best in a recent poem is a bit too
close to a line in a favourite Plath or Auden poem. Most poets
have this experience. They have to decide whether to brazen it
out and keep the line (sometimes they want to do this to show
kinship), or rewrite the line, at least so the influence is
camouflaged.

EXERCISE 20 Between the lines

The following exercise is one we've borrowed from the American poet J. D. McClatchy. He suggests you find a poem of between ten and 20 lines and type or write it out, triple-spaced. In the spaces between the lines, you should write new lines that are based on or suggested by the original ones. McClatchy comments: 'Don't be dogged. Use the original, don't merely be used by it.' After you've done this, you delete the lines from the original and work with your own lines, trying to make a poem start from them. Think of it as the first half of a poem, then write a second half that's entirely your own, extending the first part by continuing or in some other way varying the themes and images of the first.

The kind of poem you use to start you off, of course, will be critical here. McClatchy thinks – and we agree – that you should go for contemporary work because of the tone. Also it's best to go for something you don't know too well, perhaps even a poet with whose work you're not very familiar – maybe a translation. Try a few poems until you find one that gets you going.

McClatchy has an aside to his exercise that we feel makes some of the points of this chapter brilliantly clear. He quotes Igor Stravinsky: 'I have been formed in part, and in greater and lesser ways, by all of the music I've known and loved and I composed as I was formed to compose.' McClatchy then shows how unconscious borrowing may have suggested one of Robert Frost's most famous poems, 'Stopping by Woods on a Snowy Evening', quoting a stanza from Thomas Lovell Beddoes:

> Young soul, put off your flesh, and come
> With me into the quiet tomb,
>   Our bed is lovely, dark and sweet;
> The earth will swing us, as she goes,
> Beneath our coverlid of snows,
>   And the warm leaden sheet.

As McClatchy points out, Frost's line 'The woods are lovely, dark and deep' is not the only borrowing from this stanza; patterns of imagery and emotion seem to be echoed as well. He goes on to speculate that Frost may have carried the rhythm of this around in his head for years, 'a single line with a certain cadence, and that it came (unconsciously) both to shape his own line and to prompt its associated images'. What this illustrates again, of course, is the way all writers – and artists – draw inspiration and subject matter from the models they admire, and make them their own.

Immature poets borrow [T.S. Eliot said], mature poets steal.

Frequently one comes across poems in books that literally use other poems, or individual lines from them, as springboards. They are often titled: 'Poem Beginning With A Line By...'. Here are some examples: 'It is night and the barbarians have not yet come' (Derek Mahon: 'Poem Beginning With A Line By Cavafy') 'The light foot hears you and the brightness begins' (Robert Duncan: 'Poem Beginning With A Line By Pindar').

EXERCISE 21 First lines

Why don't you try writing a poem using one of the following first lines as a springboard?

- 'They are so simple, they are in another world' (D. H. Lawrence)
- 'It is difficult even to choose the adjective' (Wallace Stevens)
- 'Rising early and walking in the garden' (Robert Graves)
- 'It used to be at the bottom of the hill' (E. A. Markham)
- 'And thus she sang, all naked as she sat' (George Chapman)
- 'When the hedgehog travels furtively over the lawn' (Thomas Hardy)
- 'The bones of the artist-prince may be inside' (Elizabeth Bishop)
- 'Come here, Sweetie, out of the closet' (Sylvia Plath)
- 'Bedrooms – he'll force an entrance' (Rosemary Tonks)
- 'When I came in that night I found' (Fleur Adcock)

If you prefer, you may choose a first line yourself from an existing poem, taking your cue from the above that the lines which set a poem going can often be very quiet, with nothing extraordinary about them.

Models can sometimes be used in a very simple and straightforward way. Read this poem by George Mackay Brown for example:

Hamnavoe Market

They drove to the Market with ringing pockets.

Folster found a girl
Who put lipstick wounds on his face and throat,
Small and diagonal, like red doves.

Johnston stood beside the barrel.
All day he stood there.
He woke in a ditch, his mouth full of ashes.

Grieve bought a balloon and a goldfish.
He swung through the air.
He fired shotguns, rolled pennies, ate sweet fog from a stick.

Heddle was at the Market also.
I know nothing of his activities.
He is and always was a quiet man.

Garson went three rounds with a negro boxer,
And received thirty shillings,
Much applause, and an eye loaded with thunder.

Where did they find Flett?
They found him in a brazen circle,
All flame and blood, a new Salvationist.

A gypsy saw in the hand of Halcro
Great strolling herds, harvests, a proud woman.
He wintered in the poorhouse.

They drove home from the Market under the stars
Except for Johnston
Who lay in a ditch, his mouth full of dying fires.

The Irish poet Patrick Kavanagh said that Homer had made the *Iliad* from a local row, implying that epics can grow from parochial detail, and that the particular can stand for the universal. This poem works in exactly that way. What's striking first of all is the naming of names. You might think that's obvious but ask yourself how comfortable you feel about putting names into poems. A lot of people seem reluctant to do this. Perhaps they feel they'll make their writing too local and personal, yet look at what names have going for them. There's a nice noise to them, and they're very specific. Think of the resonance the names of places and people carry. Many of us will have listened to the shipping forecast (...Dogger, Malin, Rockall...) and twirled the knob on the old maple wireless, passing Hilversum, Luxemburg, Stralsund... We may not have known where those places were [**MS: Actually, I went to school in Malin**] but the names listed one after the other took on some of the rhythmic power of a poem. Louis MacNeice has described being in a canoe with a friend on the Isis one May morning in 1927, when a goods train came over a railway bridge:

> *We made a chant out of the names on the trucks –*
> *Hickleton, Hickleton, Lunt, Hickleton, Longbotham.*
> *This incantation of names at once became vastly*
> *symbolic – symbolic of an idle world, of oily sunlit water*
> *and willows and willows' reflections and, mingled with*
> *the idleness, a sense of things worn out, scrap iron and*
> *refuse, the shadow of the gas-drum, this England.*

In George Mackay Brown's poem you can see for yourself how distinctive-sounding each name is, marking each character out as individual, and how these individuals taken together suggest the whole community. Suggesting a way of life from the actions of a few is a classic example of what we mean by 'showing, not telling.' Those actions themselves are exemplified and not spelt out. We see what the characters did – 'Johnston stood beside the barrel'; we are not told he got drunk. Note also how the poem gets underway without any fuss. It's very uncluttered, with the simple outlines of a ballad, and the structure of a list. Lastly, the tactic of mixing humour and seriousness is one that few beginner poets are prepared to try, but the effect of doing this will lend warmth to your piece of writing.

EXERCISE 22 Community

'Hamnavoe Market' is obviously based on a reminiscence from youth or childhood. What we'd like you to do then is, very simply, to explore your own past in this way. Try to recall some activity that could be used to suggest the entire way of life of your community. Think back to where you used to live, and to the kind of people you knew. Don't be afraid to name names, or mention real events.

EXERCISE 23 Skeleton

To move from the real to the imagined, we'd like you to read the following poem by Matthew Sweeney:

Fishbones Dreaming

Fishbones lay in the smelly bin.
He was a head, a backbone and a tail.
Soon the cats would be in for him.

He didn't like to be this way.
He shut his eyes and dreamed back.

Back to when he was fat, and hot on a plate.
Beside green beans, with lemon juice
squeezed on him. And a man with a knife
and fork raised, about to eat him.

He didn't like to be this way.
He shut his eyes and dreamed back.

Back to when he was frozen in the freezer.
With lamb cutlets and minced beef and prawns.
Three months he was in there.

He didn't like to be this way.
He shut his eyes and dreamed back.

Back to when he was squirming in a net,
with thousands of other fish, on the deck
of a boat. And the rain falling
wasn't wet enough to breathe in.

He didn't like to be this way.
He shut his eyes and dreamed back.

Back to when he was darting through the sea,
past crabs and jellyfish, and others
like himself. Or surfacing to jump for flies
and feel the sun on his face.

He liked to be this way.
He dreamed hard to try and stay there.

Now, instead of imagining yourself as fishbones in a rubbish
bin, we'd like you to imagine being a skeleton on the sea bed. At
this point the questions come: how did you get there? There are
countless ways to end up on the sea bed. Think of some, starting
with the most obvious and moving on to the more outlandish.
Are you alone, or even in one piece? Are you a human skeleton?
What is down there with you – is a prawn using your left eye
socket as a front door and your right eye socket as a back door?
No detail is too much to imagine.

We'd like you to write a poem along these lines, beginning as the
model does at the end, and using a gradual flashback technique,
step by step, until the skeleton is alive again and happy; but this
happiness and all the stages until we get to it must be **shown** by
what happens in the lines, not told. Every stage must be seen
vividly, starting with the sea bed. You may choose to use the

same refrain-structure of the model or you might devise your
own structure. You can either write your poem in the first
person, speaking as the skeleton, or put it into the third person.
Finally, we'd like you to be as surprising as possible while
bringing the reader with you.

EXERCISE 24 You're a genius

Using thematic structure to kickstart you into developing a piece
of writing, as we've just suggested, should give you ideas on
how to capture some of the energy that's in poems and use it for
your own purposes. Think of it as a spark jumping across from
the original poem that may help you to start something of your
own. As an example of this tapping into a poem's energy, we'd
like you to use the following poem by the Slovenian poet Tomaž
Šalamun as a model.

Who is Who

Tomaž Šalamun you are a genius
you are wonderful you are a joy to behold
you are great you are a giant
you are strong and powerful you are phenomenal
you are the greatest of all time
you are the king you are possessed of great wealth
you are a genius Tomaž Šalamun
in harmony with all creation we have to admit that
you are a lion the planets pay homage to you
the sun turns her face to you every day
you are just everything you are Mount Ararat
you are perennial you are the morning star
you are without beginning or end
you have no shadow no fear
you are the light you are the fire from heaven
behold the eyes of Tomaž Šalamun
behold the brilliant radiance of the sky
behold his arms behold his loins
behold him striding forth
behold him touching the ground
your skin bears the scent of nard
your hair is like solar dust

the stars are amazed who is amazed at the stars
the sea is blue who is the sky's guardian
you are the boat on high seas
that no wind no storm can destroy
you are the mountain rising from the plain
the lake in the desert
you are the *speculum humanae salvationis*
you hold back the forces of darkness
beside you every light grows dim
beside you every sun appears dark
every stone every house every crumb every mote of dust
every hair every blood every mountain every snow
every tree every life every valley every chasm
every enmity every lamb every glow every rainbow

(translated by Tomaž Šalamun and Anselm Hollo)

What we find striking about this poem is that it's rampantly egotistical without being at all arrogant or superior. It's both funny and touching at the same time. We find this poem works particularly well as a model in a school environment, because kids are often told they're not quite good enough, and should try harder, and teachers sit in judgement on them. What we'd like you to do is shake off your natural modesty. We know it's a bit indecorous to praise yourself but we want you to discover powers you didn't know you had. We want you to talk yourself up in a way that will dumbfound your friends. We want you to think of yourself in relation to the celestial world, as well as this world in which we live and anything in it, and find comparisons which put you on an equal footing with the most impressive phenomena you can think of.

EXERCISE 25 You're a monster

If your reserve or your natural bent towards self-deprecation makes it impossible for you to do Exercise 24, there's another Tomaž Šalamun poem 'History' which the poet Jo Shapcott uses to kick off another similar exercise – although with one major difference. The poem begins with the lines: 'Tomaž Šalamun is a monster/Tomaž Šalamun is a sphere rushing through the air.' It then proceeds through many speculative and extravagant comparisons and/or situations until, like a big plane coming in to land, it touches down with the lines: 'This is Tomaž Šalamun he went to the store/with his wife Marushka to buy some milk.'

Keeping this imaginative range in mind, we want you to write in a similar vein about yourself. As with the previous exercise using a Šalamun poem, you'll have to put your own name in the first line (you may of course use it as many times as you wish). Once again you'll be talking about yourself, which some people have an inbuilt reluctance to do, but you'll be entering such wild, hyperbolic territory that any self-consciousness should be dispelled.

10

the co-operative approach

In Chapter 08 we spoke of the importance of getting a response to your writing, one you can trust and benefit from. We mentioned that family and friends may not be the best people to give you this. They're too fond of you to be less than kind, or simply can't give you the level of professional attention you need. One of the surest ways of getting that helpful response is by joining a writers' group.

A writers' group

What is a writers' group? It's simply a bunch of writers who meet regularly or semi-regularly to read and discuss each other's work, in a critical yet supportive environment. Sometimes these groups are private. A few friends decide that, instead of showing each other their latest poems whenever they get together for a beer or a curry, or reading them down the telephone, they'll meet in a group every so often for the express purpose of discussing each other's poems. Such groups often start small, with a handful of people meeting in one of their homes, then grow, as each member introduces new people who might be useful to the group. It is usual that one person nominally takes charge of the group, arranging convenient dates, sending out notices and so on, although his or her comments will bear no more weight than the other group members. Even with private groups like this it is important to vet the newcomers, as many groups are spoiled by dominating people of limited taste and talent, making any discussion a battle of poetic ideologies – for them, anything not rhyming or not written in iambic pentameters is not poetry, and the converse situation can also apply – until the more timid people (often the better writers) see that it's pointless to stay.

MS. In case you think we are exaggerating here, I have visited, as part of one of my residences, groups exactly like these, ruined by one or two members whom I described, in a report, as poetry's Fifth Columnists, or wearers of invisible Auberon Waugh badges, who harangue you with the unpoetic nature of contemporary poetry, and resemble nothing less than passengers in a horsedrawn coach in the slow lane of the M4.

We are not saying that it is impossible to bring a successful rhyming poem in iambic pentameters to a serious group and have it praised. It isn't, and it usually happens more than once during a group meeting, or workshop, as these meetings tend to be called; but there will be other kinds of poems brought along also, and these should not be dismissed because of the form in which the author has chosen to write them. Any decent group will be open to different approaches in the writing of poetry, and the various group-members should restrict themselves to offering opinions on the success of the poem under discussion, whatever its form, and perhaps to making suggestions towards its improvement.

An easier way in could be to look for and attend a public workshop, assuming any take place in your area. These are usually led by a professional poet, who, in effect, chairs the session, and is expected to earn his or her keep by making sure each poem gets a fair share of the time allotted, and by summing up the discussion on each poem with particularly incisive advice. There is also usually a charge for such workshops. Some of these may occupy a halfway house between a private group and a public workshop, in the sense that some regular attenders or recidivists are joined each time by newcomers who may show up only once. The standard of poems also tends to be more varied in public workshops in that people who've published widely in magazines are liable to show up together with beginners. If a public workshop is not open to such a range of participants it will be advertised as such in advance. One other major difference in public workshops is they are not always purely analytical; they can be generative, too – they can get the participants writing, via exercises of the type we are introducing throughout this book.

The benefits of attending

Whatever kind of workshop you seek out, private or public, there are undoubted benefits to be gained from attending. First, the catalyst factor: you cannot bring a poem along until you write one. This especially applies if you're a member of a group that meets regularly, and the other members are familiar with your poems. You'll want to introduce a new one (apart from anything else, it's easier to make changes – if you're persuaded they're necessary – in a poem that's fresh, rather than in one that you've written so long ago it's as good as carved in stone). It's advisable to bring along a poem that's representative, and that you're happy with, although there's an argument for bringing along something you like but don't feel is quite there yet. Maybe you feel it's too long. Maybe there's something wrong with the ending but you can't seem to be able to sort it out. The workshop can act as the barrier stage in the drafting of your poem before you make a submission to a magazine. Often, as a result of comments that people make, you will want to make changes, or even a substantial rewrite – or you may even want to dump this particular poem.

One practical piece of advice is worth mentioning here. Your poem should be well presented (typed unless this is completely impossible) and you should bring along as many photocopies as there are people in the workshop. This is to your advantage, as it is difficult to respond in detail to a poem that's been heard once, whereas if people have a copy to look over they can really feel their way into the poem.

It goes without saying that there is no point in coming along to a workshop if you are not willing to accept criticism. We have brought this point up before and will do so again. Nowhere is it more pertinent than in a workshop situation. You will learn, however, to distinguish between two basic types of criticism – one that's the opinion of someone who writes in a different way from you and can't see what you're doing, and one that chimes with the doubt in your head that you've been suppressing. This latter type of suggestion is invaluable, and any serious attender of workshops has had it on more than one occasion. You should be careful not to assume that a criticism fits into the first category. It's best to take all the comments away with you and think about them. Sometimes it's days or weeks later that you let go and admit that a criticism was apt.

There are some pieces of advice we can give here that might make the taking of criticism easier. In any decent workshop the criticism is not personal (whatever people sometimes think); it is always constructive and enabling, so think of the comments as technical tinkering, with your interest and the interest of your poem at heart. It's also good to think long term, and take the comments as applying to and influencing not just the poem under discussion, but the poems you will write in the future. (This is why we recommend that you bring along a poem that's representative, so that comments made about it are applicable to your method of writing as a whole.) In the last analysis, any comments made are that person's opinion. You can choose to take them on board or leave them, as you wish.

The big plus of a workshop is the different opinions and insights of the people there. If these add up – if all nine people think your latest masterpiece is horsedung – you'll have to reconsider. On the other hand, you may bring along a piece that you're not at all sure about (it may seem quite different to you from what you normally do) but the group can think it's the best thing you've ever written. In this way, a group can be liberating. None of us can be objective enough to always be certain immediately what is our best work. You might be so caught up with the ambition or subject matter of a poem that you neglect to notice whether it's working technically or not. You might have such a thing about camels that any poem you write with a camel in it thrills you, or you might simply be changing and unaware of this – and these can be the exciting stages of a writer's development. As Ted Hughes put it (and Wendy Cope parodied):

The progress of any writer is marked by those moments when he manages to outwit his own inner police system.

When this happens you will be glad to have it pointed out.

Choosing a group or workshop

If it's a group or regular workshop you want to join you'll have to choose carefully. You should find your level. Some workshops are an easy ride, and the criticism never strays from the gentle. This can be limiting and frustrating for someone with ambition to get ahead. Other workshops are very rigorous indeed, and you need to feel sure you can take the criticism that's offered. Some have deadweights that snarl up the workshop – we mentioned these cases earlier. The number of people in a workshop and the regularity with which it meets (if it's a recurring one) varies from group to group. Some are formal, some are informal, with wine being drunk during the discussion. Some look at a poem (usually one) by everyone present, others look at several poems by one group member each time they meet. The advantage of this is that it reinforces the point that it's not just the criticisms made about your poem that you learn from, but criticisms made of other people's poems as well. Also – and this is important – one of the joys of a workshop can be the poems other people bring along. If they're really good you'll feel envious, and this might spur you on to excel yourself in your next piece of writing.

There's one tiny practical point that might be helpful. Many workshops are done anonymously; i.e. each poem is photocopied and distributed with no name on it, so that no one can be sure whose poem it is. In a regular workshop other group members can guess (although they won't always be right) but even if they do, a convenient fiction is set up, in that people can't jump in to defend their poem so readily against all points made against it without giving away their authorship. You only have to see how rampant defensive argument can clog up a workshop to want to find ways around this. Anonymity is the neatest way, and many groups move to this approach.

If you do find a group you are happy with (and you might have to try several before you settle on one) you should keep in mind that, however important it is for you now, it is temporary. Even the best groups have a limited life. People outgrow them. Responses become predictable, people's opinions can become more clearly tied to their own developing work. Sometimes splinter groups form. Sometimes former group-members revert to showing each other new work outside the group. Sometimes they avail themselves of modern technology, and workshop their poems by e-mail. This has the advantage of bringing into play the opinions of poet-friends in Michigan or Alaska, and making your private workshop truly international.

However, we're running ahead of ourselves here. You might still be in the process of looking to join a group or workshop for the first time. How will you find such a group? Your Regional Arts Association should have an up-to-date list of any in your area that are open to newcomers. If you live in or around London – or ever visit the place – the Poetry Library in the South Bank Centre keeps updating its lists for the Greater London area. The Northern Poetry Library in Morpeth, Northumberland, is a good source of information for its area. Listings magazines (such as *Time Out*, or the *Poetry London Newsletter*) will inform you of regular open workshops. Likewise, the prospectuses of adult education colleges will tell you of any regular workshops they might offer. (A word of warning: these can fill up quickly, so check them out early in the term.) If there is a writer-in-residence in your area, and if this writer is a poet, he or she will probably offer occasional workshops (and 'surgery sessions', or one-to-ones, where the poet discusses your work with you privately). Writing courses (such as those offered by the Arvon Foundation, in Devon, Yorkshire, Shropshire and Scotland, or Tŷ Newydd in Wales) are excellent. You get a week with 15 like-minded people, two professional poet tutors and a third coming mid-week as a guest-reader, and have nothing with which to occupy yourself other than writing and thinking about poetry (think of it as an extended, live-in workshop). You might also find that some of the people on the course live near enough to you to form a group when you all go home. Another suggestion is attending poetry readings in your area (always a good idea anyway) and talking to people who turn up – the chances are that many of them will be writers themselves and may, like you, be looking for a group to join. If all else fails, or you're too shy to do any of the above, you can invite the one or two people you know who write to come to your home, and keep the group very small.

11

subject matter

'Fair is my love and cruel as she's fair,' is the way Samuel Daniel begins a sonnet. It's no surprise that she's beautiful, is it, and no surprise either to find that a beautiful woman is cruel? Those were the literary conventions of the day, and Daniel goes on to admit:

> For had she not been fair, and thus unkind,
> My Muse had slept, and none had known my mind.

(from Sonnets to Delia)

So, if she hadn't been good-looking, he wouldn't have written a poem about her? Obviously not. For a 16th-century poet, subject matter was in many ways predictable and restricted. Today, however, it's all a bit different. You'll remember that William Carlos Williams said:

Anything is fit material for poetry.

Over the last year or so our reading has borne this out. Among the subjects we have encountered are: a meeting between Martians and Earthlings, an articulate mad cow, a congress of insomniacs, a ghost bus, a 'beloved' comparing herself to a pint of stout, a hangover, the childhood of Jesus. (The poems that dealt with those subjects were written by, respectively: Edwin Morgan, Jo Shapcott, Charles Simic, Roy Fisher, Paul Durcan, Carol Ann Duffy and Robert Pinsky.) Not everybody is pleased by such diversity – but we are. What we like is, in Louis MacNeice's words, 'the drunkenness of things being various', and the way that subject matter itself can provide its own surprise. If you go around thinking that only certain subjects are fit material for poetry, you'll close yourself off from the world around you. You'll also, necessarily, limit the range of your work. Has it never occurred to you that there might be more you could write about? How many of you live in an urban environment, yet fail to reflect it in the poems you write? When did you last wade through that primrose-filled valley you've put in your poem? It's the street you cross every evening that might show you something you hadn't expected. Take this poem by William Carlos Williams, for example:

The Great Figure

Among the rain
& lights
I saw the figure 5
in gold

```
on a red
fire-truck
moving
tense
unheeded
to gong clangs
siren howls
& wheels rumbling
through the dark city
```

What makes this little poem startling is, as the title suggests, the way in which the figure on the side of the fire-truck gets picked out and not the fire-truck itself. It's a common enough scene; the interest is in the detail that's been observed. Your poems won't live unless they have the real world in them – and the real world **freshly observed**.

Finding a way to deal with the things of the world is not easy. 'In Europe,' Pablo Neruda said, 'everything has been painted.' He meant that Europe is an old culture, with the implication that Europeans may be tempted to describe their experience in terms of everything that's gone before and could perhaps fall into cliché as a consequence. When you sit down to write a love poem, all the love poems you've ever read will echo in your head. How can you find something new to say about jealousy, loneliness or grief – the universal emotions – when Shakespeare, Goethe and Ronsard have been there before you? Neruda might not have considered himself to be hamstrung by tradition, but even for a new world poet the absence of European cultural history doesn't necessarily confer an invulnerability to cliché. Whatever part of the globe you happen to occupy, our response to Neruda's remark would be: if everything's already been painted, we'll have to find new ways to paint it again.

Any poet worth the name will be impelled at some stage to write poems of love and death. These are unavoidable subjects, and not to deal with them in between the cat poems, poems in praise of tennis and the poems about your trip to Borneo would be an evasion. In order to convey the concepts 'love' and 'death' and take the measure of them in a specific and concrete way, you'll have to find what T.S. Eliot called 'the objective correlative'. This sounds a bit of a mouthful, but the idea is quite simple. Essentially it means that abstract emotion is transferred onto a concrete object. In Tess Gallagher's 'Black Silk', for example, a waistcoat takes on the weight of the grief felt for its departed wearer.

Black Silk

She was cleaning – there is always
that to do – when she found
at the top of the closet, his old
silk vest. She called me
to look at it, unrolling it carefully
like something live
might fall out. Then we spread it
on the kitchen table and smoothed
the wrinkles down, making our hands
heavy until its shape against formica
came back and the little tips
that would have pointed to his pockets
lay flat. The buttons were all there.
I held my arms out and she
looped the wide armholes over
them. 'That's one thing I never
wanted to be,' she said, 'a man.'
I went into the bathroom to see
how I looked in the sheen and
sadness. Wind chimes
off-key in the alcove. Then her
crying so I stood back in the sink-light
where the porcelain had been staring. Time
to go to her, I thought, with that
other mind, and stood still.

There are just a few details we'd like to draw attention to in this
poem. Notice how, right at the beginning, the phrase 'there is
always that to do' suggests one of those comforting, mindless
little jobs you do to mop up sorrow. There is no context yet for
this phrase, but a sensitive reader will be both intrigued and
lured on. Nothing is said about death. Then the poet smooths
the waistcoat, and its wearer is suggested by his absence:

> the little tips
> that would have pointed to his pockets
> lay flat.

The presence of the word 'sadness' in this poem seems to go
against some of what we've been saying. By linking it
alliteratively with the word 'sheen' though, the poet transfers to

'sadness' some of the concreteness of this word. It's as if 'sadness' acquires a physical property – a kind of lustre. The wind chimes of the following line add an aural melancholy – an acoustic property – that again moves it into the concrete zone. The overall effect of the poem is to focus the generalized vagueness of grief onto a simple garment.

When emotion is conveyed in this way, through the objects described, a kind of displacement is effected. The Japanese form, the haiku, works in this way. A brief description, for example, of the natural world might be suffused with emotion even though nothing is explicitly stated:

> On a withered branch
> a crow has settled –
> autumn nightfall

> (Basho; translated by Harold Henderson)

Notice that there is no metaphor here; the crow on the branch and the autumn nightfall are simply set side by side without comment. Whatever points of comparison or contrast there may be are left to the reader. In fact, the things of the world have a power over our imaginations that gives them a very specific resonance. Pablo Neruda alludes to this very articulately in the following:

> *It is well, at certain hours of the day and night, to look closely at the world of objects at rest. Wheels that have crossed long, dusty distances with their mineral and vegetable burdens, sacks from the coalbins, barrels and baskets, handles and hafts for the carpenter's tool chest. From them flow the contacts of man with the earth ... The used surface of things, the wear that the hands give to things, the air, tragic at times, pathetic at others, of such things – all lend a curious attractiveness to the reality of the world that should not be underprized.*

MS: During one of my residencies, I told a woman whose poems I'd been looking at that they showed no evidence whatsoever that the 20th century had happened, not to mention that we were at the tail end of it, or that she was in it. 'So?' she said. I said: 'We're living through the century of zeppelins, jazz bands, mushroom clouds, concentration camps, sputniks, computers and mobile phones. I can't get any sense from your poems that you've noticed.'

The list we've just mentioned will remind you that among the subjects people feel compelled to write about in their poetry is the political arena in which human affairs are conducted. That phrase 'human affairs' has a cloudy generality, of course, which should alert you, like a warning beep, to the fact that, without specificity and concreteness in your treatment of such matters, your poems will most likely end up turning into journalistic commentary. As we feel this belongs in a wider discussion of the poet's response to the world, we deal with it more fully in later chapters.

Very often the poems people bring to workshops or enter into competitions remain completely in an abstract realm, but emotions don't happen in Nowhereland. They happen in a bedsit, in a palace, on a three-masted sailing ship crossing the Atlantic. They also happen in the morning, at lunchtime and in the dead of night. Without that awareness of context, even if nothing is explicitly mentioned, your poems are going to occupy a vacuum. If they fail to intersect with the world, the interest goes out of them. If they fail to capture in some way the mood and the feel of the era in which they were written, they will inevitably suggest that everything has always been the same. Just as inevitably, none of the things of the world, none of its developments and, most surprisingly of all, nothing of what has truly happened to the writers themselves can then be brought into their poems.

Everyone has a story to tell – a story that's unique to that person. It would be foolish not to draw on this story in some way, although in the beginning young writers are often understandably reluctant to do this. In both our cases, the last thing we wanted to do in our early work was explore autobiography. We had a kind of resistance to the world that was presented to us.

JHW: When I was a teenager my teachers were always telling me 'write about what you know'. I was impatient with that advice; I wanted to break the mould and write about what I didn't know. Writing for me was an act of discovery, a way of escaping my environment, and I couldn't see anything interesting in my surroundings that was worth writing about – so how could it interest anyone else? What I later realized was that I could deal with the unknown in a convincing way only once I had come to terms with the familiar.

There is undoubtedly mileage in the advice: 'Write about what you know' – it helps to ground your writing. The process of becoming a writer is partly a process of acquiring the confidence to write about what is familiar, even though the terrain may feel too well-trodden to be interesting to anyone else. Seamus Heaney has written of how the poems in his first collection *Death of a Naturalist* were made possible by a reading of Robert Frost's poem 'Out, Out' – and the realization that what happened on a farm could be the subject matter for poems.

> ...*What attracted me was the world that Frost was writing about. Yard work, farm people, the hard rattling action of a buzz saw. It's a narrative poem about a child dying when he loses his hand in an accident with the buzz saw. And again, that kind of thing was part of my own background, a whole rural folklore of sudden deaths, tales of men going through threshing machines or stone crushers, or having their legs cut off by reaping machines. 'Awful but cheerful', as Elizabeth Bishop would say ... Frost corroborated a part of me that needed to know that the world of a County Derry farm could be given a look-in in English blank verse.*

There are various ways you can bring autobiographical material into your poem. To see some different approaches you could look at Frank O'Hara's *Lunch Poems*, for example, or at Robert Lowell's *Life Studies*, at D. J. Enright's *The Terrible Shears*, at C. K. Williams' *Tar*, at Sharon Olds' *The Sign of Saturn*, at Tony Harrison's *Continuous*, and at Carol Ann Duffy's *Mean Time*.

Every recapturing of experience, however, will, as we said in Chapter 02, probably involve a degree of fictionalization. Even at the level of anecdotal retelling of experiences, you'll find yourself instinctively reorganizing your material for dramatic effect on your listeners. As well as leaving out unnecessary details, you may also exaggerate some you want to emphasize. Any professional storyteller would do the same. In addition to exaggeration, you may also throw in details you've made up. All of this helps, paradoxically, to make the truth seem more truthful – you could say it's a kind of 'lying your way towards the truth'.

EXERCISE 26 Ghosts

The following exercise can be seen as an extreme example of this, but no more extreme than two classical works that have been presented frequently in contemporary versions over recent years – Dante's *Inferno* and Ovid's *Metamorphoses*. Basically, what we're asking you to do is imagine yourself dead, then coming back to life.

Oh, there's a bit more to it than that. You have to choose a profession that's no longer as sought after as it once was. In a workshop situation we would hand around an envelope containing little slips of paper with examples of outdated professions on them such as gladiator or gunslinger, eunuch, lamplighter, witch, knight, oracle, escape artist, or lady's maid. There are lots more, but these will give you the idea, and in the poem you will have to act in the role of someone with that profession.

First, though, you're dead. At some stage in the past you have been buried, burned or thrown to feed the fishes, and at the beginning of the poem you'll have to resurrect convincingly. How do you convince? By choosing the correct details. Ovid can give us some tips here. In the section of *Metamorphoses* where Acteon sees the goddess Diana bathing naked, and as punishment is turned into a stag by the enraged goddess, Ovid doesn't just tell us Acteon has become a stag, he shows us:

> ...Out of his forehead burst a rack of antlers.
> His neck lengthened, narrowed, and his ears
>
> Folded to whiskery points, his hands were hooves,
> His arms long slender legs. His hunter's tunic
> Slid from his dappled hide...

And a few lines later, as he's bounding across a pool, amazed at his lightness:

> ...Clear in the bulging mirror of his bow-wave
> He glimpsed his antlered head,
> And cried: 'What has happened to me?'
>
> No words came. No sound came but a groan.
> His only voice was a groan...

(This version is by Ted Hughes.)

Every stage of the process of metamorphosis is realistically depicted. Note how the senses, and sensory impressions, are being used to help the reader suspend his or her disbelief – how Acteon comes to realize he is a stag through the changes he feels happening in his body, through that astounding glimpse of the antlers, through the stag's groan instead of human words. (See also our discussion on using the senses on page 37, Chapter 05.) This is a good example of the way in which clearly imagined sensory detail can make the supernatural seem perfectly logical. The upshot of all this is that we have no trouble accepting Acteon's metamorphosis.

We would like you to try for this degree of precision. So, if you're emerging from a grave, we should see the earth or mud falling from you. At what stage will you acquire clothes again? If you're a gunfighter who's been shot and thrown into Lake Michigan, how long will it take you to notice your six-gun still functions? Remember the world may have changed radically since you were last alive in it. You may not be able to make sense of some of the things you see. You will almost certainly not be able to fit in as well as you once did, so one truth your lying will bring you to is that we do not live in the same world as that of our grandparents.

Whether your preferences are for gritty realism, or an exaggerated or 'magic' realism, you'll need to stay consistent. If you have a flying pig in the first stanza, for example, don't let it become an ordinary earthbound one for the rest of the poem. Many British poets in the not too distant past – the Movement poets, for example, and those they influenced – found realism sufficient for their purposes; others have felt constrained by this, and by the literary requirements of irony, understatement and decorum. They have looked instead at poets from South America and Eastern Europe – writers like Pablo Neruda, Cesar Vallejo, Jorge-Luis Borges, Marin Sorescu, Miroslav Holub, Vasko Popa, Yannis Ritsos – and taken their bearings from them.

Neruda has this to say on the subject:

> *The poet who is not a realist is dead, and the poet who is only a realist is also dead. The poet who is only irrational will only be understood by himself and his beloved and this is very sad. The poet who is all reason will even be understood by jackasses, and this also is terribly sad. There are no hard and fast rules. There are no ingredients prescribed by God or the Devil but these two very important gentlemen wage a steady battle in the realm of poetry, and in this battle first one wins and then the other, but poetry itself cannot be defeated.*

Stirring as this is, it's only Neruda's opinion. What we'd say is: whichever route you go is up to you. If you want to stay within the borders of realism, that's fine. On the other hand, if your inclination is to explore the territory beyond those borders, do so. However far afield your work ranges, as long as you can persuade yourself that it connects back, however obliquely, to the world and its concerns, you should not let yourself be put off by people who accuse you of indulging in whimsy. Some of the greatest 20th-century artists have worked hard to liberate our ways of seeing from faithful replications of the day to day. Yet the discoveries these artists made, far from being a denial of the world, were actually a more insightful capturing of the essence of things – much of which has to do with revealing similarities and relationships in a daring and unexpected way. When Kafka describes a man on trial, without letting us or his hero ever find out what he's accused of, he creates a mysteriously non-literal parable on the nature of guilt and punishment. Seamus Heaney has said: 'I admire works that use fantasy, treat the world as a trampoline.' Many of Edwin Morgan's poems, for example, make obvious use of fantasy but no sensitive reader would have any problems relating them to human goings on. Here is the opening of his poem 'The Video Box: 25':

If you ask what my favourite programme is
it has to be that strange world jigsaw final.
After the winner had defeated all his rivals
with harder and harder jigsaws, he had to prove his mettle
by completing one last absolute mindcrusher
on his own, under the cameras, in less than a week.
We saw, but he did not, what the picture would be:
the mid-Atlantic, photographed from a plane,
as featureless a stretch as could be found,
no weeds, no flotsam, no birds, no oil, no ships,
the surface neither stormy nor calm, but ordinary,
a light wind on a slowly rolling swell.

This poem would be described by some as surrealistic, which is a very loose, actually inaccurate use of the word. André Breton, one of the founders of the movement, said that surrealism was a response to a 'scarcity of reality'. Is it not true, in fact, that what we call reality is changing so fast that it makes many of us unsure how to deal with it in our writing? Yet these very changes are the clues we need to pick up on if we're going to write about the world in a brand new way.

12

context, mood and tone

When a women decides to leave her husband, in a novel or a play, the reader or the audience usually knows exactly why. That reader has been given all the information, realizes what's happening, and understands the context of the decision. A poem, on the other hand, must establish its context with very limited means. A situation must be pinned down as simply and surely as an artist captures a likeness with three quick strokes of the charcoal. A poem works, to a great extent, by implication, leaving a lot of the picture for the reader to fill in. A novel works more expansively: Auden, who had great admiration for the novel as a literary form, put it like this:

The novelist must be the whole of boredom.

We touched on this difference at the end of Chapter 04. As we stressed there, it's the judicious choice of detail which gives un-ambiguous pointers to the reader. Getting a poem right sometimes seems an impossible balancing act between not overstating and not giving enough to go on. Have you told the reader too little? Have you told the reader too much? – these are the questions you need to ask yourself.

Here are the opening lines of some contemporary poems:

- 'Someday I will go to Aarhus'
- 'Hitler entered Paris the way'
- 'The strangest thing I ever stole? A snowman.'
- 'Brethren, I know that many of you have come here today'
- 'We gotta make a film of this, Jack'
- 'After she left he bought another cactus'

Notice how these openings intrigue the reader. You want to know more, but a vague picture has already begun to form in your head. You feel you know a little about the situation or character that's being introduced. What the openings have in common is a hook that draws the reader into the poem, but they all work in different ways. The first opening is a vow, the second is the first half of a comparison you need to complete, the third is a question that provides its own answer, the fourth is the opening of a preacher's sermon, the fifth is a resolve in dialogue form and the sixth is a story that begins in the middle. Check out some of the poetry on your bookshelf, in your local library or bookshop, on the shelves of friends who've invited you round for a meal – find some more opening lines that grab your attention, and think about how they achieve their effects. Try writing a poem whose opening is modelled on one of those listed above, or on an opening line you've discovered yourself.

It's often said that the first and the last lines of a poem are the most important. The first line will often contain a germ of the last, and the whole poem, as it develops, must exhaust all the hints of that first line. The last line, as we suggested at the end of Chapter 08, should send the reader back to the first.

To ensure your poem is developing with sufficient clarity at all stages you should step out of your own head in the act of composition, and read the poem through the eyes of the second reader – who's everyone else – who isn't privy to the information you have in your head while you're writing. If you do this it will stop you from being too easily satisfied, and remind you that you have to persuade the reader to believe you. Too often it's here that the inexperienced writer falls down, through murkiness, or a failure to imagine well enough or sustain what's being imagined. Whichever it is, the reader loses confidence and interest in what's being said. It's a good idea, then, to be alert to the slightest hint of uncertainty, or to any suspicion, however faint, that you're copping out or being lazy. Encourage your own doubts, even if they turn out to be misplaced. You'll know later if they are or not.

One area, on which you need to focus as you work on a poem is the business of clearly establishing the emotional content that drives it. Examples of well-known poems that express feelings of grief, love, anger, fear and sadness are, respectively: Peter Porter's 'An Exequey', Yeats' 'No Second Troy', Plath's 'Daddy', Larkin's 'Aubade' and Arnold's 'Dover Beach'. The emotional charge of these poems is very clear. One might add that in order for such a direct expression of emotion to be successful it needs to be delicately handled. These poems are models of sureness and tact. Many poems, however, skirt around a particular core of feeling without appearing to state it directly, and this may be an equally valid way of operating. They may be filled with an affirming warmth, or they may be suffused with a yearning of one kind or another – an existential feeling of dissatisfaction, for example, or a wanting something more in your life, or an exile's longing for the homeland. Ultimately your poem will never be less than a vehicle for the feelings you wish to convey, and the difficulty of getting to the core of those feelings may well be related to the 'tantalising vagueness' with which Frost said the best poems begin. Getting a poem right involves crystallizing subtle variations of feeling without resorting to overstatement.

W.S. Graham says, 'Do not be sentimental or in your art.' Why does he say this, and what does he mean? Don't a lot of people find great pleasure in sentimental songs and books? Another Scot, the poet and critic G.S. Fraser, describes in his autobiography what happened when, as children, he and his sister went to see a particularly sentimental film. His sister, embarrassed by the tear-jerking nature of what they were watching, would start to suck the fingers of her gloves and they gave the name 'glove-sucky' to any film that made a too obvious play on their emotions. This shows that some people resist sentimentality. The embarrassment it makes them feel is caused by an awareness that they're being manipulated, and they don't like being manipulated, whether by films, politicians or poems. For writing to reach the level of art it needs to persuade the reader that the emotion in it is founded in the truth of the situation depicted. It has to be properly motivated. When it's not, it's sentimental – it's imitation emotion, not the real thing.

Of course, many bad poems are genuinely motivated, but they fail to persuade us because of their lack of control. Their writers don't have the means to describe what they feel, and so they resort to stock phrases and images, triteness, vague generalization and a too easy grasping of emotion. On the other hand, a poem like 'Land Love' from Douglas Dunn's *Elegies*, which is a book of poems dedicated to his dead wife, achieves its emotional effect through tonal balance and fidelity to specific detail. Here is an extract from it:

> We heard the night-boys in the fir trees shout.
> Dusk was an insect-hovered dark water,
> The calling of lost children, stars coming out.
>
> With all the feelings of a widower
> Who does not live there now, I dream my place.
> I go by the soft paths, alone with her.

As we've been stressing throughout this book, there are helpful questions you can ask yourself about what you've written. Would the first line of your poem be something you would really say to your loved one? Is what you've written overblown, or straining after grandeur, or pretentious? Think of these questions as a checklist, a specific and partial application of the frisk draft. It's a good idea to have your own bullshit detector rather than wait for other people to hold their noses.

The plot of a mid 1990s film, *Il Postino*, movingly demonstrates how one of the most common motivations for writing poetry is a desire to express love feelings for someone, and as a consequence to win their affection in return. The film is about a poor Italian postman who wants to woo a beautiful village girl and enlists the help of the poet Pablo Neruda to do so. As Neruda is commonly regarded as one of the finest love poets of the 20th century, the postman is lucky. The clear simplicity of language and unselfconscious warmth of the Neruda poems the postman borrows make a direct appeal to the unsophisticated village girl. It is the kind of language to which anyone writing a love poem should aspire – an unpretentious speaking voice in which everything said seems on first glance peculiarly slanted, and then, on second glance, wins a recognition that it's true. Here, for example, is an extract from 'I Like for You to be Still':

I like for you to be still: it is as though you were absent,
distant and full of sorrow, as though you had died.
One word then, one smile, is enough.
And I am happy, happy that it's not true.

The poem begins, as its title suggests, with a very simple, yet unexpected idea and each stanza plays through surprising variations on this, until the poem reaches the equally simple, yet somehow obliquely satisfying closure quoted above.

What we are left with, after reading a poem, is a residual aftercharge – in this case, a feeling of warmth to which the mood of the poem, its particular atmosphere, contributes. A very different atmosphere is created by Walter De La Mare's well-known poem 'The Listeners'. From its opening ' "Is there anybody there?" said the Traveller/Knocking on the moonlit door' through all the unanswered questions that follow, right up to the Traveller's cryptic final utterance ' "Tell them I came and no one answered/That I kept my word," he said' the poem establishes a mysterious, ghostly atmosphere by vividly picturing a dramatic situation while withholding any explanation of its cause.

The range of possibilities for varying atmosphere and mood from poem to poem is very wide indeed. Too often these possibilities are neglected by inexperienced writers whose work can be monotone to a degree. It is salutary sometimes to look at poetry books with an eye to seeing how much range they have. Sylvia Plath's *Ariel*, for instance, is often accused of being a one-note book, but even a cursory glance is enough to persuade the reader how various the poems in it actually are. Other fine collections which demonstrate a similar variety of tonal range, atmosphere and subject matter are Robert Lowell's *For the*

Union Dead, Elizabeth Bishop's *Geography III*, Les Murray's *The Daylight Moon* and Seamus Heaney's *The Haw Lantern*. These titles jumped out at us as we scanned the bookshelf, and if you look along yours others will surely make their own claims.

Atmosphere and narrative are, of course, inextricably linked together – the one aids and abets the other, and vice versa. Frost says:

> *It is a poem just to mention driving into a strange barn to bide the passing of a thunderstorm.*

This image is like the opening of a Hitchcock film; already in it is a clear narrative possibility, pregnant with atmosphere. 'The Listeners' that we looked at above works in a very similar way. It's a poem which seems to be part of a story whose beginning and end are missing, yet the narrative logic is clear and strong. The poem persuades you that the writer knows everything there is to know about the situation, even though he's not telling you. The poem has a quality of definiteness that reassures you that what you're getting is enough. We're not advocating that you leave details out for the sake of it. Going too far in that direction would render your poem an atmospheric blur, so it would come at the reader like guitar chords from a rock band hidden in clouds of dry ice. Narrative in poetry is always more selective than in prose, but there must always be enough detail to supply the reader with a context. Don't confuse the reader. Keep it simple, and don't lay the blame on the reader for failing to penetrate an obscurity that you have perpetrated. We could all learn from the way in which a traditional ballad keeps the tension of its narrative going. Look at 'The Twa Corbies' (in *English and Scottish Ballads*, edited by Robert Graves) and see what we mean.

Building tension in a poem is a matter of supplying alternations of crisis and release, so the reader is lured on. It's not just a simple 'What happened next?' kind of curiosity. Imagine a novel whose opening chapter consisted of 17 murders one after the other, graphically described. You would be so exhausted after reading it that you would have to take a holiday. A poem with a new incident in every line would be equally hard to take. In other words, moments of climax need to be balanced with intervals of calm.

This doesn't apply just to narrative poetry. Every poem, be it lyric, philosophical or whatever, needs to have tension built into the logic of its development. It could be the tension of a meditative self-questioning or an argument. Often when the tension is lost in a poem it's because the writer runs out of belief that what he or she is saying really needs to be said. Low-pressure writing, writing that lacks tension and drive, even though it may be perfectly competent in itself, has no inner drama, no fizz. A good poem always has drama of some sort. As Frost said:

> Everything written is as good as it is dramatic. It need not declare itself in form but it is drama or nothing.

Look, for example, at this poem by the Russian poet Anna Akhmatova:

> Three things enchanted him:
> white peacocks, evensong,
> and faded maps of America.
> He couldn't stand bawling brats,
> or raspberry jam with his tea,
> or womanish hysteria.
> ...And he was tied to me.
> > (translated by Stanley Kunitz with Max Hayward)

The structure of this poem comes from balancing the three things the 'he' of the poem liked against another three he didn't like, and summing up with a wonderfully disconnected line that is masquerading as a conclusion. You don't know to what that last line's tied – the three things he does like or the three he doesn't. It's almost a non-sequitur. Contained in the three dots before the final 'And' is an imaginary extra ten lines that would fill the story out. The fundamental structure is argumentative but there are no arguments presented, just facts, concrete details. The tension comes from the reader trying to relate the likes and the dislikes, and using them to make sense of the last line.

Notice, too, how cleverly the context is established in this poem. The reader is in no doubt that the speaker is a woman describing someone with whom she has had a relationship. All this is achieved in seven lines. The tone of the speaking voice here is playful, semi-ironic, a touch humorous and ultimately rueful. If you read this poem aloud – a practice we've already recommended – you'll notice how you automatically adjust your voice to the tonal variations in the poem. You couldn't say 'white peacocks, evensong' in the same way as you would say 'he couldn't stand bawling brats'. You would instinctively make your voice softer or harder, depending on what the words signify. When somebody says 'Don't speak to me in that tone of voice' you know exactly what they mean. Reading a poem on the page, however, you'll need to be alert to pick up the tone.

Picking up the tone of a poem, of course, is made easier when there are marked changes of register in the language. We've already touched briefly on the effects that can be achieved by this in Chapter 05. One poet who employs daring shifts of register is Kit Wright. Here is his 'Sonnet for Dick':

> My friend looked very beautiful propped on his pillows.
> Gently downward tended his dreaming head,
> His lean face washed as by an underlight of willows
> And everything right as rain except he was dead.
> So brave in his dying, my friend both kind and clever,
> And a useful Number Six who could whack it about.
> I have described this man to whomsoever
> The hell I've encountered, wandering in and out
> Of gaps in the traffic and Hammersmith Irish boozers,
> Crying, where and why did Dick Johnson go?
> And none of the carloads and none of the boozer users,
> Though full up with love and with cameraderie, know
> More than us all-of-his-others, assembled to grieve
> Dick who, brave as he lived things, took his leave.

The inversion and romanticism of line two 'Gently downward tended his dreaming head' (the kind of thing most writing workshops, and this book, try to knock out of you) comes down with a jolt on 'And everything right as rain except he was dead'. The cheerful first half of this line is upended by the second half. Later we have 'A useful Number Six who could whack it about' which sounds like something you'd hear in a pub. This juxtaposition of different kinds of language might seem alarming to someone with a more traditional view of the elegy – and in a lesser poet would be disastrous – but is actually what makes this poem so successful. You want to laugh but you can't; you never forget this is an elegy. It's another example of the benefits to be achieved by mixing humour and seriousness. None of the variations employed depart from the context the poem establishes: they all give you different perspectives on the dead friend.

EXERCISE 27 A character speaks

In conclusion, to get you writing with some of the considerations of this chapter in mind, we'd like you to undertake the following exercise. We got it from the American poet and novelist Jennifer Clements, who in turn got it from Toni Morrison. As this suggests, it is an exercise that works for prose as well as for poetry, but Jennifer adapted it somewhat, and we in turn have adapted it further to make it more suitable for poetry.

We'd like you to think of a well-known character from a literary work and answer the following questions:

- What objects does this character own?
- What does the character see when he or she closes their eyes?
- What is the character's favourite word?

After you've answered the questions, we'd like you to write a dramatic monologue in the persona of your character. Traditionally, a dramatic monologue is a poem written in the first person, and addressing an imagined listener (see Browning's famous poem 'My Last Duchess', or Carol Ann Duffy's 'Stealing', or W. S. Graham's 'Johann Joachim Quanz's Five Lessons', or Michael Donaghy's 'Black Ice and Rain', mentioned in Chapter 20 on page 185). This listener is usually addressed directly by such rhetorical devices as questions or apologies or accusations, but sometimes the addressee is more generally the reader (as in Carol Ann Duffy's 'Warming Her Pearls', Sylvia Plath's 'The Jailer', or – a more extreme example, with its own language – Christopher Reid's 'Memres of Alfred Stoker').

The first two questions above are useful precisely because they make you focus on concrete things. We suggest that to avoid the pitfalls of vagueness you choose a concrete word as your favourite one. And please don't feel you have to keep repeating it to prove that it is your favourite word.

13

writing in different modes

'Writing in different modes – why should I do that? I'm quite happy writing the way I do!'

Fine, but sometimes you can write better your own way if you try it someone else's way for a while, and pick up some of their good habits. It can be a way of extending your range as well. We touched on this subject in Chapter 09, when we introduced models. In this chapter we're going to go into it a bit more deeply, and give practical illustrations of some of the points we raised in Chapter 12.

MS: Once, when I had a new poem I wasn't sure how to read aloud, I went to an actor-friend of mine for advice. His method of helping me was to get me to interpret the poem in various ways – i.e. in an angry tone, a sarcastic tone, a sad tone, even a delighted or surprised tone. The tones he got me to adopt seemed so forced that I felt very self-conscious. I asked him what he was doing. He said that, by pulling me this way and that, some of the tones I adopted would be incorporated in my normal way of speaking the poem, which would consequently have more life in it. He turned out to be right, too.

EXERCISE 28 Questions

The mode we'd like you to try will send you back to de la Mare's 'The Listeners'. You'll remember how the haunted atmosphere of that poem is created. The traveller asks the same question twice of invisible listeners, gets no reply, then says: 'Tell them I came and no one answered, that I kept my word,' and gallops off into the night. We want you to try something similar – simply imagine a situation where someone asks questions but gets no answer, and then, after a gnomic remark, leaves. Try to resist modelling yourself too closely on the de la Mare situation or you may find yourself drawn into parody. 'The Listeners' has a rather archaic atmosphere, so you should go for a very contemporary situation to escape this. If you follow the instructions we've given, you'll find that, without having to spell it out, you cannot avoid creating an atmosphere of mystery.

If you want to ring the changes on this exercise, you could dwell for a moment on the other possibilities with which its questioning framework can provide you. For example, you could make your questions aggressive and threatening and instil an air of menace into your poem; or you could make them pleading and suppliant, or full of erotic suggestion, or just weirdly humorous. If you try several of these you'll begin to get a feel for the different tonal possibilities.

Using these fragments of dialogue forces you to adopt a persona whether you want to or not. The 'I' of the poem, remember, is not you. You need to step out of your own head and into somebody else's, just as an actor does when he or she inhabits a part. To do this properly you need to keep exploring the character you have invented for yourself. This doesn't mean you have to have a full curriculum vitae of your persona – it's quite likely that de la Mare didn't quite know who his horseman was, or what those listeners were. It was the dramatic and narrative potential of the situation which excited him into writing. Vivid yet inexplicable as the scene is, it leaves us, as readers, asking questions and wondering. The important thing to remember is that you must never break the illusion; you must make sure your readers continue to suspend their disbelief. This might seem obvious, but a fictional situation can easily be destroyed by authorial commentary. If you start off with a persona, you must sustain it and not lapse into your own voice by the end of the poem. It's especially important to keep this in mind when your poem is written in the first person.

EXERCISE 29 Professions

An excellent exercise in the use of a persona is the following, which we've stolen from Carol Ann Duffy. In the workshop situation it involves every participant taking a slip of paper from an envelope. Each slip will contain the name of a profession – for example 'surgeon', 'undertaker', 'detective', 'hangman', but also some that are unexpected, like 'rentboy', 'mime-artist', or some that are not strictly professions at all, like 'terrorist'. Reading this at home you can simply pick what profession you want, provided it is not the one you actually have. The poem you will write will be in the persona of someone with the profession you've chosen.

First, however, there are some instructions you have to follow. The poem must be written in couplets, and here is a list of what has to go on in each set:

- Lines 1 & 2: You are in a room, looking out of a window.
- Lines 3 & 4: You stop looking out of the window, but you're still in the room.

- Lines 5 & 6:   Something happens, either in the room or outside.
- Lines 7 & 8:   You have a recollection.
- Lines 9 & 10:   You leave the room.
- Lines 11 & 12:   You wish for something.
- Lines 13 & 14:   These are two free lines. You can do what you want here, but remember you have to bring the poem to a close.

Obviously the persona you've adopted will influence the details you choose for your poem, and a test of how successfully you've got into the persona is whether someone reading your poem can tell what you're supposed to be (although in the best attempts, this will not be too obvious).

What's good about the precise nature of these instructions is that you have to do something different in each couplet; you're forced to change tack continuously. So many bad poems get stuck in a particular groove of thought and rattle relentlessly on, without any deviation, until they hit the buffer of the final full stop.

You'll notice that this persona exercise is 14 lines long. As you know, this is the exact length of a sonnet, although some people insist that for a sonnet's requirements to be fulfilled there must be a regular pattern of rhyming and metrical arrangement. One of the characteristics of the traditional sonnet form is that there should be a proposition, an argumentative development of that proposition and a conclusion. The poem you will have written may not be anything like a traditional sonnet, but because of the instructions you had to carry out, it will have some of the tension of a sonnet.

EXERCISE 30 Sex and death

The next exercise we learned from the poet and mortician Thomas Lynch. In a workshop of 14 individuals (of course, more can play), each give a word that comes to mind when they think of sex. These 14 words are then employed to be the left side or right side words for a sonnet or a fourteener, at least, about mortality or death. Each line can start with one of the words (left side) or end with one (right side) but you should stick to one side or the other all the way down. If you feel you need an extra challenge, you can try to go up one side and down the other so that the last word of the first line matches the first word of the fourteenth (i.e. each word occurs twice). We're sure you can come up with 14 words of your own to do with sex. Two or more people can play, of course.

EXERCISE 31 Urgent travel

In the last chapter, we touched on how tension of some kind has to be built into the logic of a poem's development. This next exercise will be a little cliff-hanger from life. We've all, at some stage, had to be somewhere urgently. Perhaps we fell out with a partner and got an ultimatum. 'I'll be under the clock at Waterloo at 4 p.m. If you're not there, it's over.' We, dithering as usual, decide nearly too late that we have to get to Waterloo; or perhaps we've received a delayed letter, telling us that if we get to so and so's office by such and such a time we'll learn something to our advantage; or perhaps our reason for travel will be a more sombre one. Sharon Olds' poem 'The Race' is an excellent example of this. Here are the opening lines:

> When I got to the airport I rushed up to the desk,
> bought a ticket, ten minutes later
> they told me the flight was cancelled, the doctors
> had said my father would not live through the night
> and the flight was cancelled. A young man
> with a dark blond moustache told me
> another airline had a non-stop
> leaving in seven minutes. See that
> elevator over there, well go
> down to the first floor, make a right, you'll
> see a yellow bus, get off at the
> second Pam Am terminal, I
> ran, I who have no sense of direction
> raced exactly where he'd told me, a fish
> slipping upstream deftly against
> the flow of the river...

Think, then, of an urgent reason for travel. Describe the imaginary journey you undertake, focusing not on the background detail but on the pressing details of the journey itself. We don't want you to write a travelogue – you won't have time to notice what colour the carnation was in the flower-seller's hair or which of the dog's legs was missing, but you'll know that the man at the check-in desk has a scar. In other words, you'll notice only the details that can be immediately assimilated, and which are relevant to your journey. You won't notice the extraneous ones. Try to convey a progressive build-up of tension through the incidents you describe, not by littering your poem with phrases like 'panicking now', 'desperately' or 'with heart-stopping slowness'. Keep your narrative moving smoothly and don't let it sag. Remember that, however urgently motivated, your journey will reach its end, when you'll be able to relax. Try to bring your poem down to a calm conclusion.

EXERCISE 32 Souvenir

Travel needn't always be fraught with urgency or difficulty. Holiday travel should not, on the whole, be a stressful affair. Perhaps you'll bring back some souvenirs, maybe one special one. That souvenir (a voodoo mask, a dried banana flower, an earthenware Aztec flute in the shape of a bird?) will be imbued with the place you visited and the experience you had there. Maybe you've lived somewhere else and have brought something back that was very important to you. You no longer need to use it but it reminds you strongly of that other life. Elizabeth Bishop imagines Robinson Crusoe, long after his rescue from the island on which he was marooned, reflecting on something that was very important to him while he was there:

> The knife here on my shelf –
> it reeked of meaning, like a crucifix.
> It lived. How many years did I
> beg it, implore it, not to break?
> I knew each nick and scratch by heart,
> the bluish blade, the broken tip,
> the lines of wood-grain on the handle ...
>
> (From 'Crusoe in England')

We want you to imagine such an object – or maybe a real one will suggest itself – and make it the subject of a poem. By focusing on the object, you will be focusing on the experiences and the emotions of the life you led there without having to express them directly. You'll remember in Chapter 11 we mentioned what T.S. Eliot called 'the objective correlative' – the souvenir is working like that here.

EXERCISE 33 The laws

To conclude this chapter we have one final exercise. In the previous one, we asked you to use an object as a stimulus for writing. For this next task, which is a variation on one concocted by Sean O'Brien, we want you to turn to pictures. No, we're not sending you to the movies, we've done that before. This time we're sending you into art galleries. Well, not quite. But...

The world in which we live is governed by laws. We know that, but we don't spend every waking minute dwelling on it. There's the law of gravity, for example: none of us would walk off a rooftop and hope to stay up there. There's the law of libel: you can't base the most obnoxious character in your new novel on the critic who rubbished your last one (well, you can, but you'll be sued to bankruptcy if you do). There are some laws from previous centuries that have never been repealed and are theoretically still in force. One of these is that a man in London suddenly needing to pee can ask a policeman to put his cape around him so that he can urinate in privacy. Some people have to obey religious laws regarding their diet. There are social laws; you wouldn't go to an investiture at Buckingham Palace in your ripped denims. There's the law of death. We mention these to illustrate how various laws can be, and how some are more serious than others.

At this stage, in a workshop situation, we would give out picture postcards to the participants. The following exercise can be done alone, or preferably with someone else. Here are two of those cards (Paula Rego's *The Dance* and Rodin's *The Kiss*). Look very closely at them. We want you to think of each picture as a kind of trailer for a particular world. **Everything** in this world is like the picture you have selected – remember it's not the world in which you live; it's a completely different and strange world. We want you to write down at least six laws that operate within it.

When you have invented your laws, we want you to go on to the second stage of this exercise. This involves your writing a dramatic monologue, speaking as an inhabitant of your particular world. (A dramatic monologue is simply a poem in which you speak, using the voice of a persona, where the 'I', of course, is not you.) Because poetry, as we've advocated, should show rather than tell, you may not refer directly to your laws; they must, however, be implicit in your monologue so that your

Paula Rego, *The Dance*
Reproduced by permission of The Tate Gallery, London

Auguste Rodin, *The Kiss*
Reproduced by permission of The Tate Gallery, London

companion ought to be able to deduce your laws from what
you've said. You may not be able to get all your laws into your
poem, but you should try to include as many as you can. As you
write you may think of new ones that didn't occur to you in the
first stage of the exercise, and you can incorporate these, too,
into your monologue.

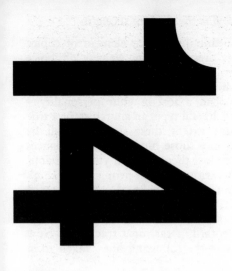

style

Style [said Samuel Wesley] is the dress of thought.

It's easy to see what he meant. Just as an element of choice comes into your day-to-day dress, the same element of choice will determine what style you adopt for your poems. What you choose to wear, of course, and the way you decide to write once you've got going, will depend a lot on your personality – whether you're a democratic liberal type, an anarchist, or a true blue conservative. To some extent these decisions will be unconsciously taken – but once those fundamental allegiances have been made, you will follow them with all your conscious skill. Styles of poetry are as various as what people wear. Think of the different impressions you'd make if you wore the following: an Armani suit, torn denims, tight black leather trousers, a bowler hat with the Union Jack on it, a see-through mini skirt, a leopardskin leotard, a sari or a track suit. Now look at the range of styles in the following lines, taken from genuine poems.

- 'I can't go there, but I know just how it will be.'
- 'Not all the women of England
  are boiling kettles
  by the tall gates.'
- 'I love you little Bo-Bo with your delicate golden lions.'
-                                    '...and the general hubbub
  of inkies and jennets and kickapoos with their lemniscs.'
- 'I see the boys of summer in their ruin.'
- 'I'd love to know what I raved that night to the night, what
                              those innocent dithyrambs were.'
- 'I *insist* on vegetating here
  In motheaten grandeur. Haven't I plotted
  Like a madman to get here? Well then.'
- 'don't think we not grateful, boss,
  how you cool the place for we comfort
  but the line shuffle forward
  one step at a time
  like Big Fraid hold we'
- 'A human is a comet streamed in language far down time, no
  other living is like it.'
-   '...but Green
  he's not thinking physics at this stage, nuh-uh,
  our boy's only trying to get himself out of bed'

Some of the poets quoted here have clearly derived their way of writing from their origins, from the way the language was used around them when they were growing up. Others have created a more sophisticated style by overlaying their original patterns of speech with a more elaborate syntax and vocabulary. Still others have substituted for the language of their childhood a language they have gleaned from books, or whatever. It's difficult to tell by what some have been influenced. As our selection goes some way toward showing, the range is as limitless as the possibilities of language itself.

The style you adopt is your business. If you trawl the poetry shelves in libraries, you'll find books exemplifying all these styles and more. You'll have to persuade yourself, though, that the style you choose is an honest reflection of your true self if it is going to persuade others. Remember, ultimately people will respond to your style, not your subject matter. As George-Louis de Buffon said: '*Style, c'est l'homme même*.' Style is the man.

Your writing style will have its origins in your background and also in the wider culture that surrounds you, so it's conceivable that elements of each of the three strands we outlined at the beginning of the last but one paragraph might be present in your style. The linguistic means you employ to write your poem will reveal your personal makeup. For example, the vocabulary you use – your diction – might be drawn from any of the following: simple, homely words, local or dialect words, arcane words, odd or outlandish words, educated words, posh words or rude words, and possibly foreign words. You'll find examples of most of these in the lines we quoted above. Obviously your style will be stretched one way or another by the way in which you accommodate these choices. Writers need to exercise a very conscious control over their diction, and any deviations they might make away from simple straightforward language have to be very surely handled. Often this is not what happens – the deviations which inexperienced writers make seem like mere inadvertence. They may have intended what they wrote, but it doesn't convince the reader; it doesn't feel like 'the best words in the best order' as Coleridge put it. One of the most important things your frisk draft will do for you is save you from yourself in this respect. You know that word you appropriated the other day – nystagmic – does it really fit your description of your mother?

Of course interesting effects can come from the mixing of registers (we looked at this in detail in Chapters 05 and 12). We're not saying you shouldn't try to achieve effects such as these – developing linguistic strategies can be very much a part of the process of finding your own distinctive voice – we **are** saying it's tricky to bring these effects off. You need to be in control of what you're doing.

Here are two exercises which will help you explore a range of tonal possibilities. The first one focuses on shifts of register.

EXERCISE 34 Different registers

Get hold of a dictionary and choose the following words:

- two scientific words
- two slang words
- two words you've never spoken
- two religious words
- two bureaucratic words.

Now put all of these words as unobtrusively as you can into a short poem.

EXERCISE 35 Tonal variations

The second exercise is to do with using variations of tone. What we want you to write is a poem in dialogue form, between Person A and Person B. Each time you have one of them speak, you must change the tone used. Incorporate (in whatever order) as many of the following tonal possibilities as you can:

- pleasant
- loving
- suspicious
- irritated
- cynical
- frosty
- hostile
- offensive
- mortified
- contrite.

Neither of these exercises is likely to result in what you would consider to be a poem, but they will help to widen your range and push you beyond the boundaries of what you normally do. Both can be considered language games, and are good to do with other people.

We're not advocating here that the style you adopt should be outlandish or spectacularly deviant. Think of the tasks we've just given you as being like the interpretative vocal exercises we mentioned at the beginning of the previous chapter – reading the same poem in different tones of voice. Just as with those, the hope here is that some of the tonal range and some of the possibilities of shifts of register these exercises compelled you to employ, albeit in a rather artificial way, will become available for your natural writing style. What you should be trying to achieve is to extend your range without sacrificing naturalness.

Often, when people think they're writing in a stylish way, all the reader can see is mannerism and overcooking. It's very natural for young writers to go looking for a new, exciting language, ignoring the one that's close to home, but what they often end up with is verbal gymnastics that convey little meaning. Our early efforts were no exception. When we were at college and gave our poems to student friends, they'd hand them back, saying, 'Very nice, but what does it mean?' Young writers are often suspicious of simplicity. Even when they do manage to get some of the meaning across, they tend to hit the reader over the head with it.

> *To hell with overstating it* [the young Seamus Heaney was advised by Michael McLaverty]. *Don't have the veins bulging in your biro.*

W.D. Snodgrass has a good example of how less can say more in a poem, how tact in handling detail can make it possible to write successfully about even the most extreme subject. He quoted Randall Jarrell's poem 'Protocols', which is about children being put to death in the gas chambers of Birkenau.

Protocols
[*Birkenau, Odessa; the children speak alternately.*]

> We went there on the train. *They had big barges that they towed,*
> *We stood up, there were so many I was squashed.*
> There was a smoke-stack, then they made me wash.
> It was a factory, I think. *My mother held me up*
> *And I could see the ship that made the smoke.*

When I was tired my mother carried me.
She said, 'Don't be afraid.' But I was only tired.
Where we went there is no more Odessa.
They had water in a pipe – like rain, but hot;
The water there is deeper than the world

And I was tired and fell in in my sleep
And the water drank me. That is what I think.
And I said to my mother, 'Now I'm washed and dried,'
My mother hugged me, and it smelled like hay
And that is how you die. And that is how you die.

Snodgrass's comment on this is as follows: 'How many poets tried to write this poem and failed? How many could not resist saying that this is evil – that it is wrong to kill children? That is not worth saying. If the reader doesn't know that by now, there is no use *your* telling him.' He goes on to show how it's an extreme tact in the choice of detail which makes Jarrell's poem work. There are no brutal guards beating the children – that side of things is excluded from the poem. This restraint – in which the children, curious yet innocent, find the trip interesting and a bit different – illustrates a complete fidelity to the experience itself. There's no propaganda, no handwringing, no expressions of horror. 'You know at once,' says Snodgrass, 'that this is no news editor trying to arouse your feelings (or his own) to the support of some particular line of action; these are merely several children who died there, who tell you exactly, simply and directly, what it was like, how it felt.' In other words, Jarrell's poem demonstrates: 'a complete removal from any ulterior motive, an absolute dedication to the object and the experience.' Whenever there's a failure of this kind of tact, this is often due to a lack of confidence in the writer: 'an insecurity which makes him shout louder and louder hoping to quiet everyone else's doubts and especially his own.'

Using tact in your writing is a matter of knowing what to leave out. We have mentioned this several times before. Look back particularly at Chapter 08 – the frisk draft – where we asked you to look through your brand new poem to see if there were any extraneous details, any lazy or superfluous adjectives, or places where you stepped in and told the reader loudly what was going on, as if the reader were somehow deaf. We're not saying that a stripped-down, austere style is the only one in which to write poems. The range of poems we've quoted shows that. We are saying that it's beneficial for all writers to learn an austere discipline, within which they'll instinctively exercise severe editorial restraint. This will be a good foundation for any stylistic freedoms you may feel you want to allow yourself later, when the confidence that comes with increased technical control tells you you can.

To end this chapter there are one or two points we'd like to make about the details of grammar, syntax and punctuation. These may strike you as tedious, but getting them right is a crucial, if unobtrusive, part of achieving a good style. Clarity is very much a matter of accurate grammar and syntax. Grammar is what holds all the parts of speech in a language together – verbs agreeing with their subjects, tenses clearly specified by temporal references, adverbs clearly modifying the verbs they're supposed to, adjectives likewise with nouns. These relationships must be treated with respect: don't think that by using an adjective as a verb you are necessarily improving the English language. The word syntax denotes the way in which you connect these parts of speech, particularly to show relationships of causality and dependency. By learning to play syntax against line-endings and stanza-shapes, as you must, you will find ways of introducing tension into your poems. The first eight lines of the following poem, 'Entropy', by Derek Mahon, illustrate beautifully what we mean by this.

> We are holing up here
> in the difficult places –
> in caves, terminal moraines
> and abandoned farmhouses,
> the wires cut, the old car
> disposing itself for death
> among the inscrutable,
> earth-inheriting dandelions.

Note how the syntax is modulated here by a cunning use of commas and that lone dash.

Ezra Pound said, as we've already noted:

> *Poetry should be written at least as well as prose.*

One area where it's easy to confuse the reader is that of pronouns, and the nouns to which they refer. For example:

> Parachuting down into the field,
> the cows look up in surprise.

The cows here are clearly not parachutists, but grammatically they are. This may seem only too obvious, but we've often encountered exactly this problem in workshops, where the syntax sends you one way and the meaning another. This is like taking what you thought was the toaster plug from a tangle of wires, connecting it up, and hearing the Archbishop of Canterbury pray at you from the radio set instead. Another problem is that of compound verbs and modal verbs in English. Take, for example, the sentence: 'It would have been nicer not to have sent those bull's testicles to your mother-in-law.' Incorporating this directly into a poem would be difficult because of the clumsiness of the grammatical construction 'It would have been nicer not to have', which makes for awkwardness. Rhythmical requirements mean that compound verb phrases like the one above seem to preclude the agility and directness with which a good poem should operate. This kind of sentence construction is more typically to be found in a certain kind of prose.

Part of what controls the intelligibility of your writing is a correct use of punctuation. You have various options in this respect. Some poets punctuate according to regular prose usage, others use a more personal system (Emily Dickinson's dashes are a well-known example of this), while some use no punctuation at all, or at any rate a very light use of it, letting the line-breaks perform that function. The thing is to be consistent. You may want to experiment with different systems – but don't employ two different systems in the same poem. Likewise capitalization at the beginning of lines is an option, although not an imperative as some would lead you to believe. You only have to leaf through a variety of poetry books to see this.

Finally you should bear in mind that the way you present your poem on the page is also a part of style. You may want to arrange your poem in one or another stanza form, or have it in a block. (But remember, as we said in Chapter 05, each unit of the poem has to justify itself.) You can use long lines or short lines, as you wish – this will be partly dictated by the requirements of your metre (see Chapter 16 for rhythm). You might want to arrange your poem on the page as a map of Ireland or rain-streaks on the window pane, but don't assume that idiosyncratic visual arrangement will compensate for any deficiencies or blandness in your text.

15

getting the rhymes to choose you

Out of us all
That make rhymes,
Will you …
Sometimes
Choose me,
You English words?

(from 'Words' by Edward Thomas)

He that first invented thee,
May his joynts tormented bee
                    Cramp'd forever;
Still may syllable jarre with time,
Still may reason warre with rime,
                    Resting never,
(from 'A Fit of Rime against Rime' by Ben Jonson)

It's in favour. It's out of favour. It's in favour again. Whatever you think about rhyme – whether you think it's beneath your dignity to use it, or whether you think it isn't poetry if it doesn't rhyme – you'd have to agree that rhyme is often what people first associate with the pleasures of verse. Poetry is a great deal about making relationships between words – which is what keeps a poem together, makes the tension, the muscles of it. Rhyme is the most obvious and physical of these relationships. We've talked about the noise a poem makes, and rhyme is the most distinctive of its sounds. The way in which the sound plays against the sense is at the heart of how a poem achieves its effect.

Use of rhyme is obviously linked to the use of metre – it defines the end of a line where it occurs and it's a sort of metrical clincher; as the rhyme falls into place you get the satisfaction of seeing the rhyme scheme work itself out. It also has the effect of binding together the lines of a stanza in a satisfactory shape. The test of ingenuity is always to see how surprising yet persuasive the rhyme word can be. To get this unpredictability, you should try to rhyme different parts of speech: 'hat' and 'at', say, rather than 'hat' and 'bat'. Different spellings set up another kind of excitement where the ear hears correspondences that are variants to the eye, for instance 'sew' and 'though'. The frictions you set up between these differences and samenesses are what give your poem its character.

Some people say English wasn't designed as a language to rhyme in – so why bother? As we've written only in English, we can't say what it feels like to try to rhyme in another language.

Rhyming possibilities in other languages appear to be much greater than in English – although we're told that, because of this, certain complicated rules are introduced there to deter too easy rhyming. There's no need for such rules in English. Try to find a rhyme for the English word love, for example; all you have are 'dove', 'glove' and 'shove' as full rhyme possibilities. (In case you're asking, 'What about 'above'?' – true full rhyme requires two words that are exactly the same apart from the initial consonants.) Our instinct would be to go for 'shove' – as a verb, not a noun.

Use of rhyme has, in the past, occasioned fits of intellectual snobbery. Thomas Campion observed (a long time ago):

> ...*the facilitie and popularitie of Rime creates as many Poets as a hot summer flies...*

He considered it is

> ...*sparingly to be usd, lest it should offend the eare with tedious affectation...*

On the other hand, the dislike of rhyme in modern writing is so widespread you might feel the ease of *not* rhyming creates 'as many Poets as a hot summer flies'. Milton called rhyme 'modern bondage' (an interesting quasi-rhyme, that) and a great many contemporary practitioners have only too willingly thrown off its fetters.

Rhyming is certainly a difficult technique to handle with confidence, especially full rhyme. One of the problems is that, for the poet, the working out of the rhyme has the effect of changing what you first thought of saying. On the other hand, this mightn't be a problem. You might find yourself saying something you didn't know you had it in you to say.

The trap awaiting the careless rhymer is, of course, the forced choice which is less than adequate. A word chosen solely for its rhyme – rather than its meaning – may not be the best word. An extreme version of this is when children sometimes get so carried away in finding a rhyme that they forget to make sense. It gets sabotaged by the children's delight in the sound they're producing. Another problem is that words like 'day', for example, or 'bread', have very many rhymes indeed, whereas other words don't have any partners at all (try finding a rhyme for 'orange' or 'chimney'). Then there are the obvious clichés of rhyme – June, moon, trees, breeze – and these patterns are only too easy to fall into. Nothing is more dulling to the ear than a succession of highly predictable and plonking rhyme words. The counterpart to this, of course, is tricksiness. Rhyme is definitely associated with cleverness; it's show-offy, and thus ideal for displays of wit. More than any other aspect of the practice of poetry it's the one people can identify as an unarguable skill. A rhymer, therefore, has to walk the narrow line between plonkiness and cleverness, and it's not always easy to do. A poet such as Tony Harrison, who is untypically committed to full rhymes, gets very mixed reactions to his work. Some people feel that, because of his rhyming, he's the only real poet writing today; others, though, feel that his work veers uneasily between seriousness and doggerel.

> I saw the charred Iraqui lean
> towards me from the bomb-blasted screen,
>
> his windscreen wiper like a pen
> ready to write down thoughts for men,
>
> his windscreen wiper like a quill
>
> he's reaching for to make his will.
> I saw the charred Iraqui lean
>
> like someone made of Plasticine
>
> as though he'd stopped to ask the way
> and this is what I heard him say:

> (from 'A Cold Coming')

These lines bring back to us the first Gulf War, and the ballad-like metre reminds us of the old broadsheet ballad response to great historical events. If, for some readers, there's a whiff of doggerel in these lines, others might respond that this is deliberately intended, as a form of ironic commentary on horror.

One of the main characteristics of rhyme, as here, is its capacity to draw attention to itself. (This is why it's the preferred mode, of course, for ironists and satirists.) Once the reader's expectation of rhyming has been set up, the movement of the verse is conditioned by the stepping stone feeling of landing on each rhyme as one goes down the page. Rhyme provides the double aesthetic pleasure of expectation followed by reassurance, followed immediately by expectation/reassurance again. The distance between rhymes is also important; the further away you get from your rhyme word, the more likely it is the reader will lose the sense of anticipation and release that comes from negotiating those stepping stones. Dylan Thomas's 'Author's Prologue' to his *Selected Poems* is a hundred line poem which rhymes inward from the first and last lines, meeting in the middle. Now, as rhyme, this just doesn't work, whatever formal assistance in composition it may have given the poet. Quite simply, you can't keep the rhymes in your head that long, so their effect gets lost.

The 'stepping stones' phenomena we've mentioned above – the 'expectation followed by reassurance' feeling that rhyme gives you – is produced by a variation on two basic strategies: endstopping and enjambement. Endstopping means that each line ends with a sense break or a sense pause. Enjambement means that the sense runs on into the next line. We can see how this works if we look at the following stanza from a poem by W. H. Auden:

> A plain without a feature, bare and brown,
>> No blade of grass, no sign of neighbourhood,
> Nothing to eat and nowhere to sit down,
>> Yet, congregated on its blankness, stood
>> An unintelligible multitude,
> A million eyes, a million boots in line
> Without expression, waiting for a sign.

> (from 'The Shield of Achilles')

In this stanza, Auden allows himself enjambement only once, in the fourth line, where inversion of the normal syntax places the verb 'stood' at the end of the line, ahead of its subject. The syntax does not allow you to pause here at the line-ending, but pushes you on to discover how, propelled by the sense of what is being said, the whole thing works itself out. There's no pause on the rhyming word. A really good rhymer will vary this technique throughout a poem, avoiding, shall we say, the very marked endstopping of the heroic couplet, as in:

> Nature and Nature's Laws lay hid in Night.
> God said, *Let Newton be!* and All was *Light*.
>> (from 'Epitaph Intended for Isaac Newton'
>> by Alexander Pope)

but also taking care not to produce too breathless an effect of running on. It's worth looking in detail, by the way, at 'The Shield of Achilles', also 'The Fall of Rome', 'In Memory of W. B. Yeats', 'Atlantis' – in fact much of Auden – to see how he uses rhyme and varies endstopping with enjambement of rhyming words for serious effect.

Louis MacNeice put the arguments for and against the use of rhyme like this:

> *The case for rhyme is that it is in itself attractive – musical – and makes for memorability (besides setting the poet a healthy technical problem). The case against rhyme is that, being obviously artificial, it suggests insincerity and that it lulls the reader into a pleasant coma. There are many ways in which one may compromise between these two schools of thought. One can use rhyme in a poem, but not continuously or not in the expected places ... One can use internal rhymes, off-rhymes, bad rhymes, 'pararhymes'; one can rhyme a stressed against an unstressed syllable. Such devices can be used for some onamatopoeic significance (a 'bad' rhyme often having a peculiar emotional effect), or less positively in order to avoid a total effect which is too pat, smug, commonplace. (I do not suggest that a complete poem of perfect rhymes need be any of these things, but it is a danger of which all poets must be conscious.)*

So, Wilfred Owen, for example, can rhyme **knive us** and **nervous**, **silent** and **salient**, **wire** and **war**, **brambles** and **rumbles**. Words can rhyme on the vowel only, and not on the consonants, as in **cord** and **gawp** (known as assonance). There can also be rhymes involving words of unequal syllables such as **recognizing** and **sing**, or polysyllables such as **histories** and **mysteries**. (The latter, known as feminine rhymes, often lend themselves more readily to comic effects.) Sometimes poets will go so far as to break a word in half in order to make a rhyme. There's no limit to what ingenuity can contrive. You see this at its most spectacular in the field of light verse and song. Who hasn't marvelled at some of W. S. Gilbert's or Cole Porter's rhymes? In the field of contemporary song-writing, Elvis Costello is famous for his deft and witty rhymes:

> So get your mind off the sweet behind of our little angel
>> (from 'Our Little Angel')

On the whole, though, it's as well to remember that ingenuity may have that 'Look Ma, no hands!' quality about it, which serious poetry (and we don't mean po-faced poetry) does well to avoid. Also, finding rhymes is by no means easy, and however you set about the task – sleeping on it, or using a rhyming dictionary – you may end up like Ben Jonson, feeling utterly frustrated with the impossible task you have set yourself.

Rhyme can also occur inadvertently. If you don't pay close attention to the sound of what you've written all kinds of discord can follow. The internal rhymes in this (invented) example:

> You watch the blue river flow past you
> And your new life passes in review

give you an uneasy feeling of excess rhyming, or over-rhyming. The reader feels, also, that the rhymes aren't quite intended (although they may have been) and one of the most important effects of rhyme is that it must strike the reader as planned, otherwise it looks like awkwardness. You also have to watch out that a rhyme doesn't pop up in an otherwise free passage of unrhymed verse. Read it through carefully and make sure that it isn't going to produce an unintentionally comic effect. If the rhyme breaks the pattern, strike it out.

Using rhyme will sharpen your ear to vowel harmonies and the possibilities of consonance (same consonant rhyming) and assonance (same vowel rhyming). Some people argue that all such effects can be included under the heading of 'rhyme'. Ezra Pound's most famous imagist poem, 'In a Station of the Metro' –

> The apparition of these faces in the crowd;
> Petals on a wet, black bough.

– doesn't quite rhyme, but look at the way 'faces in the crowd' is echoed by 'petals on a … bough'. Look too at the way the vowel in 'petals' is echoed in 'wet' and at the final sequence of vowels – **e, a, ow** – a descending sequence. This poem by Robert Graves illustrates similar effects:

Cat-Goddesses

A perverse habit of cat-goddesses –
Even the blackest of them, black as coals
Save for a new moon blazing on each breast,
With coral tongues and beryl eyes like lamps,
Long-legged, pacing three by three in nines –
This obstinate habit is to yield themselves,
In verisimilar love-ecstasies,
To tatter-eared and slinking alley-toms
No less below the common run of cats

Than they above it; which they do for spite,
To provoke jealousy – not the least abashed
By such gross-headed, rabbit-coloured litters
As soon they shall be happy to desert.

An unmistakable feature of this is the regular recurrence of 's' sounds at the ends of lines. Sometimes the 's' is strong and hissy as in 'goddesses' and 'breast', sometimes it's weak and buzzy as in 'coals' and 'nines'. A kind of 's'-rhyme effect is produced on the plurals 'lamps', 'nines', 'selves', and so on. Anyone who's ever eavesdropped on the sex life of cats will recognize the repertoire of hissing and chuffing which is mimicked here. Then we have that open 'a' vowel again, repeated internally in 'habit', 'cat', 'black', 'blackest', 'lamps', 'habit' (again), 'tatter' and 'alley', 'cats' (again), 'abashed' 'rabbit' and 'happy'. If that doesn't capture the squalling side of the proceedings, we don't know what does. We're sure Graves knew what he was doing here, but some of the internal rhymes may have been struck by happy accident through unconscious workings and association.

Let's look at a poet whose use of rhyme both does and does not draw attention to itself: Paul Muldoon.

'Why do we waste so much time arguing?'
We were sitting at the sushi-bar
drinking *Kirin* beer
and watching the Master chef
fastidiously shave
salmon, tuna and yellowtail
while a slightly more volatile
apprentice
fanned the rice,
every grain of which was magnetized
in one direction – east.

(from 'Sushi')

Notice, in this example, how rhyme is integrated with an almost prosy use of language, and how, in order to obtain a rhyme, Muldoon allows one word to have an entire line to itself. This sly use of rhyme is clearly very different from the more upfront way Tony Harrison uses it, and Muldoon has been hugely influential on younger poets itching to show off their skill and sophistication. An earlier poet who has been even more influential in this way is Robert Lowell. He has said how reading with the Beats in California in March 1957 helped to loosen his style:

> *I had a mechanical, gristly, alliterative style that did not charm much, unless … something slipped.*

One of the poems Lowell wrote after 'something slipped', as he put it, was 'During Fever', included in his collection *Life Studies*. Here's the opening of it:

Mother, your master bedroom
looked away from the ocean.
You had a window-seat,
an electric blanket,
a silver hot water bottle
monogrammed like a hip-flask,
Italian china fruity
with bunches and berries
and proper *putti*.
Gold, yellow and green,
the nuptial bed
was as big as a bathroom.

The rhymes here aren't obvious, sometimes with a lot of distance between them – for example 'bedroom' and 'bathroom'. You could call it a kind of loose stitching which holds the piece together acoustically. What is striking about this way of writing is how a completely natural-sounding and colloquial word-order communicates itself with great ease, while simultaneously alerting the reader to the subtle levels of organization that are behind it. A poem by Lowell's contemporary, John Berryman, throws rhymes at you in a rather casual, subversive way like this:

Life, friends, is boring. We must not say so.
After all, the sky flashes, the great sea yearns,
we ourselves flash and yearn,
and moreover my mother told me as a boy
(repeatedly) 'Ever to confess you're bored
means you have no

Inner Resources.' I conclude now I have no
inner resources, because I am heavy bored.
Peoples bore me,
literature bores me, especially great literature,
Henry bores me, with his plights & gripes
as bad as achilles,

who loves people and valiant art, which bores me.
And the tranquil hills, & gin, look like a drag
and somehow a dog
has taken itself & its tail considerably away
into mountains or sea or sky, leaving
behind: me, wag.

(from *The Dream Songs*)

Reading this gives you a feeling that Berryman has taken a form
and deliberately fractured it. He repeats the word 'bored' over
and over, and thus rhyming with itself (again with the word
'yearns') almost as if he's too bored to find another rhyme
(although there is an internal rhyme with 'resources'). At the
same time, he sneaks in some very surprising full rhymes – 'so'
and 'no', and finally 'drag' and 'wag' to provide a witty
emphasis, and to suggest, perhaps, that despite the boredom
there's life in the old dog yet.

EXERCISE 36 Nonsense rhyming poem

Nobody reading this book, we hope, will be unfamiliar with
Lewis Carroll's 'Jabberwocky' poem. It's what is called a
'nonsense' poem (although nonsense has a way of acquiring
meaning) and is partly made up of nonce words; words like
'vorpal', 'frumious', 'bandersnatch', 'outgrabe' and 'gimble'.
Some of Lewis Carroll's coinings have become part of the
language, such as 'galumphing'. Otherwise, Carroll uses normal
English words and structure. What we're going to ask you to do
is to use the 'Jabberwocky' model and invent some new words
of your own. They should, of course, sound as if they *might* be
English. This is really a group workshop exercise and is a little
bit more difficult to do on your own, although it can be done.
Also, you need to know – this is important – which words are
nouns, verbs, adverbs and adjectives.

If we were to list some of the Jabberwocky inventions, they
could be classified like this:

Noun	Verb	Adjective	Adverb
toves	*gyre*	*slithy*	
borogoves	*galumph*	*mimsy*	
mome raths	*outgrabe*	*frumious*	
bandersnatch			

Notice that there are no adverbs in the poem, although you could easily invent some; 'mimsily', for example, or 'vorpally'. So take a piece of paper and write down those four parts of speech; then, working as quickly as you can, invent some words to fit under the various categories. It's more fun doing this as a group, as you can then share all your inventions and have someone write them up on a board. You can also vote on whether the words are OK or not. Then you'll need to apply such criteria as: how does it sound? Can it be pronounced? Is it too much like an existing word? Does it seem a suitably *English* coining? and so on.

You now have the fundamentals of a new language. Using these invented words (all the others will be perfectly normal English words) and keeping to normal English sentence patterns, we'd like you to write a nonsense rhyming poem. It could be a Shakespearean sonnet, rhyming **abab cdcd efef gg**, or it could be in ballad form, with four-line stanzas, or any rhyming model you like. If possible, try to rhyme on the nonsense words. As you almost certainly won't have the rhyme words you need already in your list, you can now have the pleasure of inventing more new words to get the rhymes.

JHW: I gave this exercise to a group of students recently and, quite apart from the hilarity of listening to them read out what they had written – this exercise really buzzes once the glumness invoked by words like 'noun' and 'adverb' is dispelled – there was an added bonus in the comment of one of the students who said the exercise had 'taken away her fear of rhyming'.

Your nonsense words could be used for other purposes too. You could, for example, try to write something deeply serious – a love poem, for example, or a philosophical poem. No doubt you will conjure up other possibilities.

EXERCISE 37 Rhyme-led sonnet

The attraction of using rhyme is, of course, that it adds yet another level of formal organization to your language, providing a challenge that no one with poetical instincts can resist, even as it drives you insane. It would be unusual if you did not, at some time in your writing life, feel the desire to use rhyme – and we'd like to suggest that, even if you don't much care for it, you nevertheless try your hand at it. We want you to write a Petrarchan sonnet. A Petrachan sonnet rhymes like this:

- the first eight lines or octave: **abbaabba**
- the last six lines or sestet: **cdecde** or **cdcdcd** (avoiding the Shakespearian couplet at the end).

Do this exercise by writing in the rhyme words at the line endings first – before you have so much as considered what your poem will be about. You are going to let your rhyme words dictate what you're going to say, and not the subject matter. (It may comfort you to know that Shelley occasionally employed this 'rhyme-words first' method of composition. The Romantics used to play a game called 'Bout Rhymé' where two or more people would agree to use the same rhyme words and then go off and write their sonnets.) By all means use a rhyming dictionary to select rhymes that are a bit unusual, and by all means rhyme monosyllabic words with polysyllabic words, or use any variety of half-rhyme you've a mind to. Try also to bear in mind that you should select words from different parts of speech for your rhymes. Now look at your matrix and see if you can fill in the blanks. In the act of doing so, subject matter should suggest itself, but don't let yourself be governed by it to the extent of being persuaded you need to accommodate your subject by changing your rhymes. You can employ any metrical variation you like. Be daring. Try the Muldoon trick of giving your rhyme word a line all to itself. Use enjambement as Berryman does and try to avoid endstopping your lines too obviously.

EXERCISE 38 Plain sonnet

You can also tackle this Petrarchan sonnet exercise the other way around! – the normal way, so to speak – by choosing your subject matter first, and then trying to rhyme. Doing these two little tasks should tell you a lot about the relationship of sound and sense in a poem. When you do the exercise subject matter first, try to avoid comedy, or at least obvious comedy. (Using rhyme has a tendency to pull you that way.) Choose a subject that will not allow slapstick: not a sonnet to your bicycle, therefore, but a sonnet about your day job (that should keep you serious). If you haven't experimented with rhyme before, you'll find that, because the rhyme words don't necessarily come easily, the first version you'll arrive at may sound bumpy, stilted, archaic, risible, whatever. The hard work of revision begins at this stage; ironing out these wrinkles and trying to make your rhymes seem easy and unforced. The great test is: can you make your language sound perfectly natural and colloquial, and yet rhyme at the same time? Can you **naturalize** what is, after all, an unnatural linguistic device?

JHW: I recently completed a sestina that took me, off and on, over a year to write. A sestina, by the way, employs a rather peculiar kind of rhyme (perhaps, in view of the distance involved, this isn't strictly rhyme at all): it has six stanzas of six lines each and the same six end words occur in each stanza, but in a different order each time. It ends with an *envoi* of three lines in which all six words are again repeated. You might say the stanzas rhyme with each other (rather than the lines), and the rhymes in each case are the same words. My first version was written rather quickly – a commission – but I knew it wasn't right. In fact, it proved fiendishly difficult to balance the sense and the syntax against the formal requirement. Every time I looked at it, I could see where the strains were showing. When you write a sestina, once you've got your six end words you have to keep using them all through the poem and each use of the word has to seem as natural as possible; therefore no inversions, no funny word order, no archaisms, no idioms you wouldn't use yourself. The goal I set myself was to produce a poem that would allow even a clued-up reader to go through it without actually realizing it was a sestina.

The achievement of natural utterance, whatever levels of formal organization lie behind their poems, is what all good poets are striving for; but finding the natural and right-sounding rhyme is more often a matter of luck and inspiration than conscious choosing. Sometimes the rhymes come rapidly and instinctively, sometimes it can take you ages to find a rhyme, or your failure to find one can block a poem altogether. It probably strikes some people as absurd that anyone should spend time on finding a rhyme, but poets are always waiting for those happy accidents that will help them to complete a poem, and one of these could be finding that last crucial rhyme. 'The chances of rhyme', as Charles Tomlinson put it in his poem of that name

are like the chances of meeting –
In the finding fortuitous, but once found binding...

16

it don't mean a thing if it ain't got that swing

Find me good poems without rhythm. Find me warm-
blooded life without breathing. Find me in any good poet
extensive and repeated writing about metre – that which
is measured after the event, by others.

(from *The Private Art* by Geoffrey Grigson)

If you think of poets who've made pronouncements about
metre, what you usually find is that, as Geoffrey Grigson says,
these are pronouncements 'after the event'. Actual prosodists
(people who theorize about metre) are not usually poets but
academics, and although what they have to say about rhythm
and metre may be very interesting – or not, as the case may be
– it may not be of any practical help to a poet. What's actually
interesting and useful is what a poet does in his or her own
practice. Of course, there are things you ought to know. You
might feel a bit of a fool if you were a practising poet and
couldn't tell the difference between an iamb and a trochee. On
the other hand, you may well have started writing without
having the faintest idea what they are. You probably began with
a very unsure idea of what your verse should sound like: a
composite, perhaps, of everything you'd heard and read up until
that time. Most likely, you started by imitating someone else's
rhythms but then found you wanted to sound a slightly more
distinctive note and began to experiment accordingly. Finding
that individual touch, that personal fingering, is a matter of
improvization and luck, and whether or not you consider it
important to know what accentual asclepiads are (see later in
the chapter) probably has more to do with your idea of yourself
as a poet than it has to do with getting some flair and push into
your poems.

Now your home-made idea of what rhythm in verse should be
like is almost certain to be very closely related to the way you
speak. Take the sentence 'I think that John and Mary live in
town', for example. There are ten syllables, five strong and five
weak, and an alternating structure of weak and strong beats: **di
da di da di da di da di da**. The first, third, fifth, seventh and
ninth syllables, which are conjunctions and prepositions, are
weak. The even numbered syllables, which are all nouns or
verbs, are strong. It's actually an iambic pentameter.

The Shakespeare sonnet that begins 'Shall I compare thee to a
summer's day?' opens (and continues with) lines which,
metrically speaking, are just the same as 'I think that John and
Mary live in town'. There are ten syllables, and five metrical
feet, each foot consisting of one weak and one strong stress.

$$(\bar{v}\ \underline{v})v\ -\quad v\ -v\ -\quad v\quad -$$
Shall I compare thee to a summer's day?

As you'll immediately hear, it's not exactly the same, because the stresses in Shakespeare's line don't fall in quite the same places. The opening, for example, is what we call a reverse foot, the main stress falls on the 'shall' not the 'I', and if you say the two lines aloud to yourself in a natural way, you can immediately notice the rhythmic difference between 'I think that John and Mary live in town' and Shakespeare's line. This is because metre is, in fact, a simple device (although the way some people talk about it, you'd think it was the most arcane science known to man) and when a poet employs a metre, what happens is that the metrical scheme he or she employs will give rise to great rhythmical variation. In fact, the rhythmical potential of a simple metrical system is unlimited.

There are people who maintain, of course, that there is no such thing as an iambic pentameter, that the five foot line almost always breaks into a pattern of evenly-distributed stresses; that is, four accents:

Sháll I compáre thee to a súmmer's dáy?

but this ignores the fact that, whether you like it or not, Shakespeare, Wordsworth and Milton were certainly working to that abstract blueprint of five feet to a line. It's our awareness of what the pentameter is that helps us detect it beneath the rhythmical surface. If you look at Philip Larkin's poem 'Aubade', say, you'll see that, underneath the very natural, spoken quality of the language, the iambic pentameter is ticking away.

In a letter to John Bartlett in 1913, Robert Frost put forward his theory of versification, which went like this:

> *...the great successes in recent poetry have been made on the assumption that the music of words was a matter of harmonised vowels and consonants ... I alone of English writers have consciously set myself to make music out of what I may call the sound of sense. Now it is possible to make sense without the sound of sense (as in much prose that is supposed to pass muster but makes very dull reading) and the sound of sense without sense (as in Alice in Wonderland which makes anything but dull reading). The best place to get the abstract sound of sense is from voices behind a door that cuts off the words.*

He goes on to quote some real examples of overheard conversation and asks John Bartlett to imagine how these would sound **without the words in which they are embodied**. In other words, he asks Bartlett to listen, in a quite abstract way, to the succession of the stresses, the rises and falls of pitch (intonation), and the voice quality of each of his overheard utterances. He goes on:

> *These sounds are summoned by the audile (audial) imagination and they must be positive, strong, and definitely and unmistakably indicated by the context ... The sound of sense, then ... It is the abstract vitality of our speech ... An ear and an appetite for these sounds of sense is the first qualification of a writer ... If one is to be a poet he must learn to get cadences by skillfully breaking the sounds of sense with all their irregularity of accent across the regular beat of the metre. Verse in which there is nothing but the beat of the metre furnished by the accents of the polysyllabic words we call doggerel. Verse is not that. Neither is it the sound of sense alone. It is a resultant from those two.*

We've quoted this at some length as it seems to us to establish some very basic principles. What Frost seems to be referring to with the phrase 'the sound of sense' is audible speech rhythms and cadences. You can carry out some experiments for yourself, listening for the sound of sense. A good place to do this is on a longish bus journey, listening to the conversation behind you. Try fading in the sense of what you're listening to, and then fading it out, and listening simply to the noise that conversation makes. Markets, park benches and swimming pools are also excellent places for eavesdropping. Listen to the **noise** English makes in a very conscious way; but do more than that – listen to yourself. Frost concludes his letter to Bartlett with the injunction: 'Never if you can help it write down a sentence in which the voice will not know how to posture *specially*', by which he clearly doesn't mean posture in the histrionic sense. He means you should trust your special conviction that being sure of what you want to say will lead you instinctively to the right way to say it. Normally when you want to express, say, indignation, you'll do this through a particular tone of voice. You don't think about **how** you'll do this – it's an instinctive process you learned along with your mother tongue. What Frost is getting at is the idea that you should never write something that goes against this instinctive knowledge. Each of the sentences you write down should feel right and natural, enabling you to **say** it with confidence. If you think about it, it's really another way of recommending honesty as a procedure, of recommending the virtue of 'being true to yourself'.

When Frost talks about 'breaking the sounds of sense with all their irregularity of accent across the regular beat of the metre' he's saying that, if your poem doesn't have an underlying regular metre, it isn't a poem – that it's 'playing tennis with the net down' as he put it. This is a traditional view and there are many contemporary poets of established reputation who might not subscribe to this – but even the most dedicated *vers librists* would probably agree that the patterning of stressed and unstressed syllables as they occur naturally in spoken language are more deliberately patterned in most verse. What we are saying is that any kind of patterning will constitute a metre – although with the proviso that the reader must know, or be able to become aware, what that system of patterning is. Louis Zukofsky is supposed to have evolved a system for distributing 'n' and 'r' sounds in a poem according to the formula for a conic section, but if the reader hasn't the faintest idea what that means, it can't be a metre for the reader, even if it was for Zukofsky.

The way you evolve your own particular 'patterns' – however home-made they are – will need work. Whatever rules or principles you establish for yourself as a basis for composition – and everybody develops these for himself or herself, no matter how 'free' the end effect appears to be – these will constitute your own home-made prosody. Remember that the basic principle behind writing a poem is organization – at the levels of both sound and sense. The metre – the regularizing principle behind the demands of ordinary performance – can be whatever you want it to be. It could come from the classical verse tradition, or from some entirely different principle of organization, but it should be apparent to the reader.

What sets a poem off from prose is the way it's arranged on the page. There's lots of white space around it, for example. This is because the lineation reflects the rhythmic organization of the poem. If you write in regular iambic pentameters, for example, each line will have five stresses, and end on the fifth; it will then be followed by another of exactly the same length. In other words, the graphic layout enacts the rhythm. If you don't want to write in a strict metre, however, you have the problem of deciding where to break your line. Will your line break at the end of a phrase or a clause (the endstopping we mentioned in our previous chapter), or will it chop up syntactic units, precipitating the reader into the next without a pause (the enjambement we also mentioned)? On what basis do you make your decisions?

A useful exercise to help start you thinking about problems of the 'where do I break the line' variety is suggested by this found poem of Blaise Cendrars. (A found poem is a text – it might be spoken or printed – which was not originally intended as a poem. The poet, by the act of 'finding' it and framing it – that's to say setting it out as verse on the page, announces that it has become a poem.) Here, first, is the poem:

Stop Press
Oklahoma, 20 January 1914

Three convicts procured revolvers for themselves
They killed their warder and seized the keys of the prison
They ran out of their cells and killed four guards in the
    courtyard
Then they seized the young prison stenographer
And getting into a vehicle which was waiting for them at
    the gate
They departed at high speed
While the guards fired their revolvers at the fugitives
Some guards leaped on horseback and went in pursuit of the
    fugitives
Shots were exchanged on both sides
The young girl was wounded by a shot fired by one of
    the guards
A bullet killed the horse which was drawing the vehicle
The guards were able to approach nearer
They found the convicts dead their bodies riddled with
    bullets
Mr Thomas a former Congressman who was visiting the
    prison
Congratulated the girl

This was originally a straightforward newspaper report. By breaking it up into differentiated lineation, a graphic rhythmical structure has been given to a piece of prose. Thus, instead of the news report remaining a merely sequential account of consecutive events, we get a dramatic refocusing of what is being described. The slightly comic effect of this is rounded off by the satirical conclusion in the final two lines.

EXERCISE 39 Found poem

We'd like you to try a similar exercise by taking any spoken or
written text you can find and writing it out as a poem. It could
be one of those language trophies you brought back from your
bus journey, something from a newspaper, an advertisement, or
whatever sharp observation has supplied you with. As you do
the exercise, notice how the different line breaks you try out will
subtly alter the rhythmic character of the text. Each different
arrangement will affect the way your eye scans the page. What
you're doing here is, in the truest sense of the word, **editing**:
pointing up certain details, putting details in apposition to see
how they look, fragmenting or unifying parts of the text to
produce an effect of your own contriving.

This exercise will have the effect of making you think much
harder about where you break your lines, and what effects you
can get thereby. The way in which a poem looks on the page, its
graphic structure so to speak, has a marked effect on the way we
read. Even the length of a poem on the page (or on more than
one page) can affect the way a reader approaches it. Philip
Larkin, who was not a fan of long poems, claimed to experience
a sinking feeling if he noticed that the poem continued over the
page, and before starting to read, would first of all do a page
count to establish its length.

Many contemporary poets have experimented with very
unusual lineation indeed. This poem by the American poet, Ted
Berrigan, who uses wacky lineation for largely humorous effect,
demonstrates the possibilities of the genre:

60

GET THE MONEY!

that was Damon Runyon's favorite expression

the heat is coming on
like gangbusters

                   (A. Partridge
                         History of American Climate)

                   I guess that means
                   it's time to burst,
                   eh,
                       M'sieur Cloud?

                         (from 'Tambourine Life')

If this poem, chosen somewhat at random from a long sequence, reminds you of E. E. Cummings – well, it should. The ending is a bit like the Buffalo Bill poem we quoted at the beginning of this book. Still, it has a casual naturalness that is engaging. The collage of scraps of conversation echoes the way normal talk proceeds, half-abstractedly, and in a dotty, illogical way. The use of quotations, attributions and capital letters is typical of Berrigan, and although we wouldn't actually advocate this method of working now – it feels very 60s – there is, once again, a useful exercise to be got out of it.

EXERCISE 40 Anarchy on the page

Take some of those fragments of conversation you collected in Exercise 1 in Chapter 03, or from that bus journey we mentioned above. If you were so fascinated by your eavesdropping you forgot to write anything down, take a poem you've written that didn't quite come out and, using a whole sheet of A4 paper as a canvas, try to rearrange the text in a way that completely defamiliarizes it – even to yourself. Use a typewriter, a word processor, a pen or a paintbrush – whatever you feel like. Look at E. E. Cummings' experiments in typography and wild punctuation and let yourself be inspired by the anarchy of them. Get your own back on those teachers who rigidly drilled you in the rules of orthography, and employ the principle of mayhem as your guiding light. Use the whole page, placing parts of the text on the right, other parts in the middle of the page, others on the left. Use the white space of the paper around the text to allow your phrases to breathe.

After this drastic method of editing, reconstruct your original poem if you feel like it. Do you feel any differently about it? Has exploding your text in this way given you any fresh thoughts – either on content or arrangement on the page – or are you forthwith abandoning your perusal of this book in the conviction that we are anarchist saboteurs? Before you do this, hear us out. What we're actually trying to get you to do is simply to think very hard about the relationship of line-length to rhythm, and the effects that can be brought off by paying attention to such matters.

Poets, constantly experimenting with language, have found many ways of restructuring natural speech rhythms. A poem like the following one is actually written in what are called syllabics – that's to say the line-length is determined not by the number of stresses in the line but purely by the syllable count. What happens, as you read it, is that you have to play off the accentual beats against the graphic rhythm which the lines produce across the page.

Considering the Snail

The snail pushes through a green
night, for the grass is heavy
with water and meets over
the bright path he makes, where rain
has darkened the earth's dark. He
moves in a wood of desire,

pale antlers barely stirring
as he hunts, I cannot tell
what power is at work, drenched there
with purpose, knowing nothing.
What is a snail's fury? All
I think is that if later

I parted the blades above
the tunnel and saw the thin
trail of broken white across
litter, I would never have
imagined the slow passion
to that deliberate progress.

Thom Gunn

This poem has exactly seven syllables to a line, but a line-length which counts the syllables goes against the natural accentual stress-patterning of English. In French poetry – in all Romance language poetry – it's the syllables which are counted (getting more or less equal weight in pronunciation), not the accents (or stresses). Try saying a sentence like:

It would have been nicer to have read it before you reviewed it

in a fake French accent and you'll see what we mean. Chaucer, knowing both French and English (and Latin as well, of course), combined the metrical habits of both languages, virtually inventing the decasyllabic (ten-syllable) line for English. (Iambic pentameter, with its ten syllables and five accents, is sometimes referred to as syllable-stress metre.) Notice how the syllabic lineation of Gunn's poem doesn't prevent the English-speaking reader from hearing, played against this elaborate construction, what would be the normal accentual patterning coming through:

> The snáil púshes through a gréen níght
> for the gráss is heávy with wáter and méets
> over the bríght páth he mákes, where ráin
> has dárkened the eárth's dárk. He móves . . .

At the beginning of the chapter we mentioned the idea that people's perception of rhythm in verse is probably very closely related to the way they themselves talk. That sentence we quoted – *I think that John and Mary live in town* – is a good example of how iambic pentameter is almost a paradigm of the way we speak. The principle underlying accentual patterning in English is really (like metre) quite a simple one. It works like this: imagine you had to send that sentence we asked you to read in a Maurice Chevalier voice in an old-fashioned (and suitably irate) telegram, each word costing, shall we say, twenty pence. Thrifty as you are, you'd certainly write:

NICER READ BEFORE REVIEWED

which gets the message across rather neatly. In fact, these are the words you'd stress as you say the sentence aloud to someone. Ours is a language in which strong and weak stresses alternate in a fairly evenly distributed way, and the strongly stressed words are always the content words – the words, that is, that are important for the meaning. (The important words for your telegram.) The little grammatical words, the conjunctions, preposition, auxiliary and modal verbs, are correspondingly weakened. (The words you leave out of the telegram.)

When Thom Gunn lineates his snail poem syllabically, therefore, the effect is that it goes against these natural speech habits of English and as a result it reads (quite deliberately) somewhat effortfully. The line breaks slice up word groups which belong together; for example, 'a green/night' is cut after 'green' and 'heavy/with water' is cut after 'heavy'. Other phrases which have been chopped up in this way are: 'He/moves', 'All/I think', 'thin/trail', 'I would never have/imagined' and so on. As a matter of fact, this poem demonstrates something that in workshops we would tell poets to be careful of. Line breaks which leave a pronoun subject of a verb hanging at the end of a line, as in 'He moves', are to be avoided unless there is a very good reason for not doing so.

However, there is, of course, a very good reason for the poet having written as he has. Reading the poem, if we pause at line-endings as we inevitably must, we feel a hesitancy, movement against some resisting force – in grammatical terms a movement against artificial syntactic regroupings. You might say that 'the rhythm of the poem is enacting the effortfully slow progress of the snail', or 'the sound echoes the sense' or some such. Not only that, Thom Gunn also uses a very oblique form of rhyme – the verses rhyme **abcabc**. 'Green' rhymes with 'rain', 'heavy' rhymes with 'dark. He' and 'desire' rhymes with 'over', but the rhymes are so cunning, it's almost a challenge to the reader to spot them. Look through the poem carefully and you'll see how ingenious this patterning is. In stanza two 'stirring' rhymes with 'nothing', 'tell' with 'all' and 'drenched there' with 'later' and so on.

If you want to experiment with syllabic metres, you might do well to look at the work of a famous American practitioner, Marianne Moore. G.S. Fraser, in an excellent little book called *Metre, Rhyme and Free Verse*, tells us that, to get that slightly disorienting effect of syllabics, you're best advised to use a line length of odd numbers of syllables – 7, 9, 11, 13 and so on. As we've pointed out above, though, you shouldn't fool yourself into thinking you can escape the accentual matrix which underlies English. That beat will always be there.

Nor is the relationship between natural English speech rhythm and classic conceptions of metre something you should leave unexplored. W.H. Auden was a master of metrical forms – think, for example, of the stately tread of trochaic metre in his 'Elegy for W.B. Yeats':

$$- \quad v - \quad v \quad - \quad v \quad -$$
Earth receive an honoured guest

$$- \quad v \quad - \quad v \quad - v \quad -$$
William Yeats is laid to rest,

and in his poem 'In Due Season' you'll see an example of those accentual asclepiads we mentioned at the beginning of the chapter. Basically, the asclepiad is a classical metre whose line is made up of one spondee $(- -)$, two coriambs $(- vv -)$ and an iambic foot $(v -)$ at the end of the line.

```
  –     –     –    v  v    –      –    v  v  –  v –
Spring-time, Summer and Fall: days to behold a world
 –  –  v   v   –   –    v     v    –   v  –
Antecedent to our knowing, where flowers think
 –     –   –   v v  –    –  v      v     –      v –
Theirs concretely in scent-colours and beasts, the same
 –   –  – v  v  –   –     v v – v –
Age all over, pursue dumb horizontal lives
 –   –  – v v  –    –    v   v   –   v  –
On one level of conduct and so cannot be
 –   – – v v  –      –    v  v  –     v –
Secretary to man's plot to become divine.
```

Although, as we've seen, some people maintain that the old, pre-Renaissance two-stress, four-stress, or even six-stress lines (accentual patterns always seem to have evenly numbered stresses) can still be heard coming through poetry written in the classic metres, there's no doubt that metrical arrangements, which count the number of syllables as well as the stresses, provide an enormous amount of material for experiment and innovation.

Finally, we need to mention one last but nevertheless very important consideration with regard to rhythm. Many people ask us: 'What is free verse?' A very good question. The main point we would make is that 'free' in free verse means without any ostensible metre. There will be no numerical or counting procedure underlying the verse form. That doesn't mean it will lack shape or rhythm. It may, at its most basic level, be no more than a breaking up of ordinary prose phrasing into lines of even or uneven length – at its most basic, this too could constitute a prosody. The rhythmic effect will be supplied by the lineation on the page, as in the Cendrars found poem we gave you at the beginning of the chapter. The importance of line-endings and line-beginnings in free verse cannot be overestimated. There are three things that the selective placing of a word at the beginning or end of a line can influence: the rhythm, the intonation pattern and the meaning. It can also influence pacing and momentum like this:

Worn out were the buildings, I
Tell you. Worn out. Do you know how
Buildings wear out? Elm walls were
Worm-bored and warped. Rain
Through the gap. Hard stemmed

Wide weeds in the track. Door hinges
Rusted, dropped out. In the lew, strapped
War-wounded Jim wove ropes out of

Hay.

> (from 'Death of a Farmyard' by Geoffrey Grigson)

Free verse may often have some tenuous connection with the
iambic pentameter line because, as we saw, this rhythm occurs
so naturally in spoken English; or free verse may also
demonstrate a rhetorical structuring – that's to say a deliberate
cadencing through the use of repeated syntactical structures, or
repetitions of vocabulary or phrasing. Gerard Manley Hopkins
employed this device, as did Walt Whitman and D.H. Lawrence:

Not every man has gentians in his house
in soft, sad September, at slow, sad Michaelmas

Bavarian gentians, big and dark, only dark
darkening the day-time, torch-like with the smoking blueness of
> Pluto's gloom
ribbed and torch-like, with their gaze of darkness spread blue
down flattening into points, flattened under the sweep of white day
torch-flower of the blue-smoking darkness, Pluto's dark-blue daze,
black lamps from the halls of Dis, burning dark blue,
giving off darkness, blue darkness, as Demeter's pale lamps give off
> light
lead me then, lead the way.

> (from 'Bavarian Gentians' by D.H. Lawrence)

The word repetitions here have a kind of mesmerizing effect,
and the successive adjectival clauses, all in apposition to each
other, slowly build up to that injunction, the short, concluding
line at the end of the stanza. (Do look at the whole poem.) This
is what one might describe as rhetorical, although obviously the
rhythmic structure is actually a compound of all the features we
have mentioned so far – the regular beat of the accents, the
lineation, the echoings of the syntax. In fact, as we can see,
poetic rhythm, as it is experienced by the reader, actually comes
from an enormous complex of different features. Here's an
example from an older poet, producing a quite dissimilar result,
this time marshalling a regular metre, stanza arrangement,
syntactic effects and word repetition to get its effect:

When people say 'I've told you fifty times'
They mean to scold and very often do;
When poets say 'I've written fifty rhymes'
They make you dread that they'll recite them too.
In gangs of fifty thieves commit their crimes,
At fifty love for love is rare, 'tis true.
But then no doubt it equally as true is
A good deal may be bought for fifty louis.

(from 'Don Juan' by Lord Byron)

As you develop your craft, of course, your skill in manipulating these kinds of detail will grow. Through application and reading, you'll widen your appreciation of the rhythmic variety that is possible in the writing of verse. You should try, as we've said, to experiment with different kinds of metre as well as with varieties of free verse. You should aim to cultivate a tacit understanding in your head of the need for an interplay between some ordering principle of rhythm and everyday spoken language. This is the source of that articulate energy by which a poem lives or dies. If you have no rhythmic matrix in your head when you write, your lines will have no buzz. That matrix, as we've said, can take any shape or form: it might be trochaic dimeter, or it might be a stanza pattern of alternating long and short lines, or it might begin every line with the rhetorical formula: 'I remember'. Whatever you choose it'll be a kind of sounding wall against which you can bounce your lines.

Something else, too, that might help you is aiming to capture the rhythms of the world around you in your writing. To do this, first of all you'll have to listen to the fundamental ground bass of the age in which you live. This means reaching down into yourself as well. You have to listen to **you**. You have to find out what you've unconsciously internalized. It's a psychological process as well as a matter of craft or technique. If you're not prepared to do this or take the risks associated with it, the muse will never toss you a poem.

One of the most exhilarating books we know on the subject of writing poetry is by the Russian poet Vladimir Mayakowsky, who, although he ends with a rather disingenuous disclaimer, had this to say about incorporating the rhythms of the modern age into his work:

In order to write about the tenderness of love, take bus no. 7 from the Lubyanska Square to Nogin Square. The appalling jolting will serve to throw into relief for you, better than anything else, the charm of a life transformed. A shake-up is essential for the purposes of comparison...

I got further with my poem about Esenin on the short journey from Lubyansky Passage to the Tea Marketing Board (I was on my way to settle my account) than on all my voyagings. Myasnitsky was a sharp and needful contrast: after the solitude of hotel rooms, Myasnitsky was packed with people; after the silence of the provinces, there was the cheerful hubbub of buses, cars and trams; and all round, as though challenging the old lamplit villages, were the offices of electro-technical firms.

I walk along, waving my arms and mumbling almost wordlessly, now shortening my steps so as not to interrupt my mumbling, now mumbling more rapidly in time with my steps...

So the rhythm is trimmed and takes shape – and rhythm is the basis of any poetic work, resounding through the whole thing. Gradually individual words begin to ease themselves free of this dull roar...

Where this basic dull roar of a rhythm comes from is a mystery. In my case it's all kinds of repetitions in my mind of noises, rocking motions, or in fact of any phenomenon with which I can associate a sound. The sound of the sea, endlessly repeated, can provide my rhythm, or a servant who slams the door every morning, recurring and intertwining with itself, railing through my consciousness; or even the rotation of the earth, which in my case, as in a shop full of visual aids, gives way to, and inextricably connects with, the whistle of a high wind...

Rhythm is the fundamental force, the fundamental energy of verse...

A poet must develop just this feeling for rhythm in himself, and not go learning up other people's measurements: iambus, trochee or even this apotheosized free verse...

I know nothing of metre...

(from *How Verses Are Made* by Vladimir Mayakowsky)

17

translation

In the Village of my Forefathers

One hugs me
One looks at me with wolf eyes
One takes off his hat
So I can see him better

Each one asks me
Do you know who I am

Unknown old men and women
Usurp the names
Of boys and girls of my memory

And I ask one of them
Tell me old chap
Is George Kurja
Still alive

That's me he answers
In a voice from the other world
I stroke his cheek with my hand
And silently beg him to tell me
Whether I am alive still too

(Translated by Anne Pennington)

As the title of this chapter, and the translator's name below the poem will have led you to expect, the above poem was not originally written in English, but even without the clue of the title, if you'd read the poem alertly you'd have guessed anyway. It's by Vasko Popa, and was written in Serbo-Croat in the early 1970s. What are the qualities that reveal it's a translation? One of the first things you may have picked out is the name, George Kurja, which isn't an English name by origin, of course, but then there are towns throughout America inhabited almost exclusively by European immigrants. Maybe you were struck by the casual way the dead are allowed to speak in the poem – this wouldn't happen in a typical British poem of the same period. Then there's the tone: deadpan and objective, about something nobody has any right to be objective about – the question of whether they're alive or dead. The poem also has a noticeable 'folktale' character, and suggests the quality of an older way of life, where people, leaving their village for the city, might return years later and find the friends of their youth grown old. The poem's magical-realist quality (what the Serbian/American poet Charles Simic describes as 'elemental surrealism') is grounded, therefore, in reality.

You can find many more recent poems written in English that share an imaginative territory with this way of operating, and this has to do with the influence poetry in translation has had. Such poetry has been widely available since the 1960s when Ted Hughes and Daniel Weissbort started their *Poetry in Translation* series. In 1975, the influential anthology *Another Republic*, edited by Charles Simic and fellow-American Mark Strand introduced North American readers to the poetry of Europe and South America. In Britain, the Penguin *Modern European Poets* series flourished briefly in the 1970s, while smaller publishing houses on both sides of the Atlantic made available and are still making available a wide range of new translations from even the most obscure languages. Is it any wonder that many English language poets have either consciously or unconsciously been influenced?

MS: It was the belief in this influence, and its liberating effect on English language poetry, that partly motivated the anthology *Emergency Kit* that I co-edited with Jo Shapcott; or rather, the influence made itself clear to us as we gathered the poems and realized how many recent foreign language poets (our anthology has poems written only in English) effortlessly achieved the fresh angle we were looking for. Still, we were delighted by the number of English language poems we came across that displayed a subversiveness, a gift for exaggeration, an imagistic power – that often operated in an oblique and parable-like manner too similar to the procedures of foreign language poetry (much of it written under oppression and needing to fool the censors) to be, we felt, mere coincidence.

The effect of the above Popa poem, on us at least, gives the lie to the idea that to translate is to betray, or *traditore*, *traduttore* as the Italians put it, or as Robert Frost said, 'Poetry is what gets lost in the translation.' It has to be said, though, that not every poem comes across equally well in another language. The concreteness, the spareness and precision of Popa's language assist the process of translating here. Even when you suspect a translation is giving you less of the original poem's power, it can still broaden your range of possibilities and ultimately benefit you as a writer. Curiosity about poetry in other languages is something you should develop in yourself, even if you've never thought about this. There's no better remedy against insularity and provincialism.

Reading poems in translation is one thing; attempting to translate them yourself is another. Why should you want to do this? The practice of translation helps you to get inside a poem in a way that no reading or classroom analysis can achieve. Of course, close reading and discussion can be extremely fruitful, we would be the last people to deny that – but the process of translation allows a 'hands on' approach to the poem you're interested in. It's qualitatively different. Translation will often reveal to you just why a particular poem has stood the test of time, and why it is still read as eagerly today as it was when it was first published.

Robert Lowell puts a couple of other reasons for translating in the introduction to his *Imitations* (versions of poets from Homer to Pasternak, via Baudelaire, Rilke, Montale and many others): 'This book was written from time to time when I was unable to do anything of my own.' He then goes on to say that he sees the process as being beneficial to his craft: 'My Baudelaires were begun as exercises in couplets and quatrains...' Most poets who from time to time engage in translation find that the technical problems they have to deal with – finding the word or phrase that exactly conveys the meaning of the original, attempting to come up with an equivalent rhythm or rhyme scheme, deciding on an appropriate line-length and stanza shape – are a rehearsal for the technical difficulties they will encounter in their own work. Occasionally translation can have a central importance to the way a poet writes. Miroslav Holub, another poet who comes across well in translation, said, not long before he died, that he no longer completed his poems in Czech until he saw drafts from his American translator.

JHW: Some poems of mine were translated into French a while ago. The translator sent me a list of questions about the poems. As a result of trying to answer these I saw I had been clumsy, or had left what I thought were interesting ambiguities – I had, in fact, been self-indulgent – and then I realized that clarity is, after all, what you really want. I changed my original poems as a result of this and sent them back to her.

Let's look in detail at a few of the problems you'll almost certainly encounter if you sit down with that long-loved Rimbaud poem and attempt to give it its definitive English version. First there's the rhyme – you might find this so hard to handle that you're tempted to do without it, but will the poem lose too much without the rhyme? You'll have to weigh up the difficulties of the task you've set yourself. For example, rhyme is easier to manage with long lines, or with a shortish poem; if you have a long poem with short lines, you're in trouble. In the latter case you may find yourself reinventing the entire contents, and it could begin to feel like trying to solve a diabolical crossword puzzle.

Translating Rimbaud is actually a temptation many poets find impossible to resist, but the way he comes out in English displays an intriguing variety. Here's the penultimate verse of his celebrated poem 'Le Bateau Ivre' ('The Drunken Boat') and translations of that stanza by Robert Lowell and Samuel Beckett respectively. It's quite a long poem and runs for 25 quatrains in its entirety. Lowell chooses to translate a part of the poem, cutting ten stanzas without comment, and to rhyme, although not quite so wholeheartedly as Rimbaud did. Lowell rhymes **abca**, Rimbaud rhymes **abab**. Beckett, on the other hand, translates the whole poem and doesn't bother with rhyme, which allows him to be much more literal. Here's the original first, with a literal translation below it, and then the two versions:

Rimbaud   *Si je désire une eau d'europe, c'est la flaque*
        (If I desire one water of Europe, it's the pool)
        Noire et froide òu vers le crépuscule embaumé
        (Black and cold where toward the scented dusk)
        Un enfant accroupi plein de tristesse, lâche
        (A child, squatting, full of sadness, launches)
        Un bateau frêle comme un papillon de Mai.
        (A boat, frail as a butterfly of May)

Lowell   Shrunken and black against a twilight sky,
        our Europe has no water. Only a pond
        the cows have left, and a boy wades to launch
        his paper boat frail as a butterfly.

Beckett   I want none of Europe's waters unless it be
        The cold black puddle where a child full of sadness,
        Squatting, looses a boat as frail
        As a moth into the fragrant evening.

Both (the complete) versions make interesting poems in their own right. They do, however, illustrate the problems a translator has to solve. It's impossible to judge, for example, what the original has lost by being only partly rhymed in one case, and not rhymed at all in the other. Lowell's departures from Rimbaud's poem are very surprising in places: 'only a pond / the cows have left' suggests a pool of cow pee, and there's no mention of cows in the original. (Probably Lowell is remembering an image of 'hysterical herds of cows' which Rimbaud uses in stanza 11 of his poem.) Lowell also shifts the focus of the stanza. The original begins with the idea of '*une eau d'Europe*' – 'Europe's waters' in Beckett's version – and the boy using them as a puddle to launch his boat. Lowell shifts parts of speech around so that 'shrunken and black' describes Europe, not its waters. The word 'shrunken' is derived, perhaps, from '*accroupi*', which means 'squatting'. The whole image of the boy crouching beside a pool to launch his boat has been transformed in Lowell's energetic and verbally forceful style: the boy 'wades to launch his boat', for example. Who is to say that it was not the pressure of having to find a rhyme that caused Lowell to make these changes? Beckett's version, by contrast, seems rather mild. Another interesting point to notice is the changes which French word order force the translator to make (adjectives after the noun, for example).

It's partly the inspiration afforded by the original poem which produces variations in the translated end-product, and partly, also, a matter of structural differences between the two languages. In German, for example, words tend to have more syllables than English words, and a literal version of a poem into German would tend to stretch the lines in an ungainly way. Good translators have to find their own methods for making the lines come out approximately the same length and work rhythmically. Whether they cheat or not – for example, by dropping words they consider unnecessary, or can't accommodate easily – as long as they're faithful to the requirements of the language they're translating into, they will have gone some way towards making a real poem in the new language. One stratagem employed, as we've seen with Lowell's Rimbaud, is to lift a part of speech and put it somewhere else. Here's another illustration, this time going from English into German:

old horses grow shaggy
and flies hunker down
on curtains, like sequins
on a dead girl's ball gown.

(from 'The Idyll Wheel, May' by Les Murray)

Margitt Lehbert has elegantly translated this quatrain as follows:

alle Pferde werden zottig
und Fliegen kauern grün und blau
auf Vorhängen, wie Ziermünzen
auf dem Ballkleid einer toten Frau.

In order to get the rhyme, she has added the phrase 'grün and blau' (green and blue) to describe the flies, and reversed the position of the nouns *'Ballkleid'* (ball gown) and *'Frau'* (girl) in the last line, also in order to get the rhyme. This may look easy, and a bit cheeky, but you have to realize it's inevitable if you're going to end up with a version that reproduces the rhyme scheme and *lives* in the new language.

Good translators shouldn't end up with a version that's half as long again as the original text. Then there's the appearance of the poem on the page to consider as well. If the poet chose not to write a ragged poem but one which looks like a block, that's an important choice and the translator should take it into account, and not have lines sticking out all over the place like fishing rods out of every window of a car. On the other hand, a poem that's ragged in the original needs to be ragged in the translation; you can't tidy it up because you disapprove. However, the raggedness needn't correspond exactly to where it was ragged in the original.

Translation work means you have to be alert to all the possible meanings a word might have, and be particularly on the lookout for uses of slang and idiom. Imagine the ludicrous effect of translating the line 'He fell into the bath, legless' as 'He had no legs and fell into the bath'. This obviously has to do with having an imperfect knowledge of the foreign language, and some might argue it's better to have no knowledge at all, and rely on a prose crib, or get assistance from a native speaker. Actually, we would feel uneasy about translating from a language completely unfamiliar to us because we'd want to know for ourselves how the original poem sounded. Of course, many translators do work from languages they can't speak, but what this might mean in terms of loss of musicality is always difficult to estimate. Musical effects in one language are notoriously difficult to reproduce in another, whereas concrete images and the thought content of a poem are more easily captured in a translation.

However, Stanley Kunitz, who confesses he does not know Russian, has this to say about a translation he was making of a poem by Anna Akhmatova (with the aid of a Slavist, Max Hayward):

> *The so-called literal version is already a radical reconstitution of the verbal ingredients of a poem into another linguistic system – at the expense of its secret life, its interconnecting psychic tissue, its complex harmonies ... The rendering is conscientious, but the lines are only a shadow of the original text, incapable of producing its singular pleasures. The object is to produce an analogous poem in English out of available signs and sounds, a new poem sprung from the matrix of the old, drenched in memories of its former existence ... what it said, how it breathed, the inflections of its voice. The Russian poet Nikolai Zabolotski had another figure for the process. He said it was like rebuilding a city out of the evidence of its ruins ...*

Sometimes the task of translation is made complicated by the knowledge or learning of the poet. Margitt Lehbert comments: 'Les Murray *knows* a great deal, he reads books on everything imaginable, and he incorporates this knowledge into his poetry.' She gives the example of a poem narrated by a snake, where the reader learns how the snake experiences the world through its sensory apparatus.

> *If you don't know that some snakes can see infra-red through a heat organ, and you read a poem about the perception of a heat-glowing, melon-shaped something lapping dark segments up, it sounds completely bizarre. But once you realise what's happening you can understand the visual images being described, and translate these back into German. You have to understand what's going on to translate.*

This is an extra-textual problem. Specific local or cultural references also belong in this category. Would it be clear in the context of your translation, for example, that 'Woodbine' (or the foreign language equivalent) was a cigarette? When Seamus Heaney, in his poem 'A Postcard From North Antrim', lists a whole series of things he considers represent 'independent, rattling, non-transcendent / Ulster – old decency'

> ...Old Bushmills
> Soda farls, strong tea,
> New rope, rock salt, kale plants,
> Potato-bread and Woodbine.

he presents his translator with a problem. Do you try to find the cultural equivalent of these in your language, or do you resort to notes at the bottom of the text? If you're translating a springtime song from New Zealand with the title 'September', do you change the title to 'May'? One shouldn't insult one's readers by assuming they know nothing, in these days of global travel, of other cultures and languages.

The strength of Seamus Heaney or Les Murray is in the detail. In contemporary poetry in English their kind of concrete specificity is highly valued, whereas in some other literary cultures the tendency is to lean towards a more generalized, abstract mode of expression. When Seamus Heaney won the Nobel Prize, for example, one reviewer in Germany accused him of being too local for such an international award, for being not typical of international modernism. Likewise, Les Murray was described in another German paper as being 'bucolic', a quaintly reductive word to describe the richness, the fascination with the human and the natural world, that typifies his work. We mention this merely to underline the fact that one cannot predict how poetry will be received in another language and culture, no matter how well translated or how esteemed the poet is in his or her own culture.

The translator's perception of the poem he or she is translating will, of course, influence the finished version. One of the most crucial factors in translation is recapturing the tone of the original. Robert Lowell in his introduction to *Imitations* quotes Boris Pasternak:

> ...*The usual reliable translator gets the literal meaning but misses the tone... and in poetry tone is, of course, everything.*

Lowell wrote that he had been reckless with literal meaning, but had laboured hard to get the tone. The question of strict, literal accuracy versus free versions or imitations is vexing. We saw the different results these two approaches produced when we compared Beckett's and Lowell's versions of Rimbaud above. In the first mode, the translator aims to be as self-effacing as possible, so as not to get in the way of the original voice (Beckett). In the second mode, the translator will allow him or herself a considerable degree of freedom, so the poem becomes as much part of the translator's opus as the original poet's (Lowell). In this latter instance the original poem will have acted, in part, as a catalyst for a new poem of the translator's. In the most extreme cases the poem will be called, for example, 'After

Nerval', but the poem you read will be a very long way after Nerval. All it may have in common with the original Nerval poem is one shared image. This is not to say that the new poem might not be a good one – it just won't be, in the strict sense, a translation from Nerval. Furthermore, poets have recently been coming up with spoof translations which sit brazenly in their books purporting to be derived from Welsh or Polish poets who have never existed. The Irish poet Paul Durcan, who happily does exist, has responded to paintings as if they were texts of which he had to make versions in English, and there is a Les Murray book, in which he tries to imagine the language animals would use if they could speak, called *Translations from the Natural World*. In a way, writing a poem in itself could be considered a kind of translation, in that one starts with dimly perceived notions and hard to crystallize feelings and tries to get hold of them, and move from Frost's 'tantalising vagueness' into clarity.

Here, to conclude, are three very different kinds of translation exercise.

EXERCISE 41 Translation

If you know a foreign language, or have a smattering of one, pick any poem you know and like in that language and try to translate it, bearing in mind that you can be strict or free, that you can use rhyme or not, and that above all you should try to capture the tone of the original. Don't restrict yourself to just one of these options. If you find that a free version is starting a poem of your own, go with it. (For those of you who have no foreign language, we recommend using a book of original texts with prose cribs in English.)

EXERCISE 42 Homophonic translation

This is an exercise in homophonic translation. Here is a poem in Romanian:

Camera

Îi dă o forfecuţă de tăiat unghii
bărbatului dezbrăcat.
Va zbura
şi-l va uimi
cînd ea va pleca.

O cîntărește pe pîntece;
e ușoară și uscată.

E zgomotoasă.
E sigur că o aude venind
cînd o strînge ușor
pe piele.

We want you to translate it. Don't tell us you don't know the language – that's irrelevant – and don't rush out to buy *Teach Yourself Romanian*. There are two ways of approaching this exercise: try saying the poem aloud. Are there any sounds that suggest English words? Do some of the words look like English words slightly askew on the page? You should also aim to reproduce stanza shapes and approximate line-lengths. Your English version should be the same length as the original. You should allow yourself to be led by any cadences or repetitive effects you suspect you have found in the original. Above all, let your mind off its leash.

EXERCISE 43 Translating a painting

We mentioned earlier the poems that Paul Durcan has written in response to paintings, as if they were texts he was translating. Overleaf is a reproduction of a René Magritte painting that hangs in the Tate Gallery, London.

We want you to use this picture as a springboard for a poem. Try to focus on the things in the picture as if they were words in a foreign language of which you have to make sense. In particular, what is the meaning of the six things embedded in the stone, and how do they relate to the person in the picture? You can choose to write as this person (using the first person) or write it in the third person, standing back, telling the story. Be as fresh and original as you can, and be alert for any clichéd or too easy interpretations.

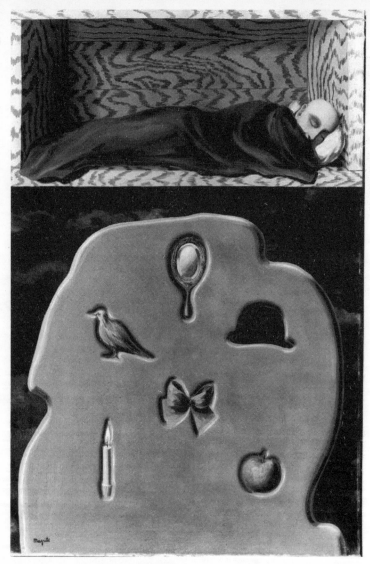

René Magritte, *The Reckless Sleeper*
Reproduced by permission of The Tate Gallery, London

18

writing for children

What is a children's poem? Is there such a thing? Charles Causley, in a Radio 4 interview a few years back, said:

A children's poem is simply one which a child can comprehend as well as an adult. It has to be a poem, not a jingle, not a silly collection of rhymes – a real poem.

And somewhat earlier W. H. Auden said:

While there are some good poems which are only for adults, because they presuppose adult experience in their readers, there are no good poems which are only for children.

Before you read any further, then, it is as well to take these words on board. Some people think writing poems for children is a doddle, something you can dash off while waiting for your breakfast in bed, or at least when your inspiration is in too short a supply to fuel a real poem. If you read a lot of the stuff that comes on the market, aimed at children, you could be forgiven for continuing to think like that. Most of it is pretty feeble, patronizing in the extreme, usually silly or 'yukky' (an adult's idea of being childish), and overly dependent on rhyme, ineptly done. In short, badly written. Some publishers out there ought to know better – and they ought to remember that children are capable of more; that they don't have to be fobbed off with lowest-common-denominator stuff.

However, if you're diligent in your reading you will find that enough of the real stuff is out there, too, for you to be able to relax and from which to take your bearings. Who's good, then? Charles Causley would be one of the first names in that roll-call. Other names would have to include Ted Hughes, Gareth Owen, Roger McGough, Kit Wright, Philip Gross, Jackie Kay and Richard Edwards. Brian Patten, Michael Rosen and Allan Ahlberg have proved hugely popular with children. Adrian Mitchell's unpredictability is welcome and refreshing. Norman Silver, especially in his earlier books, has homed in well on teenage concerns. John Agard and Grace Nichols have published a string of books alive with dialect-laced language. John Mole and the late Roy Fuller have brought out excellent work. In Canada there is Dennis Lee, and in America there is Jack Prelutsky and Shel Silverstein, and earlier there was Theodore Roethke. Then there are all the anthologies, although you have to be even more choosy about these. Most of them are dull, predictable and theme-led to a hair-pulling-out extent. If you're diligent, however, you'll find some that are surprising and excellent.

If the names in that last paragraph mean anything to you, you'll have noticed that most of them write poetry for adults, too. Given Charles Causley's comment in our opening paragraph, this is no coincidence. What these poets have learned is craft, and this serves them well, whether they're writing for children or adults. Craft is what is lacking in the bulk of the children's poetry published. You may also have noticed that most of the above poets are alive, and their publications recent. This may give you the impression that children's poetry is a new phenomenon. In the last couple of decades it's certainly been a growth industry, but there have been some extremely able practitioners in earlier times. Many of you will have encountered, in your youth, Robert Louis Stevenson's *A Child's Garden of Verses*, A. A. Milne's *Now We Are Six* and *When We Were Very Young* and Hilaire Belloc's *Cautionary Tales*. The wonderful nonsense verse of Edward Lear and Lewis Carroll is widely and justifiably known, and we mustn't forget Walter De La Mare. Here is a poem from his perennial *Peacock Pie*, first published in 1913, and reprinted many times since:

The Sea Boy

Peter went – and nobody there –
Down by the sandy sea,
And he danced a jig, while the moon shone big
All in his lone danced he;
And the surf splashed over his tippeting toes,
And he sang his riddle-cum-ree,
With hair a-dangling,
Moon a-spangling
The bubbles and froth of the sea.
He danced him to, and he danced him fro,
And he twirled himself about,
And now the starry waves tossed in,
And now the waves washed out;
Bare as an acorn, bare as a nut,
Nose and toes and knee,
Peter the sea-boy danced and pranced,
And sang his riddle-cum-ree.

This poem is a good one to look at in order to answer the questions with which we opened this chapter. Yes, there is such a thing as a children's poem, at least in the sense of what it can and cannot be, and this poem illustrates some of those qualities.

The protagonist is a child, which is often the case (but by no means essential) in children's literature. The poem has a simple, stark clarity, with a strong narrative element. It is not only rhymed but very musical – so musical it would be easy to imagine it turned into a song. Children's poetry doesn't have to rhyme, any more than adult poetry does, but it's fair to say that, because the noise of a poem is very important to a child (think of nursery rhymes, playground skipping rhymes, etc.) rhyme is a more pressing option when you write for children. This still doesn't excuse bad rhyme, or rhyme that alone dictates where the poem goes. Often you'll find that, when a children's poem doesn't rhyme, it employs other noise effects, such as a chorus or refrain structure, or at least it'll be strongly rhythmical.

However, if we may bring your attention back to 'The Sea Boy', there are one or two other points still to notice. One is the mystery of the situation, and the way the reader is left with it. There is no attempt made to explain why Peter did his moonlit jig on the beach, or to inform us whether this was a one-off or a frequent occurrence. We have touched on this in previous chapters – the need for poetry to ask questions, not provide answers, to let the reader's imagination fill out the story. This is arguably even more vital in poetry aimed at children, whose imaginations are so vibrant and unforced. We are all born with imagination, Franz Kafka said, but most of us, by the time we're nine or ten years old, have lost it or have had it driven out of us. You also need to take note of the language in which the poem is written. There is no word in it that would baffle or lose a child.

This brings us to the central necessity in writing poems for children: as you write you have to think both as an adult and as a child at once. We have all been children. Anyone arriving in this world, fully-formed, at the age of 21, or created in the lab, like Frankenstein, would have problems – but our childhoods were long ago. It is useful, therefore, for aspiring children's poets to have regular contact with children – either their own, or other people's. Many successful poets for children will tell you that it was the experience of working in schools, encouraging children to write, seeing once again the different logic children have and the ease with which they can be imaginative, that first got them writing for children.

What is this different logic? You could say, simply, that for children the boundaries of realism and non-realism blur naturally. Again, it's that imaginative capacity of which Kafka spoke. Nothing is too much to be imagined. Think of the games children, even young children, play. Think of their literature: *Pinocchio*, *Peter Pan*, *The Wind in the Willows*, *Flat Stanley*, *The BFG*, to name but a few old favourites. Also it is worth mentioning here the part the sinister plays in all this – but, maybe because of their innocence, the sinister is not as real or as threatening for children (in their games or literature, at least) as it is for us. It's often mixed with humour. Think of the roadrunner in the cartoon of that name getting up and running away after being flattened by a steamroller.

Children's writers have often treated the sinister in this cartoon-like way. Elements of dark surrealism feature in many books that are children's favourites. Look at Dahl (we mentioned *The BFG* but most of his books fit equally well, and they're hugely popular with children), or Belloc's *Cautionary Tales*. This doesn't stop some adults taking such literature over-literally.

MS: I have a poem (that children find funny) where a boy stuffs a cat inside a snowman, and it was once removed from a radio programme by a BBC producer, because he didn't want children throughout the land stuffing cats into snowmen. I challenged him to find me a cat that would sit there quietly and allow itself to be immersed in a snowman; if he did so, I'd grant he had a point. He refused to give way. The next radio programme I did, with a different producer, featured the poem. I saw no tabloid articles about cat snow-murders.

Such literary custodians who slap a veto on subject matter they imagine to be dangerous confuse black with sick humour, see absurdism as symbolism, and show no understanding of that different logic children have. No one who thinks that way would ever make a children's poet. We don't mean to imply by this that a children's poem must necessarily exist beyond the borders of realism; just that, for the best practitioners, the non-realist is always an option – or, at least, what Elizabeth Bishop called 'the surrealism of everyday life'.

To return to our central point, then, in the act of writing poems for children you have to see through the eyes of a child while controlling these images and perceptions with your adult mind. You have to go back and ransack your childhood for the kind of images that were potent to you then, while at the same time updating those images to fit the modern world. No matter how imaginative you are in your poems, if they aren't filled with the things of the modern world – and the things a child would notice – children will not relate to them. This is why it's often said that a children's poet is still partly a child, or at least the child in them is still active, so perhaps it's not so much a going *back* to childhood. P. L. Travers in a *Paris Review* interview wrote:

> *I can, as it were, turn aside and consult it [James Joyce once wrote, 'My childhood bends beside me.']. If we're completely honest, not sentimental or nostalgic, we have no idea where childhood ends and maturity begins. It is one unending thread, not a life chopped up into sections out of touch with one another.*

It may be, however, that not everyone can do this, or that not everyone who writes poetry has it in them to write for children. It's tempting to say it's possible to tell which poets can. Here's an early poem by Theodore Roethke that's not considered a children's poem:

Child on top of a Greenhouse

The wind billowing out the seat of my britches,
My feet crackling splinters of glass and dried putty,
The half-grown chrysanthemums staring up like accusers,
Up through the streaked glass, flashing with sunlight,
A few white clouds all rushing eastward,
A line of elms plunging and tossing like horses,
And everyone, everyone pointing up and shouting.

The clarity of this and the simple dramatic structure, not to mention the child focus, make it unsurprising that Roethke went on later to include children's poetry in his oeuvre – a rare development for someone of his stature in those days. Robert Frost never, to our knowledge, wrote poems specifically for children, but a poem of his such as 'The Runaway' which opens like this:

> Once, when the snow of the year was beginning to fall,
> We stopped by a mountain pasture to say, 'Whose colt?'
> A little Morgan had one forefoot on the wall,
> The other curled at his breast. He dipped his head
> And snorted to us. And then he had to bolt...

would grab a child's attention straight off; and the Sylvia Plath of *Crossing the Water*, poems which are full of curiosity and big-eyed awe towards the world ('...I think of the lizards airing their tongues / In the crevice of an extremely small shadow...' –

from 'Sleep in the Mojave Desert') would surely have written more seriously for children if the literary climate at the time had been more accommodating of the venture, or if she had lived longer to watch her children grow.

Many of you won't have to be told that children's poetry isn't for everyone. Some of the sneeriest reactions to the enterprise of writing for children come from fellow-poets, as if the activity is a dissipation of energy and intellectually worthless. Then there's the dearth of critical response – if poetry is marginalized in the literary review pages, children's poetry is extra-marginalized. Few of the literary editors give space to it, even when they review children's fiction, non-fiction and picture books.

If all this doesn't deter you, and you still want to have a go at writing poems for children, let's re-cap what you have to keep in mind. First of all, as the Auden quote early on had it, don't 'presuppose adult experience in your readers'. Some subject matters are obvious no-nos: overt reference to sex; upfront political messages (with the possible exception of environmental concerns, or responses to bad stuff in the news, although even here children don't like it too preachy); a high intellectual content, couched in words you'd find in Heidegger or the boardgame *Balderdash* (although the odd unfamiliar word isn't a bad thing for an alert, inquisitive reader, provided it's precise in its context). Clarity and musicality are a good idea – also, although not prescriptively, some element of mystery. It's good to remember the kinds of questions children repeatedly ask and to put these into your poems (questions you usually don't or can't answer in life, either). Tap into their curiosity about the world, and into their playfulness, their zest.

Perhaps it's time to look at another children's poem, a contemporary one this time, by Kit Wright:

Pride

Two birds sat in a Big White Bra
   That swung as it hung
   On the washing-line.

They sang: 'Hurray!' and they sang: 'Hurrah!
   Of all the birds we're the best by far!
   Our hammock swings to the highest star!
   No life like yours and mine!'

They were overheard
  By a third
  Bird

That swooped down onto a nearby tree
  And sneered: 'Knickers! It's plain to see
A bird in a tree is worth two in a bra.
  There's no bird *half* so fine!'

And it seemed indeed that he was right
  For the washing line was far too tight
And old and frayed. As the laundry flapped,
  The big wind heaved and the rope ... *snapped!*

You should have heard
  The third
  Bird.

He cried: 'Aha!
  For all their chatter and la-de-dah,
  They didn't get far in their Big White Bra!
  If there is a bird who's a Superstar,
  It's me, it's me, it's me!'
Down to the ground
  He dived in his glee

And the Big Black Cat
  Enjoyed his tea.

It's easy to see from this how a good children's poem can be two poems simultaneously – one for children and one for adults.

MS: One comic illustration of this is a poem I wrote about a dog on a beach, coveting a second dog's white spots. When I showed it to a friend immediately after writing it, he said that for kids it might be a poem about a dog but for adults it was a poem about sex. It was entirely unintentional, but as it was high summer and I had been apart from my wife for ten days, I saw he had a point.

Charles Causley puts some of his children's poems into his adult collections as well as the children's collections in which they first appear. Even when poets who write for both don't do this, many will tell you that there is an inevitable cross-influence between their children's and adult poems. Writing the children's poems can be liberating for the adult poems – liberating imaginatively.

Writing the adult poems can help prevent you from patronizing child readers when you write for them.

And it's important not to forget the children in all this. They are, after all, the readers one writes for first – they are, ostensibly, the only readers. No amount of critical praise or technical adroitness can help a children's poet when he or she stands up in front of two or three hundred kids in a school hall; you're either going to get and keep their attention or you're not. Such readings can be daunting – much more so than most adult readings – and they have to be approached very differently, as a newcomer to the circuit quickly finds out; but they can be immensely rewarding as well, when the kids stay quiet enough to listen and maybe make an appreciative noise after the odd poem, by banging on the floor, for example. You'll find that it'll be one of the nasty poems.

EXERCISE 44 The bad box

We'd like to end this chapter with a writing exercise. It's a variation on an exercise Kit Wright does with children in schools, one based on his poem 'The Magic Box' (the last poem in *Cat Among the Pigeons*). What Kit asks the children to do is imagine a box on the floor, a magic box, which can be as big as you want it to be, and into which you can put things you wouldn't normally put in a box. What might these be, he asks them? The children are liable to say a car, an elephant, a house and so on. They'll all fit in if the box is big enough, Kit says. Eventually one child will suggest something different, like 'the sky', and they'll be away. Here is the opening of Kit's poem:

I will put in the box

the swish of a silk sari on a summer night,
fire from the nostrils of a Chinese dragon,
the tip of a tongue touching a tooth

and he goes on to fill his box with more wonderfully precise and surprising things, with the refrain 'I will put in the box' recurring three more times, then a stanza telling us what his box is made of, and a final stanza telling us what he'll do with the box. We could, of course, have quoted you the whole poem, but instead we'll give you our variation on the exercise, which is, instead of 'The Magic Box', 'The Bad Box', and our inferior poem as an example.

The Bad Box

I will put in the box
the cooks responsible for school dinners,
ads in the cinema and all tabloid newspapers,
the leaders of the Bosnian Serbs.

I will put in the box
hijackers and bombers who blow up planes,
people who smoke in no-smoking compartments
or whose personal stereos leak rap.

I will put in the box
windowboxes full of chrysanthemums,
crooked ministers and racist policemen,
poems that are vague, and bad rhyme.

My box will be a sphere
of cast iron, two foot thick,
with red lead chains coiled around it.

I will electrocute my box
until it's molten and glowing,
and all fused together,
then I'll catapult it into orbit –
it might become a small moon.

We have obviously stuck fairly rigidly to Kit's original structure (we spoke about using models earlier), just substituting a list of bad contents for his magical and gentle list; and it's easy to come up with a variety of things you dislike, some important and dangerous, some trivial. The twelfth of Adrian Mitchell's *Thirteen Secrets of Poetry* is: 'Pile up your feelings on a poetry plate/Write about something you really hate!'

We want you to give us your own bad box, being as precise and surprising as you can (nothing vague like 'war' or 'disease' – *what* war, *what* disease?), writing as a child and as an adult simultaneously. You can stick to the rigid structure we've borrowed, or you can invent a new structure of your own. Remember that, when you come to what your box is made of, you'll have to make it very tough to make sure that the nasty lot you've put in there doesn't get out – and getting rid of it is every bit as tricky as nuclear waste disposal. Then, when you've written it, find a child on whom to try it out. It may not be an *echt* children's poem, but it'll be a step on the way.

19

getting published

You may think, once you've accumulated a few poems you feel are successful, that all you have to do is place them in an envelope and send them to the poetry editor at Faber & Faber. Before you do so you should realize that Faber & Faber receive, on average, 50 poetry manuscripts a week, and although it is on record that some people have gone straight into publication this way, your chances of being accepted are actually very small indeed. The more usual way to proceed is to try small magazines first.

How do you know which magazines to send to? The best tactic is to read as many as you can find which are likely to be interested in the kind of poetry you write. It's no good submitting your polished domestic narratives to a magazine that specializes in concrete poetry, or your abrasively hilarious social satires to a magazine that publishes only intense Celtic lyricism. You also need to consider that magazines will vary, not only in the kinds of poetry they print but also in levels of production and distribution. The best way to find out about these magazines – and there is an enormous number of them, frequently shortlived – is to visit a specialist poetry library or poetry bookshop where they will be on display. If you do not have direct access to one, you'll have to write off to one, or to the Poetry Society (which you might consider joining) to obtain a list of magazine addresses. Any small magazine editor will be happy to send you a copy in return for a cheque, and actually you should aim to subscribe to at least one or two magazines with which you can identify.

Poetry magazines come in all shapes and sizes. The roneo'd broadsheet is probably the most basic level of production. After this come staple-bound and perfect-bound productions. In these days of desktop publishing, such magazines can reach a higher degree of professionalism in their presentation than was formerly possible. Some magazines restrict themselves to printing poetry; others (especially the more established) will include reviews, criticism, fiction and non-fiction. Then there are the literary and general periodicals, which may have regular poetry slots, and the broadsheet newspapers, some of which publish the occasional poem. The advantage of getting a poem into the latter, in particular, is that you may be unusually well-paid; the smaller poetry magazines are generally not in a position to pay much, or at all, but they are easier to get a poem into.

It's important to know how to make your submissions properly. At the risk of being banal, here are some basic tips:

- Type your poems, single-spaced, on one side of an A4 page. If your poem runs to more than one page, make sure you number the pages, and make clear it's the same poem.
- Do not send your entire *oeuvre* at once. Choose three or four of your best poems, but try to pick those that show a range of what you can do.
- Write your name under each poem. You do not want your favourite appearing attributed to someone else.
- Send a **short** covering letter. Resist pointing out at length to the editor the excellence of your poetry.
- Enclose a self-addressed envelope with sufficient stamps to ensure the return of all your manuscripts. Don't assume the envelope will come back much lighter. You ought to send international reply coupons if you're submitting abroad, but better still, if you can manage it, are stamps from the country to which you're sending.
- Some magazines take longer than others to consider submissions. Give the editor time to make up his or her mind. It's perfectly acceptable after three months, say, to write a gentle reminder.

At the outset, unless you are extremely lucky, you will have to cope with rejection. This is a fact of any writer's life. The rejections you get will probably take one of three forms: a printed slip; the same printed slip with a brief comment on it; or, most encouragingly, a letter. The bare printed slip tells you nothing, although, more likely than not, it means the editor doesn't think very highly of your efforts. It's just possible, however, that the magazine has enough poems for the time being and the editor isn't accepting any more poems of whatever standard. If the editor has seen any merit in your work, he or she might scribble a comment on the printed slip. For example, they might write 'Please send more', or 'Sorry not to like this quite enough' or maybe something specifically relevant to the pieces you sent. Rejection is never pleasant, but you have to develop certain strategies for dealing with it. In the beginning you may find this extremely difficult.

MS: I used to take to my bed for two days and speak to no one.

JHW: If the editor sent back my poems with a disparaging comment, I would immediately fire off a 15 page letter of self-justification, verbal abuse and concealed threat.

We know, however, from talking to editors (and from dabbling in magazine-editing ourselves) that editors are not usually in the business of satisfying sadistic impulses by rejecting you. What makes an editor's day is opening an envelope and finding poems he or she can't wait to publish. If they've taken the trouble to send you comments, despite rejecting your poems, you should take the trouble to try to work with what they've said, despite how distasteful and shortsighted it may seem. Don't immediately bin any observations you've been sent. Simmer down for a few days, then read them again. They may just contain an acute critical observation from which you might benefit. Even when poems are taken, the editor may enclose a critical comment along with the acceptance: 'Not very keen on the verbless sentences', for example, or 'What's all this coffin stuff?'. What the editor is doing here is warning you about stylistic mannerisms you may be developing without noticing. In a workshop or surgery situation criticism is easier to take because it is delivered in the context of a personal and constructive engagement with your work. Here is a comment made by an unpublished writer, after a surgery session with a poet-in-residence, which illustrates how the personal approach can make criticism much easier to assimilate:

> *Of course, I hoped secretly that X would tell me that I was a brilliant, undiscovered poet. No such luck! He didn't waste any time in praise, and yet I left feeling far from disappointed. What he gave me was in some ways more valuable: an hour of intense concentration on my work, criticism that was both detailed and dynamic, and very concrete suggestions for improvements that left me aching to get back home and start writing again.*

The writer went on to say that it was the illuminating honesty of the session that left no room for sentiment or ego. It's too unrealistic to expect a magazine editor to respond in such a thorough and enlightening manner. Away from the personal situation, comments on the page, delivered by someone you've never met, can seem harsh and negative. Sometimes it clearly is and you'd be right to feel offended.

JHW: I once got a single pencilled sentence on a rejection slip: 'This poem is neither considered nor considerable.' A gratuitous remark which, as you can see, I still remember.

MS: Once in the 1970s, when I was beginning to publish in magazines, an American editor told me that four lines in the

middle of a 35 line poem was the whole poem, and offered to publish the four lines under the poem's title. With some misgivings I let him.

This latter is unusually drastic editorializing and you may feel you couldn't agree to such a proposal. One the other hand, some people expect editors to rewrite their poem for them, which isn't a good idea either. You must be the first and most important editor – the one who decides when your poem is finished.

Remember that, whoever rejects your work, it's one person's opinion and their taste may not be infallible. Get a second opinion, and a third. If 25 editors in a row reject the same poem, maybe it's not one of your best. We all have failed poems, and it may take us a while to see they are failures. The best thing to do with these is line your bottom drawer with them and forget about them. If there was anything good in them to start with, you may find images and phrases reappearing in later successful poems. Think of them as poems that weren't ready to be written at the time you tried them first.

When your first poem is accepted, this will be the beginning of a confidence-building process that you will need if you're going to function as a writer. We're not saying that you need outside confirmation in order to build up confidence but it helps. Sometimes the sequence of acceptances and rejections can be very bewildering. You may be lucky enough to start with a series of acceptances which give way in turn to a series of rejections. You have to learn to cope with the wobbles that invariably affect your progress.

Submitting your poetry to magazines is an invaluable way of testing it on the outside world. The way in which it is received may influence the way you write, in the sense that if a certain kind of poem keeps getting accepted you will begin to write only that kind of poem. This may strengthen you by showing you what you do well, but the drawback is that it may limit you, may stop you exploring different ways of writing that could broaden your range.

Once you've appeared in a number of magazines you'll begin to establish a profile. In most cases you'll need this kind of exposure before editors at major publishing houses will consider taking you on for book publication. A number of magazine appearances might, if you're lucky enough, elicit a letter asking if you have a collection the editor might consider. The young

Seamus Heaney, for example, was approached by Faber & Faber after some poems of his appeared in an issue of the New Statesman. This is unusual, to say the least.

You should be wary of rushing into book publication, even though this might be a tantalizing prospect. When a full collection is published, the writer can be reasonably confident of getting review coverage in the newspapers and the media generally. If those reviews are bad, however, it can be difficult to retrieve a reputation that has been damaged at the outset. A pamphlet, on the other hand, is unlikely to be widely reviewed and can be regarded as a kind of trial publication.

MS: The biggest audience I ever attracted in Dublin was before I'd published a book. After the reading Thomas Kinsella approached me, said some friendly things about the reading, but advised me not to be in too much of a hurry to publish a first book. Most poets published too soon, he said. Unfortunately, I didn't heed his advice. I felt this crazy urgency to publish a book before I was 30, and my first book does little for me now.

A word here about vanity publishing. You will often see newspapers and magazines advertisements soliciting your manuscripts. Typically, they will say 'Authors wanted' or 'We want your manuscripts'. If you send your manuscript you may well receive an immediate offer of publication, provided you contribute a sum to cover the cost of the production. What's wrong with this? you might ask. Well, if your work is any good, you shouldn't have to pay for publication. The speed of acceptance might in itself suggest that little or no editorial discrimination has been exercised. What's more, you always need to remember that book publication involves a lot more than printing and binding a text. A book has to be marketed, publicized and distributed. Review copies have to be sent out and readings are usually set up for the author. Only reputable publishing houses have the experience and commitment to do all this. Once a vanity publisher has produced your book it's over to you, no matter what you have been promised.

This may not matter to you. You may just want to preserve those memories of the fleeting affair you had with that escaped German prisoner of war, but in that case why not really publish the book yourself? Go to a reputable printer and ask for an estimate of what it will cost you; or, alternatively, your grand-nephew may be a wizard at desktop publishing. He may be itching to get his hands on your book. It's never been easier to publish yourself, but think seriously about what you're going to do with those books when you get them. They can really clog up a cellar.

You'll almost certainly be tempted to enter a poetry competition, of which there are now hundreds. Winning one of these has proved to be a shortcut to book publication for some. It's best to think of the whole phenomenon as being like bingo: There are too many uncertainties. Some of the judges' predilections, for example, may make them favour only one type of poem.

JHW: I was a judge in a major competition once. There were four judges. It became clear to me during our deliberations that one of the judges had excluded all poems from his initial selection that were not illuminated by Christian belief. I concluded from this that at least a quarter of the entrants had as much chance as the orchestra on the Titanic.

Poetry competitions

If you do decide to go in for a competition you would do well to bear the following ten guidelines in mind.

- Most competitions are anonymous, so do not put your name on the bottom of the page. Even if the competition organizers Tippex it out it can still be read if the page is held up to the light, and the judge might be your biggest enemy.

- Don't exceed the stipulated maximum line-length and assume the quality of your entry will inevitably overcome petty restrictions.

- Do not be tempted to use a weird typeface in the hope of making your entry stand out, although there is some argument for putting the title in bold.

- Give your poem a good title – keep it snappy, specific and a little surprising. Avoid clichéd titles such as 'Fettered Hearts' or 'Song of Dawn'. And bear in mind a title should do more than just sum up what the poem is about.

- Remember, the judges will be looking for contemporary language. No 'thees', 'thous' or 'perchances'.

- If the competition has a theme, stay focused on it. You'd be amazed how many people enter themed competitions and write about something completely irrelevant. Don't, however, be constrained to the point of predictability. We've just judged a competition where the theme was slavery. Few of the entrants found a fresh angle to the subject matter.

- Consider the judges. Do you know their work? Given how they write, are they likely to appreciate your poem about polar bears having sex on a dislocated ice floe?
- Do not think of entering a poem that you have workshopped with the poet who is judging the competition. It will inevitably be disqualified.
- Do not enter a poem that has been published before, even if it was only in the parish magazine. Likewise, do not enter a poem that has been submitted elsewhere. We both know of cases where winning poems have been disqualified for these very reasons.
- It might be a good idea, before entering a competition, to analyze a number of poems that have won competitions. Some people claim there are particular qualities that characterize a competition-winning poem.

It's best not to presume that you will inevitably win. No matter how good your entry is, and however much your friends have been urging you to fire it into that competition, you'd do well to remember that the whole competition phenomenon is rather like bingo.

20

ipoems and cyber verse

Let us quote you the beginning of a letter from the project manager of the 2003 Poetry International (Rotterdam) website. He wrote:

> *Dear Poet,*
>
> *The internet is a wonderful thing, but it is also a mess. Type 'poetry' into your search engine and you'll get well over a million hits. Naturally, what the genuine poetry maniac is looking for is a well-organized website presenting poets and poems from countries all over the world. This website is here: **www.poetryinternational.org**. It's a worldwide forum for poetry.*

We've checked out this site and he's not exaggerating. As well as the central domain (Poetry International's headquarters in Rotterdam), there are individual country domains, each connecting to the centre, and each presenting a range of poetry and poetry-related information from that country. For example, you'll find Croatia there, the Ukraine, South Africa, Morocco and Argentina, and the number is constantly growing. Taken together this adds up to a comprehensive overview of what's happening in poetry globally. One obvious effect of such international cooperation is the facilitation of translation, and this is a chief aim of the Poetry International site. You will also find the Defence of Poetry lecture series, given and simultaneously published online during the annual Poetry International Festival in which 'poets of world-renown defend their discipline'. The homepage tells you how to access an archive of poets, audio files and a collection of video material, *camera poetica*, that is quirky and fun.

MS: You'll find me up there, walking round a circular room in the house of an eccentric nineteenth-century Dutch doctor, reading a poem about a lovesick skeleton to a series of skulls, one human, the rest animal: cow, anteater, sheep and warthog.

JHW: I just tried to find Matthew but all I got was a black screen. Why do I always have to download a new media player to see (or hear) something new?

MS: Luddite!

Translation is also a feature of an even more impressive German site at **www.lyrikline.org**. This site is noteworthy for its clarity and ease of use. Click on a country's name, and a list of poets from that country will appear. Click on a name and you will see a photograph of the author, a short biography, ten poems (usually), translations of these poems in whatever languages there are translations available, and an audio file of the poems being read by the author in the original language. There may also be a video file. Of course, you may wish to look up an individual poet, regardless of country, in which case you simply click on a letter of the alphabet and scroll down till you find his or her name. This might also be a good way – should you be a teacher of poetry – to locate the poem you need to kickstart that difficult workshop in Finland. You could be lucky. It just might be one of the ten. Naturally, as this is a German site, the emphasis is on German poets, but it is truly international and expanding all the time.

Other good poetry sites are:

• www.contemporarywriters.com
This British Council site provides a searchable database of writers (poets, novelists, dramatists etc.) with profiles, critical perspectives, interviews, photographs, etc.

• www.writersartists.net
This is an agency website where a number of writers and artists are represented, including biographies, bibliographies, sample reviews, forthcoming appearances for readings and workshops, examples of work and, usefully, weblinks that take you to other important sites featuring that particular writer or artist.

• www.thepoem.co.uk
Like most of these sites, this a non profit-making organization dedicated to furthering contemporary British and Irish poetry. It is run by Edward Barker, son of the poet George Barker. It features poets of the month and a permanent archive.

• www.poems.com
This American site ('Poetry Daily') features a daily English language poem, picked either from new collections or from current issues of poetry magazines. The poems are up for a day, then go automatically into a back archive, where they can be easily accessed. The poems are not just American but from anywhere in the English-speaking world. In addition to this, they feature a weekly prose item on some subject connected with poetry, also drawn from new books or magazine issues. These can also be found in the back archive.

• www.webdelsol.com
If you click on this site you enter a world of poetry whose ramifications seem endless. Here you'll find the names of poets, poetry magazines, upcoming poetry conferences, and general

poetry chit-chat. It is fair to say that the emphasis here is mainly, if not exclusively, on American poetry.

• www.poetshouse.org
Another American site, founded by the distinguished American poet and one-time Laureate, Stanley Kunitz, in 1985. This excellent website features a collection of 50,000 volumes of poetry that can be accessed free of charge.

Here are a few more American sites:

• http://www.poetryfoundation.org
• http://www.poets.org
• http://www.poetrysociety.org

And a couple of Australian ones:

• http://www.austlit.com
• http://home.vicnet.net.au/~ozlit

Back in the UK, you might like to try and access the following website:

• www.poetryarchive.co.uk

This site was created by British Poet Laureate, Andrew Motion, and like all these sites is constantly being added to and developed. It holds an extensive repertory of both contemporary and historic recordings of poets reading their work, plus the original texts, biographies and critical appraisals. Motion comments: 'We've done it to conserve voices that might otherwise be lost. We've done it to demonstrate that the sound of a poem is as important to its existence as whatever the words might mean when we read them ... It is fascinating to hear a poet reading their own work, hearing their accent, hearing their idiom, seeing where they place the emphases and so on.'

• www.poetrykit.org
This is basically an online information guide for poets looking for markets for their work, similar to *The Writers' and Artists' Yearbook* (UK) or *Poet's Market* (US) – see the index for more on these. Here you will find lists of magazines, poetry publishers, and constantly updated information regarding competitions, poetry organizations, and a host of other practical (and worldwide) links. You can also find individual poets' home pages listed here.

• www.poetrysociety.org.uk
This is the website of the UK Poetry Society. It gives you information about all the Society's doings, including the current issue of *Poetry Review*, the newsletter, the National Poetry

Competition (you can download entry forms from the site, you can even enter online). If you happen to be teaching poetry writing in schools, for example, you will find something very useful here: 'Poetry Class – Kids' Poetry Sites', in which poets provide exercises to get young people writing. The exercises might even start you writing, just as we hope those in this book have done. There are lots of links provided to other interesting and useful sites for teachers. For example, the American poet Billy Collins has a sprightly site called **180** which presents the poems he's chosen for each of the 180 days of the American High School year. You can find these at **http://www.loc.gov/poetry/180/**

- **www.poetryireland.ie**

This is the website of Poetry Ireland, and gives details of poetry goings-on in Ireland, as well as featuring a bi-monthly newsletter.

The above examples are, broadly speaking, sites for source material and information. There is a also a very interesting and contemporary commercial site at **www.57productions.com**. The most striking feature of this is what is named iPoems. On the principle of iTunes downloads, you can listen to, watch, and then purchase downloads of an array of writers and performers. These range from performance poets such as Jean 'Binta' Breeze and Benjamin Zephaniah, to 'book' poets such as Tony Harrison and Michael Donaghy. There is also a Poetry Jukebox here that functions just like a jukebox in a bar – search through performers and poets and play the poem you want to hear. There is also a slightly less extensive repertoire of video clips that you can also activate, watch and purchase for download if you wish. Much of this material is also available on CD.

MS & JHW: We've just watched the late Michael Donaghy recite his powerful, dramatic monologue 'Black Ice and Rain'. Try it!

There are also good poetry and poetry-related webzines, and these include, for example: *Jacket Magazine, 3ammagazine, nth position, X Magazine, Terrible Work, Stride, Qualm and Proof.* A full list is available from **www.poetrylibrary.org.uk**.

Some of these magazines have both a print edition and a web version. *Jacket Magazine* has no print edition, and is edited by the well-known Australian poet, John Tranter. It features interviews, reviews, long essays, in-depth considerations of specific poets, and, of course, poems. It is intellectual, lively, and a serious contribution to poetry discourse. One striking aspect of this magazine is that it builds as you watch it. When a new number appears it will only have a few slots filled, at first. Then over a period of time the issue is fleshed out until it is complete. You can find it at **http://jacketmagazine.com/00/home.shtml**.

nthposition runs stories, essays and poems, as well as reviews. It is famous for having produced the broadside *100 Poets against the War*, a polemic against the war in Iraq. We should stress, though, that the poetry does not have to have a political slant. *Terrible Work* features reviews of contemporary poetry. *3ammagazine*, heavily weighted towards prose, though with some poetry, has editors on both sides of the Atlantic, and features poems, stories or extracts of longer prose works and in-depth interviews – all of which go onto a back archive when a new edition of the magazine goes online.

A further website dedicated to finding poetry and poetry-related material online is run by Peter Howard at **www.hphoward.demon.co.uk**.

We should also mention that the Poetry Library has established a free access site to the full-text digital library of twentieth- and twenty-first-century UK poetry magazines from their collection, at **www.poetrymagazines.org.uk**.

Amongst the print magazines you can now find online (selected editions) are: *Ambit, Angel Exhaust, Magma, Modern Poetry in Translation, PN Review, Poetry Review, Poetry Wales, London Magazine, Smith's Knoll* and *The North and The Wolf.* Two of these – *Magma* and *The Wolf* – also provide mp3 audio files for some of the poets featured in their pages.

On the subject of magazines on the internet we should mention that august periodicals such as the *Times Literary Supplement* and *The London Review of Books*, both of which publish poems and reviews of poetry frequently, put their issues online and keep a back archive. This material, however, is only available to subscribers.

The Guardian newspaper is one of the few national dailies to continue to review poetry in depth. As well as commissioning general essays on subjects to do with poetry, it also publishes a poem of the week. All this material can be accessed in *The Guardian* online, as well as an onsite poetry workshop conducted by a known poet. It costs nothing to visit this site – **books.guardian.co.uk/poetryworkshop**.

JHW & MS: We have both contributed workshop exercises here and they can be accessed through the archive provided there together with our comments on a selection of the poems submitted.

Some poetry publishers have their own websites. The most sophisticated of these that we have identified so far is that of 'Salt'.

JHW: The speed at which Salt works is breathtaking – especially if you're used to the gentlemanly pace of traditional publishing houses. I emailed the text of a new book, a retrospective volume called *The Ship*, to the publisher and within a day it was advertised on the Salt website, complete with author's photo, sample text, audio files and a complete contents list.

MS: I have been waiting five years for my Dutch bilingual selection to appear.

Salt has an excellent website which also directs you to the weblogs of poets and writings on poetry from all kinds of sources. Here are some more sites to be explored:

- http://www.saltpublishing.com/blogs/
- http://ronsilliman.blogspot.com
- http://www.ubu.com

Similarly, Youtube (a wealth of video content), Myspace and Facebook are also worth exploring, though the sheer amount of material is sometimes bewildering, and not always easy to navigate.

Much activity in the poetry field would remain invisible were it not for the internet, and websites and journals such as those we have just drawn your attention to. But these are examples of the relatively small amount of gold amongst the dross. In fact, lurking in the deeps of cyberspace, as the letter from Poetry International suggests, are to be found examples of the lunatic, the maudlin and the deviously exploitative. In the first category, for example, you will find the poetry of Betty the Budgerigar (we're not making this up). The sitemaster says, 'It takes a concentrated effort to understand her, but just follow the words I have provided with the recordings and that should help' and goes on, 'It takes some people a bit of practice to get adjusted to the budgerigar's accent.' We have listened attentively to the admittedly rhythmical squawking, and we have to concur. In the maudlin category, we would put most of the sites devoting themselves exclusively to love poetry – and, as you will find, there are many of these. Here is a cornucopia of the breathtakingly clichéd, the cloyingly sentimental and the utterly obvious. We don't doubt the sincerity of the poets contributing to these sites but we hope this book has made clear there is more to writing poetry than being sincere.

And the devious? Well, one site that looks like a very promising place for a new poet to start searching for information and opportunities is the innocuous-sounding **www.poetry.com**. Poets, whether previously published or not, are invited to submit poems on any subject and in any style, provided they're 20 lines or less, to regular competitions for cash prizes. We took the liberty of entering something on your behalf. We wrote a short poem together entitled 'The Wigwam of the Baroness' and submitted it, under the pseudonym Bill Gerard-Wright. Almost immediately, it was sent back to us, formatted, with each line centred, making it look '*good*'. Then a notice flashed up on the screen that we were the one millionth visitor to the website, and should contact the prize department. As Today's Winner we could call a toll-free number, and if we did so within the next four minutes we would receive $3,000 and a Bahamas cruise vacation. The countdown began. We did not touch the phone. The next thing that happened was an email to Bill, saying his poem was being reviewed by the editorial staff for acceptance into the International Library of Poetry and Poetry.com's Open Amateur Poetry Contest, as well as the Poets' Choice: Rate my Poem Contest. A follow-up email would come in two weeks. We were also told that while waiting we should vote on current Poets' Choice: Rate my Poem Contest entries. We did, and are sorry to say that we were unable to award anything a higher vote than the minimum 1. We would love to have had the option of zero.

Whether or not we 'win a prize', we can be fairly certain a publication will be offered for a fee – vanity publishing, in other words. This highlights a real problem with the web in general; it's too easy to exploit the poet's natural desire to see his or her work published. We have always insisted throughout this book that you should submit your poems to magazines or periodicals where you can expect a serious and informed appraisal of your work. There's no substitute for doing this, even though it may take time and disappointments before you find an editor who is sympathetic. Too many websites offer to post up poems regardless of quality, sometimes for payment, sometimes not. The driving impulse behind a site such as Poetry International is the need to establish some form of quality control: critical assessment, editorial appraisal, peer group commentary etc.

MS: In 1998 I was poet in residence for the electronic publisher Chadwyck-Healey. Each fortnight I had to come up with a masterclass, focusing on some technical aspect of writing poetry (not unlike what goes on in this book), and a surgery, where I'd

choose one of the poems submitted and comment on it critically and, I hope, constructively. These poems were available on a bulletin board that also held comments on any aspects of the site, sometimes including responses by the chosen poets to what I'd written about their work, or opinions from other people that ran contrary to mine. Often there'd be comment on poems I hadn't chosen. At the end of the residency it was really buzzing as a site.

Although Chadwyck-Healey (now Proquest) still have a site, they no longer have a poet in residence, unfortunately, but the fact that such a facility was offered once doesn't mean it won't be offered again. In the meantime, we've given you some other site addresses to get you started, although we're fairly certain that those of you who are computer users will already have this information at your fingertips. The addresses we've suggested provide links to countless more sites. Remember, though, these sites change constantly. You'll want to find your own favourites (you almost certainly already have) and you'll undoubtedly discover that some of the sites we've listed will have vanished (or become inaccessible) by the time you read this. Keep looking though. You're sure to find new ones.

The question is: does the web make the book superfluous? Those still firmly operating in what they like to think of as the Gutenberg Galaxy believe not. To them, there's no substitute for reading from a well-made book, while sitting in a deckchair in a garden, with a glass of wine to hand, or while travelling somewhere on a train, munching a salmon and cucumber sandwich. The thought of scrolling down text on a monitor (possibly surrounded by the clutter of other work) is anathema to them. They'd prefer to read the newspaper. But for the convert to a sleek and elegant site such as Lyrikline (as we both were instantly when we saw it demonstrated at a prizegiving ceremony in Berlin Mitte) the internet offers serious alternative possibilities, suggesting it is time it was recognized that both are possible.

We'll leave the last words on this to that prophet of global communication, Marshall McLuhan. He said, in *Understanding Media*, 'Since all media are fragments of ourselves extended into the public domain, the action upon us of any one medium tends to bring the other senses into a new relation.' In other words, it is as yet impossible to gauge the full impact of this new medium, the internet, on poetry. The ending of this chapter is still being written.

21

reading aloud

He was not a splendid reader, merely decent to his own lines, and he read from that slouch, that personification of ivy climbing a column, he was even diffident, he looked a trifle helpless under the lights. Still he made no effort to win the audience, seduce them, dominate them, bully them, amuse them, no, they were there for him, to please him, a sounding board for the plucked string of his poetic line, and so he endeared himself to them. They adored him – for his talent, his modesty, his superiority, his petulance, his weakness, his painful, almost stammering shyness, his noble strength – there was the string behind other strings...

This is Norman Mailer writing about Robert Lowell reading to a public anti-Vietnam War meeting in Washington in September 1967. What is illuminating about this cameo is how Lowell gets his effects in a completely non-actorly manner. The slouch (no posture-training at drama school), the diffidence, the stammering shyness – and yet the audience adored him. Lowell wouldn't have come across as effectively as he did if he hadn't first of all been 'decent to his own lines'.

This is what anyone contemplating getting up in front of an audience has to learn to do – to be decent to their own lines. It's partly a matter of being confident, of course, that your own lines can stand up orally. It's also, and more crucially, a matter of using the fact that you wrote the poems in your voice to help you find a way to put them across to an audience. What kind of relationship your poems have to your own speaking voice, your accent, will not be clear to you in the beginning but will become clearer as you develop into your own distinctive style of writing. Reading your poem aloud can magnify that distinctive voice for the hearer. In any case, as we said in Chapter 05, voicing your poem to yourself in the privacy of your study should be an integral part of the process of composition. Reading poems successfully aloud to an audience, of course, is also a basic matter of being clearly audible, not mumbling behind a spit-stained book raised like a shield between you and your audience.

As we hinted at in the first paragraph above, there is a difference between the way poets and actors generally read poems. Most actors think poets can't read their work aloud. Poets know that most actors can't read poetry properly. There are enough exceptions, of course, but generally actors exaggerate the effects of a poem, giving it an unnatural and somewhat precious emphasis.

MS: I've heard it put that actors skate down the vowels of a poem, while poets step from consonant to consonant. I can't remember whose wisdom this was, but around the time it was said to me it rang true. I'd just had to endure hearing an actor murder a Yeats poem, 'The Song of Wandering Aengus', by elongating the vowels as if they were elastic bands: 'I went oouut to a haaazel wooood because a fiiire was in my heeead...' The effect was ridiculous.

At the same time it's worth saying that there are many poets out there who have not learned to be decent to their own lines, and that any poet new to reading aloud could learn from a good actor. What you would learn is how to enunciate the whole word, not lose half of it, and how to project your voice to the back row of the audience. Also how to pace the poem – which lines to give more emphasis to than others, when to speed up, when to slow down – and obvious things, such as when there's a whisper in a poem you should whisper that line to the audience, when there's a shout you should shout. In short, you would be learning how to be more dramatic, without being histrionic and without being less true to yourself and your writing voice. You would be giving your poem a chance to work in the oral/aural medium.

It's worth saying as well that not every poet has a desire to get onto the reading circuit. For some it reeks of showmanship and has nothing to do with the writing of poetry. One poet who usually declined invitations to read his poems aloud was Philip Larkin. In an interview with *The Paris Review* he said the following:

> *I don't give readings, no, although I have recorded three of my collections, just to show how I should read them. Hearing a poem, as opposed to reading it on the page, means you miss so much – the shape, the punctuation, the italics, even knowing how far you are from the end. Reading it on the page means you can go at your own pace, taking it in properly; hearing it means you're dragged along at the speaker's own rate, missing things, not taking it in, confusing 'there' and 'their' and things like that. And the speaker may interpose his own personality between you and the poem, for better or worse. For that matter, so may an audience. I don't like hearing things in public, even music. In fact, I think poetry readings grew up on a false analogy with music: the text is the 'score' that doesn't 'come to life' until it's 'performed.' It's false because people can read words, whereas they can't read music. When you write a poem, you put everything into it*

that's needed: the reader should 'hear' it just as clearly as if you were in the room saying it to him. And of course this fashion for poetry readings has led to a kind of poetry that you can understand first go: easy rhythms, easy emotions, easy syntax. I don't think it stands up on the page.'

(from *Writers at Work: The Paris Review Interviews* edited by George Plimpton)

What Larkin is objecting to here may be the Barnum and Bailey Circus Extravaganza elements in some types of poetry readings (and we don't have to speculate on what he would have thought of performance poets). But personality, surely, is what comes through in the voice of the poem. We don't see what is wrong about having that personality impose itself at a reading. A comically extreme presentation of this prejudice against poetry readings is given by Flann O'Brien:

I was once acquainted with a man who found himself present by some ill chance at a verse speaking bout. Without a word he hurried outside and tore his face off. Just that. He inserted three fingers into his mouth, caught his left cheek in a frenzied grip and ripped the whole thing off. When it was found, flung in a corner under an old sink, it bore the simple dignified expression of the honest man who finds self-extinction the only course compatible with honour.

(from *The Best of Myles – Myles na Gopaleen* by Flann O'Brien)

Although there are many poets who are only interested, like Larkin, in publishing their poems so that people can read them on the page (and it's fair to say that publication is still a priority for most poets), we would nevertheless like to emphasize that poems can be taken in aurally as well as visually. The work of many poets reaches a future reader first at a poetry reading. An audience-member hears the reading, likes it, and buys a book. In this way the reading acts as a sampler of the poet's work for someone who doesn't know it. If the person in the audience is a fan who has read the poems many times but has never heard them read aloud by the poet, the reading can offer new insights because of the way in which the poems are delivered – or simply through the introductions and asides the poet gives. Both ways of taking in a poem – visually and aurally – are important and can be seen to be complementary. If, despite this way of looking at matters, you still persist with the view that you don't want anything to do with readings, fine. You should bear in mind, however, that people who earn a living as successful poets make a sizeable proportion of their income from readings – and that's not just from the reading fees but from the booksales at the event.

Readings, of course, come out of the oral tradition. Despite our print-based and increasingly computer-dependent culture, there is still a strong oral tradition in many parts of the English-speaking world. Africa, the Caribbean and Ireland are a few places that spring immediately to mind.

JHW: You can find this tradition in England, too. I remember my first readings in the 1960s took place in the framework of a folk club. There'd be a lot of heavily bearded men and interestingly pale girls. Someone would sing a Dubliners' song to a guitar, someone else would tell a story in Lincolnshire dialect, then I'd read my poem. Not quite the Albert Hall, perhaps, but there was often a very high level of performance, especially with the storytellers.

Radio is also part of the oral/aural medium, and although actors, unfortunately, read a great deal of the poetry which is broadcast, there are also possibilities for poets to read their own work. There has long been a tradition of poets recording their own work as well, on record, tape and, lately, CD. In most cases only prominent poets have recorded in this medium, but with the increase in popularity of poetry in performance, this outlet has already tentatively begun to become available to more poets.

It has to be said there are poems that lend themselves more than others to being read aloud to an audience. Such poems are generally at least accessible enough to yield something to an audience on a first hearing. Poems that are dense and complex, although they may intrigue part of the audience and make them want to read them on the page, may very well pass the majority of the audience by. At the closest end of accessibility, of course, is what is called performance poetry. Most of this is written to be performed, rather than read in a book (although some performance poets sell well in book form also). The characteristic of this poetry is that it engages the audience directly, employing such devices as upfront humour, topical subject matter, political concerns or possibly love lyricism, and sometimes audience response. It is performed in a dramatic, showstopping manner and is usually spoken from memory rather than read from a text. The book may be in the poet's hand but is little more than a prop. Sometimes there will be a musical element to the performance (dub poetry is an obvious example here). The skill with which the performers connect with the audience is reflected in their often large followings.

One democratic and competitive offshoot of performance poetry is the poetry slam. At a slam, poets perform original work alone or in teams before an audience, which serves as judge. The work is evaluated as much on the manner and enthusiasm of its performance as its content or style, and many slam poems are not intended to be read silently from the page. It encompasses a very broad range of voices, styles, cultural traditions and approaches to writing and performance. One of the goals of slam poetry is to challenge the authority of people like us who might say we think we know what constitutes literary quality. Slam poets wish to break down the barriers between poet/performer, critic and audience. Only the poets with the best scores advance to the final round of the night and this ensures the audience gets to choose who they want to hear more from.

You don't have to be a performance poet, though, to engage with an audience and send them home purring. More and more 'book' poets are learning to put themselves across in a manner that can illuminate and magnify the text on the page. Many of us have had the experience of hearing poets read their work aloud, and know that we can read their work years later and still hear the voice, the tones and inflections, and the rhythms that the poet employed. This can actually be a considerable enrichment of the text. Nor is it a bad thing for a poem not to surrender all its effects on first hearing. Further pleasures can be gained on a subsequent reading.

A poem [as T.S. Eliot said] *can communicate before it is understood.*

MS: A dramatic example of this was a children's reading I did as part of the Salisbury Festival a few years back. The reading had been advertised as being for children of eight years and over, but when I got to the library I saw that the majority of the audience was five years and under. Alarmed by this, and the fact that none of my poems is suitable for that age group, my instinct was to run. I wasn't allowed to, however, and embarked on the reading with foreboding, only to discover with surprise that the little kids stayed (fairly) rapt throughout. I could put it down only to the effect the noise of the poems and their delivery had on them.

If you've got a sufficient body of work together that you're confident with, and that you've roadtested on your patient partner and friends, you may decide you want to present it in performance. How should you prepare yourself? First of all, be realistic. How many people have heard of you outside Skelmersdale? Don't expect to be invited straight-off to read at the Purcell Room, on London's South Bank, and attract an audience of 200. You're more likely to appear in a grotty upstairs room of a pub, or in the organizer's sitting room, and apart from a couple of true friends, the audience is likely to consist of the organizer and his 80-year-old mother who'll probably doze off and snore half-way through your best poem. A worst case scenario that both the authors of this book have experienced is quite simply no audience at all until a couple of cleaners are roped in reluctantly to provide one.

Still, things get better. The more widely known you become, the more your audience will grow – first locally, then further afield. With practice you'll also become a better performer. Even poets who are well-known readers of their work weren't always good at it, and may even have had some disastrous early experiences. You'll probably be no exception. You will need to work constantly at improving the way you read.

EXERCISE 45 Wigwam

There are techniques that can be learned. Projection of your voice is not just a matter of loudness, which by itself is no guarantee that the meaning of your words will get across: it's a matter of knowing how to vary levels of volume and pitch for dramatic effect. It's also a matter of articulating each word clearly and distinctly, and not running one word into the next or skipping over some. Here's a little exercise to illustrate what we mean. Say the words 'wigwam', 'peremptory', 'cannibalism', 'blackguard' and 'alcohol', rolling each sound in the words around in your mouth as if they were sweets. Then make up phrases containing these words, and say them aloud in a similar way, varying the type of emphasis you put on each word. If you say, for example, 'The Baroness bought a wigwam', ask yourself which are the words that are most stressed. In how many ways could you vary the emphasis in the phrase? What would be gained by these variations?

If you have a regional accent, learn to incorporate this into the way you read; don't feel you have to sound like a BBC newsreader. As long as you clean up your enunciation, work at putting a little variety into your delivery and availing yourself of as much of the vocal range as possible, without exaggeration, the potential for sounding good, while still being yourself, is there.

Part of the business of projecting well involves holding eye-contact with the audience. Because your head will be up from your book, your throat will be open and your voice will carry. Eyeballing your audience is also a way of keeping their attention. You may not have committed your text to memory but a degree of familiarity with it enables you to lift your eyes from the text for longish stretches of it.

One common fault of people new to poetry reading (and some people not so new either) is the tendency to drop their voice at the end of a line or a whole poem. This may have something to do with the way in which they look down to find the next line, or the next poem they're going to read. In the process they forget their responsibility to the line or poem they're actually saying. They forget, too, their responsibility to the audience.

A word here on pacing. Just as not every word or phrase in your text is equally emphasized, not all lines are necessarily read at the same speed. The pacing of your delivery will reflect the ebb and flow of whatever inner drama your poem has. With practice (and advice) you'll learn to recognize those passages you read slowly, and those passages where you quicken up. We've already mentioned how important it is, during the act of composition, to read your poems to yourself. Reading them to an audience will further highlight any weak bits. You will also, like Robert Lowell at the start of this chapter, be using the audience as a sounding board, and their response will tell you a lot about the success and failure of your poems. Getting feedback from the audience in this way is not only valuable for your work, it can also increase your self-esteem, and your belief in what you're doing.

In addition to considering points of technique regarding the reading itself, you'll need to think about the manner of presentation. If you expect the reading you do to be properly organized, so that the event is as rewarding for the audience as a night out at the theatre, your part in the proceedings must also be professional. When poetry readings turn out to be shambolic and chaotic, as they unfortunately often are, it confirms the public perception that poetry isn't a serious enterprise. You may not be responsible for the organization but you can at least ensure you do your bit properly. We've drawn up a list of things to keep in mind.

- Do you know which poems you're going to read, and in what order you're going to read them? Have you made a list so you won't forget, or did you leave your books on the train?

- Are you going to introduce your poems briefly and intriguingly, or are you going to explain so much the poem will be redundant? Maybe you'd better jot down some of the things you might want to say.
- Have you over-fortified yourself? Is your speech slurred? Will you be able to avoid falling into the front row of the audience?
- Is there a microphone? Is it still set for the previous reader who was 6 feet 8? Have you used one before?
- Are you so overdressed for the lights that you're dripping with sweat? Is your mode of dress appropriate for the venue and the event?
- Do you intend to read your poems with your back to the audience (the way Miles Davis used to play his trumpet to the audience in the 1960s), or do you fancy the idea of reading lying down, or in the lotus position? Are you sure this isn't a gimmick?
- Are you prepared for hecklers, people who throw pints of beer at your feet or who ask you daft questions?
- Are you going to ignore the organizer's instruction to read for a maximum of 20 minutes and read your entire book, thinking that's what the audience has come for?

What we're getting at here is matters of general etiquette – in short, respecting your audience and your public role as a performer. If somebody asks you, for example, 'Why do you write poetry?' you may feel there's no point in answering this. More likely, though, you'll try.

Finally, a word on how your own reaction to your reading can sometimes be subjective. Here is Franz Kafka's account of a reading he gave from Kleist's novel *Michael Kohlhaas* on 11th December 1913.

> *In Toynbee Hall read the beginning of Michael Kohlhaas. Complete and utter fiasco. Badly chosen, badly presented, finally swam senselessly around in the text. Model audience. Very small boys in the front row. One of them tries to overcome his innocent boredom by carefully throwing his cap on the floor and then carefully picking it up, and then again, over and over. Since he is too small to accomplish this from his seat, he has to keep sliding off the chair a little. Read wildly and badly and carelessly and unintelligibly. And in the afternoon I was already trembling with eagerness to read, could hardly keep my mouth shut.*

Max Brod, who was also at this event, gives a slightly different account.

> *Actually ... the reading was a much less melancholy affair than Kafka's account would indicate. Kafka, needless to say, read wonderfully; I was present at the reading and remember it quite well. It was only that he had chosen a selection that was much too long, and in the end was obliged to shorten it as he read. In addition, there was the quite incongruous contrast between this great literature and the uninterested and inferior audience, the majority of whom came to benefit affairs of this kind only for the sake of the free cup of tea that they received.*

22

poetry prizes and festivals

One of the developments in poetry over the last 20 years is the emergence of glitzy poetry prizes and we've been asked to write about this. We want to say upfront that prizes are no concern of a true poet, especially one just starting out, finding his or her muse. We are saying – as we have been throughout this book – that what's important is to learn the nuts and bolts of craft and technique. The rest will happen or not happen, as the case may be. Prizes are no measure of a poet's worth. They do not validate what he or she has achieved. Prizes are for others – publishers, journalists, representatives of the culture industry etc. If, after establishing yourself as a poet, you become a candidate for a prize, and miraculously win, the only possible response is to take the money and run. And to take the accolades with the grain of salt they deserve. Will a poem of yours be included in the Oxford Anthology of English verse for 3007? Now that would be something worth having.

A point worth making here is that we do not consider competitions in the same light. Poets have always enjoyed a bout of peer-group rivalry, and it's natural to want to pit your poetic craft against your colleagues in the guild, but please note what we have said on this subject on page 179.

To get back to the prizes, the biggest, in the UK, are the Forward Prize, T. S. Eliot Prize, the Costa Book Award (Poetry), previously known as the Whitbread Prize, and in Ireland, the Irish Times Poetry Now Award. These are worth considerable sums of money (£10,000 for the first two UK awards, £5,000 for the Costa poetry category, but £25,000 if you win the Costa award outright, and €5,000 for the Irish award), and can really bring the spotlight onto the winner, procuring for him or her invitations to all the festivals, and ensuring his or her book gets maximum review coverage. In part, the emergence of these prizes is a spin-off from fiction's older Booker Prize, but it is fair to say that the latter generates a lot more publicity, which seriously increases book sales. Poetry simply doesn't interest enough people. Still, winning one of the poetry prizes can make a difference to a book, and to a poet.

Modelling themselves on the Booker Prize, the Forward and the Eliot prizes first announce a shortlist – the Eliot shortlist being longer than the Forward – then some months later, at a public event, where it is hoped all the shortlisted poets will attend, the winner is announced. The Eliot Prize goes one step further in having, the previous evening, at a London Theatre, a brief reading by each of the shortlisted poets in turn.

The performance, however, and perhaps contrary to the expectations of the audience, has no influence on the award. The live announcement of the prize, with the winner and the losers present, so that the disappointment of the losers is as visible to the reception-attenders as the elation of the winner, may supply media drama but it is not comfortable for the poets. Better, to us, is the Irish Times model (which is also how the German poetry prizes operate) where the winner is announced before the prizegiving ceremony. It seems, somehow, more humane.

JHW: I was shortlisted for the Eliot Prize in 1997. The paranoid atmosphere of the event – that at least is how I felt about it – seemed heightened by the fact that the preliminary reading took place at the Almeida Theatre where a production of Gogol's 'Dead Souls' was running. I couldn't help thinking the atmosphere resembled a model for corrupt, Soviet cultural production, and wrote a satirical piece about human vanity for a book about writers' humiliating experiences. Some idiots felt insulted – but I don't regret writing it.

Whatever the format of the prize announcement, the same strictures we mentioned in Chapter 19 in relation to poetry competitions apply here: the decision of whom to shortlist, or award the prize to, is totally dependent on the judges' predilections. A different set of judges would very probably award the prize to a different poet. There are always announcements that astonish the poetry world, just as there are announcements that are completely predictable.

The Forward Prize has two innovations – as well as the main prize, there is also a prize for the best first collection (£5,000), and another for the best individual poem (£1,000) – both of these with announced shortlists also. The individual poems are submitted by the periodicals where the poems first appeared, which brings in another uncertainty – the periodicals might have kept back a poem that might have appealed more to the judges. How can the category 'Best Individual Poem of the Year' be justified when only a handful from the countless published ones are considered for the prize?

A long-established poetry prize worth mentioning is the Geoffrey Faber Memorial Prize, worth £1,000, and given bi-annually to a volume of verse. The Society of Authors administers the Eric Gregory Awards, which grant substantial sums of money (£4,000 in 2006) to poets who are under 30. This can be a huge confidence boost but it's no guarantee that those poets will stay the course, as a look online at a list of those successful will verify. The Society of Authors also supervises the long-running Cholmondely Award which is given in recognition of a body of work and is worth £2,000. There are also Authors' Foundation grants one can apply for, to help finish books.

MS: Just before I was 30, I sent in an application for a Gregory Award. I was turned down, on the grounds that I was born in the Republic of Ireland. I replied, saying I was born in Lifford, bang on the border with Northern Ireland, and only there because my mother had been playing cards, and winning, and left too late to reach the nursing home in Derry she had been booked into. The Society of Authors was unmoved.

And we'd like to lament one extinct poetry prize that we'd welcome seeing restarted – the one-time Prudence Farmer Award that was given, once a year, to the best poem published in the *New Statesman* magazine, with an entertaining judge's report published in the issue announcing the prize.

There are countless awards and prizes out there. For a full list, with previous winners, you can consult the British Council website at **www.contemporarywriters.com/awards**.

The other obvious development in the visibility of poetry in the last 20 years is the proliferation of poetry festivals, where an assortment of poets who have already acquired reputations is invited to come and read. Previously, there were longer-established literary festivals – such as the famous Edinburgh Festival – but a purely poetry festival is something different. The most prominent poetry festivals are the Aldeburgh Poetry Festival, the Ledbury Poetry Festival, and more recently, in Scotland, the Stanza Poetry Festival in St Andrews. Any visitor who attends a festival of this kind will be astonished by the large crowds who attend the events, and clearly revel in them. The reason is very simple – the poetry readings are not put on at the same time as a reading by a big-time novelist (as invariably happens at the literary festivals that embrace all genres), and because there are no novelists there, or TV chefs, the audience discovers what an enjoyable event a poetry reading can be.

MS: These mixed-genre literary festivals can sink the poetry readings. I was invited to read at the Hay on Wye festival one year, and was having a butterfly-drowning beer on the grass beforehand when eight people came up to me, one after another, to say they'd be coming to my event if it didn't clash with a reading by Ian McEwan. I wondered what was the point of my being there.

The true poetry festivals are excellent occasions for buying books, and after hearing a poet you like, it's very important to follow up by reading the poems on the page. There is usually an excellent, wide-ranging display of poetry books such as few shops can offer these days. We urge you, if you have the opportunity, to visit one of these festivals to pick up the atmosphere and the buzz, the conversation in the bar afterwards, and the opportunity to talk to the poets themselves.

There are other smaller poetry festivals, probably the most prominent being the Dun Laoghaire–Rathdown Poetry Now Festival, which claims to be the only remaining Irish and International festival solely devoted to poetry. The festival in Kings Lynn handles the poetry/prose divide very simply by having two festivals at different times of the year, one for poetry, one for prose. The poetry festival used to, at least, operate with a certain style – the invited poets were met on the platform at Kings Lynn station (which is an end-of-the-line stop) by a bagpiper and bottles of champagne. Only the small festivals would bother with a detail like that.

As well as festivals, of course, there are established reading series, with programmes printed in advance, which can be seen as long-drawn-out festivals. One of these takes place at the Wordsworth Trust, in Grasmere, making a connection with the Romantic poets. Another key centre over the years has been the South Bank Centre in London, which also hosts the Poetry International Festival every two years, bringing poets from everywhere, and organizing translations of foreign language poets. They also have smaller one-off festivals.

MS: In 1995–96, when I was Writer-in-Residence at the South Bank, they hosted a Festival of the American South. This began with a paddleboat going up and down the Thames, with Dixieland jazz playing, and mint juleps flowing. It was a poetry and prose festival, and included the best poetry reading I have ever heard. This was the now-dead poet James Dickey who came in, wearing black leather and red shades, and opened with a poem about going to the zoo dressed like that and standing in front of the panther's cage. The panther stood there, transfixed, but when Dickey took the shades off, the panther got bored and walked away. When the shades went back on the panther was interested again. At the end of the poem, Dickey took the shades off and said to the audience, 'Hell, wasn't that good?'

When a reading is as terrific as that one, the divide between performance poets and 'book' poets (Dickey was definitely the latter) disappears. As we have said before, in Chapter 21, more and more 'book' poets are learning how to put their work across well in front of an audience, and one can always go back to the books and take the poems in with the eye afterwards – which is not what one can always say about performance poets. But there are audiences for both.

JHW: I remember having to read after a reggae poet at the international festival in Medellin, Colombia. He had the huge audience laughing, beating time, dancing and chanting and I wondered how I was going to follow him. I swigged an entire bottle of the ubiquitous Chilean red they drink in Colombia and launched into my poems. I hope I gave a reasonably fired-up account of myself – but my predicament does illustrate the divide between purely 'performance' poetry, which tends to be a crowd-pleasing entertainment, and 'book' poetry, which can entertain but also stimulate more complex responses.

23

ars poetica

I had now met all those who were to make the nineties of the last century tragic in the history of literature, but as yet we were all seemingly equal whether in talent or luck and scarce even personalities to one another. I remember saying one night at the Cheshire Cheese when more poets than usual had come: None of us can say who will succeed or even who has or has not talent. The only thing certain about us is that we are too many.

(from *Autobiographies* by W. B. Yeats)

This might seem a sobering start to the last chapter of a book in which we've been examining ways of helping you to become a poet, yet the fact is there would be no culture of poetry at all without many people writing and reading poems. Seen from this perspective, the winning of honours and literary prizes and the divergences of reputation in people who started as equals – who might even have been seen initially as belonging to the same group – is a separate issue. We have advocated that you should seek the company of other poets for mutual support and criticism (they won't all be glad to see you, but some will). Poetry is a marginalized art and the solidarity of a peer group is crucial. Yeats also said, around the same time as the quotation above:

I am growing jealous of other poets and we will all grow jealous of each other unless we know each other and so feel a share in each other's triumph.

Implicit in Yeats' remarks, of course, is the idea that all these poets were serious about their craft and that success was a possibility. If you *are* serious about your craft and make this evident in what you write, you'll go a long way towards answering the jeers of those who accuse poetry of being nothing more than self-indulgent posturing. If, for example, you are commissioned to write a poem and read it at a conference of psychiatrists, and you carry off this assignment in such a way that your audience can see you have not only written a well-crafted piece but have also engaged clearly and intelligently with their concerns, you'll have done yourself a favour and the image of poetry a favour as well. It may help, of course, to be in deep analysis in order to write a poem like this, or to have Freud's *Interpretation of Dreams* as your preferred bedtime reading. There usually has to be some intersection between a commission and your own interests for the result to be successful.

There are some poets who would strongly argue that poems have no business in the marketplace and that to take on the writing of a poem that hasn't arisen from your own inner promptings is a kind of prostitution. The relationship between the poet and the world is a vexed one. Do you insist that poetry should be spontaneous, or can it on occasion be done to order? Leaving commissions aside, are there subjects you should avoid – political subjects, for example? Poets in Northern Ireland in recent decades have been accused of exploiting the situation if they write about the Troubles and of copping out if they don't. Sometimes when poets find themselves on the edge of deep political divisions, they discover they are expected to produce propaganda for the side to which they ostensibly belong. Here's an interchange from a Seamus Heaney poem 'The Flight Path', which he describes as having taken place on a train from Dublin to Belfast in 1979:

> 'When for fuck's sake are you going to write
> Something for us?' 'If I do write something,
> Whatever it is, I'll be writing for myself.'

The implication of this, we feel, is that Heaney has not, in his reply, ruled out the subject matter of the Troubles, but that if he does deal with it at all, it will be on his terms – it will be his own private response as a poet to the situation. This kind of thing annoys people. Why don't poets take up clearly defined positions? they ask. It's another version of that question we echoed in Chapter 02: why can't you poets say what you mean?

The fact is, it's dangerous, on occasions, to say what you mean. At the beginning of Shelley's famous poem 'The Mask of Anarchy' these lines occur:

> I met Murder on the way –
> He had a face like Castlereagh –
> Very smooth he looked, yet grim;
> Seven bloodhounds followed him.
>
> All were fat; and well they might
> Be in admirable plight,
> For one by one, and two by two,
> He tossed them human hearts to chew
> Which from his wide cloak he drew.
>
> Next came Fraud, and he had on
> Like Eldon, an ermined gown;
> His big tears, for he wept well,
> Turned to millstones as they fell.

And the little children, who
Round his feet played to and fro,
Thinking every tear a gem,
Had their brains knocked out by them.

This was written as a passionately indignant response to the Peterloo Massacre of 1819 and was sent for publication to Leigh Hunt, editor of *The Examiner*, who judged it prudent not to publish it at the time in case it inflamed the population. It's interesting to speculate that Britain might be a republic now if it had been. Opinions differ, of course, as to the power poetry has to change things. Yeats believed there was a possibility it could.

I lie awake night after night
And never get the answers right.
Did that play of mine send out
Certain men the English shot?

(from 'The Man and the Echo')

But here is Auden in his elegy for Yeats:

...mad Ireland hurt you into poetry.
Now Ireland has her madness and her weather still,
For poetry makes nothing happen: it survives
In the valley of its saying where executives
Would never want to tamper...

(from 'In Memory of W.B. Yeats')

And here is Paul Muldoon on Yeats:

As for his crass, rhetorical

posturing, 'Did that play of mine
send out certain men (*certain* men?)

the English shot...?
the answer is 'Certainly not'.

If Yeats had saved his pencil lead
would certain men have stayed in bed?'

(from '9 Middagh Street')

The fact is, whether or not poetry makes anything happen, to try to exclude the political altogether would seem to us to make it difficult to engage fully with life in the way we've been saying, from the very first page of this book, a poet should.

Besides, poetry doesn't have to deal with politics in a rhetorical, head-on fashion. Some of the Eastern European poets, as we've already mentioned, found oblique ways of dealing with subject matter that has to be described as political. Here's a poem by Vasko Popa:

Imminent Return

In a cell of Beckerek prison
I spend the day with a Red Army man
Who'd escaped from a prison camp

Any moment the door may open
And he'll be taken out
And shot in the yard

He asks me to show him
The quickest way
To Moscow

With breadcrumbs on the floor
I build the towns he'd pass

He measures the distance with his finger
Claps me on the shoulder with his great hand
And rocks the whole prison with his shout

You're not far my beauty

                        (translated by Anne Pennington)

Popa was imprisoned by the Nazis during the war and this poem draws on that experience. The harnessing of a kind of domestic simplicity and the brutal yet unstated fact of execution is chilling because the life that is soon to be cut off is so richly and understatedly suggested. It's not so much politics as human tragedy that is the subject of this poem.

You may object that you've never been thrown in a foreign jail and no one has ever threatened to execute you, so how can your poems be interesting? Our answer to this is: don't insult your own experience, learn to trust it, listen to the authenticity of it. It's not the experience that makes a poem but what the writer does with it, how the writer's imagination transforms it. Scattered throughout this book are many examples of poems where unremarkable subject matter is made to resonate in an unexpected way.

Perhaps the best way to consider poetry's subject matter would be to reflect on these remarks made to the American poet Hart Crane that we found in John Unterecker's introduction to his *Complete Poems*. When he first came to New York as a young man Crane was looked after by a slightly older artist friend of his parents, Carl Schmitt, who had just returned from a year's study in Paris. Fascinated with the possibilities of integrating traditional theories of art with the innovative ideas he had picked up in Europe:

> *Schmitt opened his studio to the young writer to talk of his notion that all of the arts operated in what he called an 'area of expediency,' a zone that he saw as balancing the opposed material of ugliness and beauty (he drew a horizontal line to represent them) and the spiritual elements of good and evil (an intersecting vertical line). No true art, he argued, could exclude any of the four elements, though it might, of course, be weighted toward any one of them. Illustrating his ideas with his own work and with trips to galleries and to the studios of friends, he persuaded Crane that the key to great art was a complex set of balances in some ways similar to the reconciliation of opposites that Coleridge had defined as central to the art of poetry.*

EXERCISE 46 Multimedia approach to writer's block

We want to try to get you to engage with your own experience in a fashion that will prompt you to explore territory you've not visited before, even though it's under your nose. The following exercise is one we've borrowed from Thomas Lynch. He calls it 'Multimedia Approach to Writer's Block'. Take:

- one item in the room
- one item from outside
- one item from a newspaper
- one item from TV.

Put them together in a poem using self-imposed formal restraints (e.g. same word rhymes). The arbitrary conditions of this and the straitjacket of the rhymes set you a challenge that helps to focus your concentration. It might sound impossible to do, but here's what Lynch himself did with his own recipe:

A Note on the Rapture to his True Love

A blue bowl on the table in the dining room
fills with sunlight. From a sunlit room
I watch my neighbour's sugar maple turn
to shades of gold. It's late September. Soon...
Soon as I'm able I intend to turn
to gold myself. Somewhere I've read that soon
they'll have a formula for prime numbers
and once they do, the world's supposed to end
the way my neighbour always said it would –
in fire. I'll bet we'll all be given numbers
divisible by One and by themselves
and told to stand in line the way you would
for prime cuts at the butcher's. In the end,
maybe it's every man for himself.
Maybe it's someone hollering All Hands On
Deck! Abandon Ship! Women and Children First!
Anyway. I'd like to get my hands on
you. I'd like to kiss your eyelids and make love
as if it were our last time, or the first,
or else the one and only form of love
divisible by which I yet remain myself.
Mary, folks are disappearing one by one.
They turn to gold and vanish like the leaves
of sugar maples. But we can save ourselves.
We'll pick our own salvations, one by one,
from a blue bowl full of sunlight until none is left.

EXERCISE 47 Commissions

Those of you who take the pure line that no matter how famous
you become you would never accept a commission can skip this
next exercise. We want you to imagine we are representatives of
the Glassblowers' Federation. We are celebrating 1,000 years of
glassblowing and we want a poem on the subject to be read out
at our annual conference and to be printed in our Federation
Newsletter; or we are the educational wing of NASA and we
want poems that will be launched in an Earth Pod to a distant
galaxy. The poems should aim to tell possible intelligent life
forms what life at the Second Millennium is like on our planet.

There are no further conditions attached to either of these commissions; only that your efforts are unlikely to be remunerated if they're at all predictable.

How you set about undertaking a commission varies from writer to writer.

MS: My tactic is to forget about it and hope that a message is sent to my unconscious so that when I come to write a poem it might orient itself vaguely in the direction of the commission. The poem might be a bit oblique, but I feel the people who commission poems would always prefer something lively to something that met the commission's requirements head-on but was stilted, dead (which is how I've come to regard all my early efforts where I made myself sit down and write...). The advantage of this method is that, if I get a poem, it's likely to be a real one. The disadvantage is that half the time I forget about it too well and get no poem.

JHW: Rather than talking about commissions generally, I'd like to try to focus on the ones we've given you. Glassblowing suggests bubbles, refractions, coloured tints, fantastic shapes. I'd brood over these, over the process itself – molten liquid followed by transparent chewing gum followed by that fracturable, delicate end-product. I'd press my metaphorical nose up against the glassblower's cabinet and contemplate what's inside – all those chirpy little figurines. The thing is: you have to ruminate over a subject until its essence becomes a thing you might grasp. And what features of the way we live might be of interest to, say, a superior life form with a hundred-year attention span? My poem's going to be so short the alien won't even notice it, unless the poem carries the energy of a zap gun. I'd agree with Matthew that you have to let your unconscious solve some of the problems. I certainly wouldn't turn down a challenge.

What we're doing with these exercises, as with all the exercises throughout this book, is trying to nudge you from being an occasional poet in to being more of a professional one. There's nothing wrong with being an occasional poet, but you don't have to wait until the Queen reaches her 100th birthday before you write your next poem. Regular attempts at writing will, as we've said, keep your hand in, even if nothing comes of them.

When we use the word 'professional', of course, we don't necessarily mean you'll be paying cheques received from poetry into your bank account straightaway. What we're talking about is adopting a professional **approach** – working at all aspects of your craft, giving yourself a chance to develop as fully as possible whatever talents you might have. In short, we're urging you to be ambitious, while being realistic about what you can achieve at any given moment. Learning your craft is more than just knowing about metaphors, iambs, syllabics and sestinas; it's about acquiring the instinctive surefootedness that will enable you to achieve the effects you want. It's also about developing an alertness to those inner promptings which may lead unexpectedly to a poem.

We'd like to finish with excerpts from two poems, the first by Archibald MacLeish, from his poem 'Ars Poetica'.

> A poem should be equal to:
> Not true.
>
> For all the history of grief
> An empty doorway and a maple leaf.
>
> For love
> The leaning grasses and two lights above the sea –
>
> A poem should not mean
> But be.

And here are lines from two sections of John Heath-Stubb's long poem of the same name:

> A poem is built out of words;
> And words are not your property.
> They are common counters, involved
> In private chaffering, and international transactions;
> They have been tossed into the caps of beggars, and plonked
> On the reception-desks of brothels.
>
> You have got to make language say
> What it has not said before;
> Work against language. It is your enemy.
> Engage in a bout with it.
> But like a Japanese wrestler
> You will overcome by not resisting

* * * *

So through patience, perseverance, luck and that sort of thing
(I can only wish you luck)
You may arrive at an actual poem –
An interjected remark
At a party which has been going on
For quite a time (and will, we trust, continue);
A party at which you are not
A specially favoured guest
And which you will have to leave before it is over.

Let us hope the others will occasionally recall it.

But to you it will seem a little world.
You will look at your creation and see that it is good.
In this you will be mistaken:
You are not, after all, God.

I have defined poetry as a 'passionate pursuit of the Real', and undoubtedly it is that; no science or philosophy can change the fact that a poet stands before reality that is everyday new, miraculously complex, inexhaustible, and tries to enclose as much of it as possible in words. That elementary contact, verifiable by the five senses, is more important than any mental construction. The never-fulfilled desire to achieve a mimesis, to be faithful to a detail, makes for the health of poetry and gives it a chance to survive periods unpropitious to it. The very act of naming things presupposes a faith in their existence and thus in a true world, whatever Nietzsche might say. Of course there are poets who only relate words to words, not to their models in things, but their artistic defeat indicates that they are breaking some sort of rule of poetry.

CZESLAW MILOSZ

last words

Now that you've graduated from our Academy you should be ready for a vicious writing exercise we've saved until last. We found it in Richard Hugo's book *The Triggering Town*, and he got it from Theodore Roethke, whose pupil he was.

Richard Hugo was a much under-rated American poet who had many germane things to say about the writing of poetry. In a self-interview, for example, he likened a poet to 'a drummer alone in the ballroom of a deserted hotel. If he plays well enough a passer-by might prick up his ears and step inside to see what is going on, but he can only play the way he likes because when he starts, at least, he is the only one listening. Solipsism will never be a crippling problem because, by its very existence, language implies more than one person lives. Talking to yourself is not insane, it is only primitive. During the composition of a poem it's best to know you don't have a friend in the world.'

EXERCISE 48 Voodoo

Now we'd like you to take your drum kit into that hotel, and go manic. Here's the music sheet: take five nouns, verbs and adjectives from the following lists:

Nouns	Verbs	Adjectives
tamarack	to kiss	blue
throat	to curve	hot
belief	to swing	soft
rock	to ruin	tough
frog	to bite	important
dog	to cut	wavering
slag	to surprise	sharp
eye	to bruise	cool
cloud	to hug	red
mud	to say	leathery

Now write a poem as follows:

- Four beats to the line (can vary)
- Six lines to the stanza
- Three stanzas
- At least two internal and one external slant rhymes per stanza (full rhymes acceptable but not encouraged)
- Maximum of two end stops per stanza
- Clear English grammatical sentences with no tricks (all sentences must make sense)
- The poem must be meaningless.

Richard Hugo commented that the final item was 'a sadistic innovation' of his own.

This exercise is a difficult one, but it's one of the most rewarding we know. The problems of actually doing the exercise are so great that, while you are focusing on those problems, other problems, such as: 'I know what I want to say, if only I could find the words!' simply vanish. In this exercise you have been given the words and a number of quite complex technical problems to solve, and you are freed from worrying about how you want to say what you really want to say. With problems like that put aside, you can say, as Richard Hugo puts it, 'what you never expected and always wanted to say'.

In the course of our research for this book we tried the exercise, on a hot July afternoon in Berlin, fortified by rosé wine. We're sure you'll handle it better.

British MA courses in creative writing

The last ten or 15 years has seen a considerable growth in the teaching of poetry through MA degree courses in the creative writing programmes of universities. More and more people clearly think they need the life-swerve of joining a creative writing course. Perhaps they do, but remember that completing a course in poetry writing is not a guarantee that you are going to be able to write the epic poem of the new century. Far be it from us, however, to try and dissuade anyone from applying – even though one poet we know recommends reading this book as a substitute for taking a creative writing course.

In order to gain admission to one of these courses, you will have to submit a portfolio of your best work, and possibly go for an interview. Some of these courses (at the University of East Anglia, for example) have been running for a very long time and have prestigious alumni. The competition for entry here will obviously be much greater than at some other colleges. It is also now possible (at the University of Manchester, for example) to take a course by email – distance learning, as the jargon has it. In some cases, you will find poets running the courses – Jo Shapcott and Andrew Motion at Royal Holloway in London, for example, or Sean O'Brien and W. N. Herbert at Newcastle University. In other cases, it is a little hard to gauge what qualifications for teaching poetry people have. In the United States a situation has arisen where there are countless diploma'd teachers of creative writing who, so far as one can see, do not exactly have a track record in publication. This may increasingly come to be the case in Britain. Before you select a college, therefore, do try and find out who is teaching on the course you're aiming for. If they are writers and you don't know their work, read it. Does it speak to you? If it does then maybe you will find their teaching congenial, too. If, on the other hand, it seems to run quite counter to what your idea of poetry is, be careful.

JHW: At a reading I gave some years ago, a poet whose work I had read in magazines approached me and told me he was studying for an MA in poetry. He complained that his tutors were all of an 'avant garde' persuasion, and that they were pressuring him to move his work in that direction.

We feel very strongly that courses of this kind should be 'enabling' courses, free of the poetry politics that so confuses audiences on the contemporary scene. You need a course which will help you to achieve the best *you* want to achieve, and not the mythical best someone else wants you achieve. Another danger of such courses is that they will start to produce factory-built poets in whom the capacity for surprise will have been quality-controlled out. We have talked to some tutors, and can report that they are aware of the problem – but this may not always be the case. You should, therefore, be very choosy about which courses you apply for.

The advantage of a poetry year like this (if you can afford it), is that it will make you take your own work seriously. You will be working with a peer group who are also, no doubt, ambitious, and this will bring home to you a sense of where you stand as a writer, and focus your ideas about what you really want to do. We have, broadly speaking, summed up most of the advantages such a course will bring you in our Chapter 10 on 'The co-operative approach'.

Below, we list just a few MA programmes that are known to us. We have been unable to find a website that lists all known courses in Creative Writing, but practically every institution of higher education in the UK now runs courses in this area. In any case, we suggest you trawl through the internet looking for a course that seems to suit your needs. Then read the small print carefully.

- Royal Holloway, University of London, English Department, Egham, Surrey TW20 0EX
- University of Newcastle-on-Tyne, English Department, Newcastle-on-Tyne NE1 7RU
- University of Glamorgan, Pontypridd: School of Humanities and Social Sciences, Pontypridd, Mid-Glamorgan CF37 1DL

- Sheffield Hallam University: Dept of English Literature, Montgomery House/The Mews, Gate M, Collegiate Crescent, Sheffield S10 2BP
- University of East Anglia: School of English and American Studies, Norwich NR4 7TJ
- University of St Andrews: School of English, St Andrews, Fife KY16 9AL
- Warwick University: Dept of Creative Writing, Coventry CV4 7AL
- University of Manchester: Dept of English Language and Literature, Oxford Rd, Manchester M13 9PL.

These are books we've read that seemed to say, at the time we read them, something really germane about the craft of poetry. These are books which, whatever their origins, don't have too much of a whiff of the classroom about them – that's to say they're written, in the main, for the general reader. It doesn't pretend to be an exclusive list; it's a personal selection of books that have been important to us.

The Shaping Spirit   A. Alvarez
Chatto & Windus
Still a lively and accessible book.

The Dyer's Hand   W. H. Auden
Faber & Faber, 1963
Masterly.

Robert Frost on Writing   Elaine Barry
Rutgers University Press
A judicious selection of letters that will surprise you. Says more in less than everybody else.

Content's Dream – Essays 1975–1984   Charles Bernstein
Sun & Moon Press, 1986
Bernstein is the High Priest of the American avant garde L-A-N-G-U-A-G-E poetry, as it's called. Although his poetry is deliberately quite devoid of anything you might describe as 'meaning' ('towards the unreadable poem'), his critical writing is actually quite interesting. British writers don't have the time (or the money) to go in for this kind of theoretical work, by and large, which is a pity, in a way, as much British poetry does seem to take place in somewhat of an intellectual vacuum.

Manifestoes of Surrealism   André Breton (trs. Richard Seaver, Helen R. Lane)
University of Michigan Press, 1972
Re-read this now and blink. Breton may have been an old poseur, but by God he had something to pose about.

Under Briggflatts   Donald Davie
Carcanet Press, 1989
Donald Davie was an academic, and given to some rather startling prejudices, but when you read this book, and realize what a scrupulous and warm judgement he exercised, you forgive him for any crankiness. This is a very good, although by no means complete, account of some post-war British and Irish poetry.

Introduction to English Poetry   James Fenton
Penguin, 2003
Useful information about formal structures and techniques.

Metre, Rhyme and Free Verse   G. S. Fraser
Methuen, 1970
Others have tried to write this book, more recently too, and failed. An extremely clear, enlightening and attractively personal account of a complex subject.

The White Goddess   Robert Graves
Faber & Faber
Completely mad and utterly irresistible. Did Graves really read all this stuff? Holy cow! We particularly like this quote: 'No poet can hope to understand the nature of poetry unless he has had a vision of the Naked King crucified to the lopped oak, and watched the dancers ... stamping out the measure of the dance...' The last two sentences of Graves' introduction read: 'How you come to terms with the Goddess is no concern of mine. I do not even know that you are serious in your poetic profession.' Quite.

Contemporary Poetry and Postmodernism   Ian Gregson
Macmillan Press Ltd, 1996
An academic book, but up to the minute and always clear, interesting and persuasive. Very readable.

The Private Art – A Poetry Notebook   Geoffrey Grigson
Allison & Busby, 1982
Just that, a notebook, but fascinating in the way it jumps around, giving us insights and asides from one of the grouchiest poet-critics of recent decades.

The Truth of Poetry   Michael Hamburger
Anvil Books, 1996 (Reissued)
For an easy to read account of the development of
'international modernism' – the kind of thing that makes
Philip Larkin turn in his grave – this can't be beaten. Highly
intelligent and horridly well read, it should give you ideas for
further reading that will take you well into the millenium.

Metaphor   Terence Hawkes
Methuen, 1972
Apparently, Terence Hawkes would rather watch *The Bill* on
television than read anything worthwhile – like Shakespeare,
say – in the evening. He is, after all, a professor of literature,
and needs to wind down after all that daily deconstruction.
Still, this is, like G. S. Fraser's book about metre, an
approachable and well-documented book.

The Redress of Poetry – Oxford Lectures   Seamus Heaney
Faber & Faber, 1995
Preoccupation – Selected Prose 1968–1978   Seamus Heaney
Faber & Faber, 1980
*The Government of the Tongue – The 1986 T. S. Eliot
Memorial Lectures and Other Critical Writings*   Seamus Heaney
Faber & Faber, 1988
These three books show Seamus Heaney to be as impressive a
critic as he is a poet, and whoever or whatever he's writing
about – be it Sylvia Plath or his own early years – he keeps his
focus on the makings of poetry.

Conviction's Net of Branches   Michael Heller
Southern Illinois University Press, 1985
This is a quasi-academic book, about 'the objectivist' (mainly
American) poets. It's a thoughtfully presented and lucid
account of a poetic method which constitutes a bracing
antidote to some kinds of 'poetic discourse' offered to us today.

Strong Words: Modern Poets on Modern Poetry   ed. by W.N.
Herbert and Matthew Hollis
Bloodaxe, 2000
A comprehensive selection of poetical manifestoes.

Poetry in the Making   Ted Hughes
Faber & Faber, 1967
Originally a series of programmes on BBC Radio and intended
as a text and anthology for the classroom, or as a general
handbook for the teacher. A landmark work in its time, and
still widely used and admired.

Poetry and the Age   Randell Jarrell
Faber & Faber, 1973
Always intelligent, always urbane, always making suggestive
connections.

The Poetry of Ezra Pound   Hugh Kenner
Faber & Faber, 1951
Well, this *is* an academic book, actually, but written with great
verve and wide-ranging intellectual curiosity.

Maldoror 'Les Chants de Maldoror'   Lautréamont (Isidore
Ducosse) (trs. Alexis Lykiard)
Thomas Y. Crowell & Co., USA, 1972
*'Poetry happens to be wherever the stupidly mocking smile of
the duck-faced man is not.'* Not something you can argue
about, really. André Gide's comment on this book was: 'Here
is something that excites me to the point of delirium.'

Inside Out   ed. by JonArno Lawson
Walker Books, 2008
A vibrant anthology of children's poems with a difference:
each poet has written an enlightening commentary on how
their included poem came about.

Collected Prose   Robert Lowell
Faber & Faber, 1987
Essays, interviews, critical appreciations, fragments of
autobiography – essential gleanings from a hugely influential
figure. We love the quote about his own early poetry, that it
had 'a timeless, hackneyed quality'.

Curiosities   William Matthews
The University of Michigan Press, 1988
Wide-ranging, lively essays from one of the most engaging of
contemporary American poets. Includes 'A Poet's Alphabet' –
here is L: ' "L" is for limitations, and how artists wrench them
into strengths.' Heartening.

The Strings are False – An Unfinished Autobiography   Louis
MacNeice
Faber & Faber, 1965
A superbly readable account of the forming of a poet, with
frequent illuminating asides on poetic craft.

Modern Poetry   Louis MacNeice
Oxford University Press (2nd edition 1968)
Here the advice is given head-on. Trenchant and persuasive –
assuming you can get hold of a copy.

How Are Verses Made?   Vladimir Mayakovsky
Cape Editions, 1970
Short, pithy, unputdownable.

The End of the Poem: Oxford Lectures on Poetry Paul
Muldoon
Faber & Faber, 2006
The procedure of this weirdly kaleidoscopic book might be
best summed up by the ending of a Muldoon poem which goes
'... which made me think/of something else, then something
else again.' Interesting, but watch out for the anagrams.

The Language Poets Use   W. Nowottny
London, 1962
An academic book, first of all, but not at all classroomy. Full
of insightful things.

The De-Regulated Muse   Sean O'Brien
Bloodaxe Books, 1997
Essays on contemporary poetry by one of the sharpest, most
readable critics around.

52 Ways of Looking at a Poem   Ruth Padel
Chatto and Windus, 2002
The Poem and the Journey   Ruth Padel
Chatto and Windus, 2007
52 Ways of Looking at a Poem is a valuable book for anyone
who writes poetry, teaches it, or simply wants to enjoy it. *The
Poem and the Journey* is a follow-up to this, looking at 60
further poems, and connecting the experience of reading
poems to the problems of everyday life.

The Joy of Bad Verse   Nicholas T. Parsons
Collins, 1988
Unusual book, in that it focuses only on notoriously bad poets
– McGonagall is here (naturally) but also a host of lesser-
knowns, including Julia A. Moore 'The Sweet Singer of
Michigan', about whose work Mark Twain had this to say: '(it
has) the touch that makes an intentionally humorous episode
pathetic and an intentionally pathetic one funny.' Hilarious
and (we hope) salutary reading.

Poetry and the World   Robert Pinsky
Ecco Press, NY
A book very much on American themes, but worth reading.
His essay on 'The Responsibilities of the Poet' – see his

discussion on the Frank O'Hara poem 'Ave Maria' – is particularly good value.

Poets at Work – The Paris Review Interviews   ed. by George Plimpton
Viking Penguin, 1989
From the horse's mouth, as you might say. From where else would a punter want to hear it?

Selected Letters of Ted Hughes   ed. by Christopher Reid
Faber & Faber, 2007
Includes dazzling responses to other poets, throwing light on their work and their methods, and urging them to greater things.

Mortification   ed. by Robin Robertson
Fourth Estate, 2003
Sometimes hilarious, sometimes grizzly accounts of writers' public humiliations, including quite a lot of the poets mentioned in this book. Pure *schadenfreude*.

Emergency Kit: Poems for Strange Times   ed. by Jo Shapcott and Matthew Sweeney
Faber & Faber, 1996
Well, we'd have to recommend this, wouldn't we? Seriously, in its focus on the fresh angle, very much a companion work to the book you're reading. Check it out. A poem-oriented anthology, not a poets' league table like so many recent anthologies. We're not saying these other anthologies are no good; on the contrary, we strongly recommend you to get hold of as many as you can. The great advantage of anthologies is that you get a lot of poets for your money, and if the editorial selection has been done well, you also get a reasonable overview of the current scene. Most anthologies are compiled from a particular ideological standpoint, which accounts for the fact that books with titles like 'the new British poetry' or 'The New Poetry' may hardly duplicate each other at all. (A plus for the book buyer.) We also think you should be reading what poets are doing in other languages as well as in your own. If you have a smattering of another language, look for a bilingual selection of work in that language. Otherwise, reading anthologies that just have translations into English will give you some idea of how differently poets in other cultures write.

In Radical Pursuit   W.D. Snodgrass
Harper, Colophon Books, 1977
Lectures on the craft of poetry, written with feeling and
commitment.

The Nightfisherman: Selected Letters of W.S. Graham   ed. by
Michael and Margaret Snow
Carcanet, 1999
Full of insights into his own craft, and his dealings with fellow
poets and his publishers. This selection of letters (1938–85)
allows a glimpse of his often turbulent life.

Poetry: the Basics   Jeffrey Wainwright
Routledge, 2004
A guide, like this book, to how poetry works.

*I Wanted to Write a Poem: The Autobiography of the Works
of a Poet*   William Carlos Williams
New Directions, USA, 1958
Described as a 'talking bibliography', this is Williams' own
account of how he came to write his poems. He describes how
he narrowly averted major success when his book *White Mule*
appeared. Praised by reviewers, it sold out quickly, but the
boss of New Directions, James Laughlin, had gone to New
Zealand on a skiing trip, so no reprinting could take place to
take advantage of the huge interest. 'The whole thing blew up.
I was heartbroken but there it was – I had to take it.'

Letters to James Laughlin   William Carlos Williams
New Directions
Unguarded comments, at off the cuff moments. Offers
interesting sidelights on the relationship between a poet and
his publisher.

And, finally, books more specifically targeted at poets
themselves:

The Practice of Poetry   edited by Robin Behn and Chase
Twitchell
Harper Collins, 1992
Writing exercises from American poets who teach. More from
the horse's mouth – from a whole stable of horses this time.

The Way to Write Poetry   Michael Baldwin
Elm Tree Books, 1982
The Way to Write   John Fairfax & John Moat
Elm Tree Books, 1981
Writing Poems   Peter Sansom (Bloodaxe Poetry Handbooks 2)
Bloodaxe Books, 1994

Getting Into Poetry   Paul Hyland (Bloodaxe Poetry Handbooks 1)
Bloodaxe Books (new edition 1996)
Two older and two newer books out of the many for poetry practitioners. They're like the book you're holding in your hand this minute – but each (as we'd all like to think) with its own individual touch.

How to Publish your Poetry   by Peter Finch
Allison & Busby, 1984
Full of practical commonsense.

The Triggering Town   Richard Hugo
W. W. Norton & Co., 1979
A very engaging book, funny and personal, amazingly prescriptive one minute, and candidly on the defensive the next. Was reissued in 1997.

The Writer's Handbook
Macmillan (published yearly)
The Writers' and Artists' Yearbook
A & C Black (published yearly)
Both these two books have poetry sections which are regularly updated. Currently there is a good introduction to the poetry scene by John Whitworth in the W. & A. Yearbook, and an equally useful one in the W. H. by Peter Finch. Both these books provide you with addresses of poetry libraries, small press magazines and poetry presses. Quite indispensible. (You don't, of course, have to buy them every year. Matthew's W. & A. Yearbook is dated 1974!) There's a specialist American publication which might also be of interest, called:

Poet's Market
Bugeja & Martin
Writer's Digest Books (published yearly).

The Penguin Rhyming Dictionary   Rosalind Fergusson
Penguin
We don't tend to use it much, but there's no reason why you mightn't find it perfectly useful.

Oxford Companion to 20th Century Poetry   edited by Ian Hamilton
Oxford
It makes entertaining reading, although you shouldn't believe what it says about us.

Dictionaries, thesauruses, etc: if you haven't got at least one work of language reference on your shelf, we really have to conclude you're not serious.

Oh, last thing – really – and not a book recommendation this time. You might like to know that the Romanian poem in Exercise 42, page 160 (homophonic translation exercise) is actually a translation of a Jo Shapcott poem from her book *Phrase Book* (Oxford, 1992). Which poem? See if you can find out.

The lines quoted on page 116 are from poems by, in order, Eiléan Ní Chuilleanáin, Selima Hill, Allen Ginsberg, Paul Muldoon, Dylan Thomas, C. K. Williams, Rosemary Tonks, Edward Baugh, Les Murray and August Kleinzahler.

The opening lines quoted on page 98 are by Seamus Heaney, Sharon Olds, Carol Ann Duffy, Ian Duhig, John Hartley Williams (website: **www.johnhartleywilliams.de**) and Matthew Sweeney respectively.

ndex of exercises

index

teach yourself®

From Advanced Sudoku to Zulu, you'll find everything you need in the **teach yourself** range, in books, on CD and on DVD.

Visit **www.teachyourself.co.uk** for more details.

Advanced Sudoku and Kakuro
Afrikaans
Alexander Technique
Algebra
Ancient Greek
Applied Psychology
Arabic
Arabic Conversation
Aromatherapy
Art History
Astrology
Astronomy
AutoCAD 2004
AutoCAD 2007
Ayurveda
Baby Massage and Yoga
Baby Signing
Baby Sleep
Bach Flower Remedies
Backgammon
Ballroom Dancing
Basic Accounting
Basic Computer Skills
Basic Mathematics
Beauty
Beekeeping
Beginner's Arabic Script
Beginner's Chinese Script
Beginner's Dutch

Beginner's French
Beginner's German
Beginner's Greek
Beginner's Greek Script
Beginner's Hindi
Beginner's Hindi Script
Beginner's Italian
Beginner's Japanese
Beginner's Japanese Script
Beginner's Latin
Beginner's Mandarin Chinese
Beginner's Portuguese
Beginner's Russian
Beginner's Russian Script
Beginner's Spanish
Beginner's Turkish
Beginner's Urdu Script
Bengali
Better Bridge
Better Chess
Better Driving
Better Handwriting
Biblical Hebrew
Biology
Birdwatching
Blogging
Body Language
Book Keeping
Brazilian Portuguese

German
German Conversation
German Grammar
German Phrasebook
German Starter Kit
German Vocabulary
Globalization
Go
Golf
Good Study Skills
Great Sex
Green Parenting
Greek
Greek Conversation
Greek Phrasebook
Growing Your Business
Guitar
Gulf Arabic
Hand Reflexology
Hausa
Herbal Medicine
Hieroglyphics
Hindi
Hindi Conversation
Hinduism
History of Ireland, The
Home PC Maintenance and
  Networking
How to DJ
How to Run a Marathon
How to Win at Casino Games
How to Win at Horse Racing
How to Win at Online Gambling
How to Win at Poker
How to Write a Blockbuster
Human Anatomy & Physiology
Hungarian
Icelandic
Improve Your French
Improve Your German
Improve Your Italian
Improve Your Spanish
Improving Your Employability
Indian Head Massage
Indonesian
Instant French

Instant German
Instant Greek
Instant Italian
Instant Japanese
Instant Portuguese
Instant Russian
Instant Spanish
Internet, The
Irish
Irish Conversation
Irish Grammar
Islam
Israeli-Palestinian Conflict, The
Italian
Italian Conversation
Italian for Homebuyers
Italian Grammar
Italian Phrasebook
Italian Starter Kit
Italian Verbs
Italian Vocabulary
Japanese
Japanese Conversation
Java
JavaScript
Jazz
Jewellery Making
Judaism
Jung
Kama Sutra, The
Keeping Aquarium Fish
Keeping Pigs
Keeping Poultry
Keeping a Rabbit
Knitting
Korean
Latin
Latin American Spanish
Latin Dictionary
Latin Grammar
Letter Writing Skills
Life at 50: For Men
Life at 50: For Women
Life Coaching
Linguistics
LINUX

Lithuanian
Magic
Mahjong
Malay
Managing Stress
Managing Your Own Career
Mandarin Chinese
Mandarin Chinese Conversation
Marketing
Marx
Massage
Mathematics
Meditation
Middle East Since 1945, The
Modern China
Modern Hebrew
Modern Persian
Mosaics
Music Theory
Mussolini's Italy
Nazi Germany
Negotiating
Nepali
New Testament Greek
NLP
Norwegian
Norwegian Conversation
Old English
One-Day French
One-Day French – the DVD
One-Day German
One-Day Greek
One-Day Italian
One-Day Polish
One-Day Portuguese
One-Day Spanish
One-Day Spanish – the DVD
One-Day Turkish
Origami
Owning a Cat
Owning a Horse
Panjabi
PC Networking for Small
  Businesses
Personal Safety and Self
  Defence

Philosophy
Philosophy of Mind
Philosophy of Religion
Phone French
Phone German
Phone Italian
Phone Japanese
Phone Mandarin Chinese
Phone Spanish
Photography
Photoshop
PHP with MySQL
Physics
Piano
Pilates
Planning Your Wedding
Polish
Polish Conversation
Politics
Portuguese
Portuguese Conversation
Portuguese for Homebuyers
Portuguese Grammar
Portuguese Phrasebook
Postmodernism
Pottery
PowerPoint 2003
PR
Project Management
Psychology
Quick Fix French Grammar
Quick Fix German Grammar
Quick Fix Italian Grammar
Quick Fix Spanish Grammar
Quick Fix: Access 2002
Quick Fix: Excel 2000
Quick Fix: Excel 2002
Quick Fix: HTML
Quick Fix: Windows XP
Quick Fix: Word
Quilting
Recruitment
Reflexology
Reiki
Relaxation
Retaining Staff

Romanian
Running Your Own Business
Russian
Russian Conversation
Russian Grammar
Sage Line 50
Sanskrit
Screenwriting
Second World War, The
Serbian
Setting Up a Small Business
Shorthand Pitman 2000
Sikhism
Singing
Slovene
Small Business Accounting
Small Business Health Check
Songwriting
Spanish
Spanish Conversation
Spanish Dictionary
Spanish for Homebuyers
Spanish Grammar
Spanish Phrasebook
Spanish Starter Kit
Spanish Verbs
Spanish Vocabulary
Speaking On Special Occasions
Speed Reading
Stalin's Russia
Stand Up Comedy
Statistics
Stop Smoking
Sudoku
Swahili
Swahili Dictionary
Swedish
Swedish Conversation
Tagalog
Tai Chi
Tantric Sex
Tap Dancing
Teaching English as a Foreign
  Language
Teams & Team Working
Thai

Thai Conversation
Theatre
Time Management
Tracing Your Family History
Training
Travel Writing
Trigonometry
Turkish
Turkish Conversation
Twentieth Century USA
Typing
Ukrainian
Understanding Tax for Small
  Businesses
Understanding Terrorism
Urdu
Vietnamese
Visual Basic
Volcanoes, Earthquakes and
  Tsunamis
Watercolour Painting
Weight Control through Diet &
  Exercise
Welsh
Welsh Conversation
Welsh Dictionary
Welsh Grammar
Wills & Probate
Windows XP
Wine Tasting
Winning at Job Interviews
Word 2003
World Faiths
Writing Crime Fiction
Writing for Children
Writing for Magazines
Writing a Novel
Writing a Play
Writing Poetry
Xhosa
Yiddish
Yoga
Your Wedding
Zen
Zulu

teach
yourself

creative writing
dianne doubtfire

Creative Writing is the ideal practical handbook for any aspiring author. Using exercises to explore topics, it will encourage you to develop, direct and edit your creative ideas in addition to giving you invaluable guidance on how to present work for publication.

The late **Dianne Doubtfire** was a successful author of both fiction and non-fiction. This edition has been fully revised and expanded by Ian Burton, a former pupil of Dianne's and a published author and lecturer in creative writing.

teach
yourself

writing a play
lesley bown & ann gawthorpe

Writing a Play covers both the creative and practical elements, with plenty of interactive exercises and examples. Covering everything from character development to stagecraft, it explains how to write for both amateur and professional theatre, with plenty of advice for taking it further.

Lesley Bown and **Ann Gawthorpe** are prize-winning writers. They have been writing together for more than ten years, producing many plays for amateur and professional theatre groups, as well as broadcast productions.

writing for magazines
lesley bown & ann gawthorpe

Writing for Magazines offers everything you need to write for any type of magazine. From finding your inspiration and working to a word count, to conducting interviews, submitting work and getting published, it offers both creative guidance and practical advice with plenty of interactive exercises.

Lesley Bown and **Ann Gawthorpe** are journalists and prize-winning writers. They have been writing together for many years, and are the authors of **Writing a Play** in addition to many articles, screenplays, novels and scripts.